On Replacement

Jean Owen • Naomi Segal
Editors

On Replacement

Cultural, Social and Psychological Representations

Editors
Jean Owen
London, UK

Naomi Segal
Birkbeck, University of London
London, UK

ISBN 978-3-319-76010-0   ISBN 978-3-319-76011-7 (eBook)
https://doi.org/10.1007/978-3-319-76011-7

Library of Congress Control Number: 2018940698

© The Editor(s) (if applicable) and The Author(s) 2018
This work is subject to copyright. All rights are solely and exclusively licensed by the Publisher, whether the whole or part of the material is concerned, specifically the rights of translation, reprinting, reuse of illustrations, recitation, broadcasting, reproduction on microfilms or in any other physical way, and transmission or information storage and retrieval, electronic adaptation, computer software, or by similar or dissimilar methodology now known or hereafter developed.
The use of general descriptive names, registered names, trademarks, service marks, etc. in this publication does not imply, even in the absence of a specific statement, that such names are exempt from the relevant protective laws and regulations and therefore free for general use.
The publisher, the authors and the editors are safe to assume that the advice and information in this book are believed to be true and accurate at the date of publication. Neither the publisher nor the authors or the editors give a warranty, express or implied, with respect to the material contained herein or for any errors or omissions that may have been made. The publisher remains neutral with regard to jurisdictional claims in published maps and institutional affiliations.

Cover illustration: Still from ITV mini-series *Rebecca* (dir. Jim O'Brien, 1997)

Printed on acid-free paper

This Palgrave Macmillan imprint is published by the registered company Springer International Publishing AG part of Springer Nature.
The registered company address is: Gewerbestrasse 11, 6330 Cham, Switzerland

*This book is dedicated
to Ross, with love
and to the irreplaceable Scarlet*

Acknowledgements

This book grew out of a conference held in December 2016 at Birkbeck, University of London, in association with Birkbeck Research in Aesthetics of Kinship and Community (BRAKC) and the Birkbeck Institute for Social Research (BISR). We would like to extend a special thank you to Andrew Asibong, Nathalie Wourm, Maddison Brown and Melissa Butcher for all their support.

For permission to reproduce the images in the book we thank the Center for Jewish Film, Archivi Alinari Firenze and Lita Stantic Producciones.

Contents

1 **Introduction**   1
Naomi Segal and Jean Owen

Part I   What is replacement?   13

2 **'An eye for an eye' or 'a mile to a mile': versions of replacement**   15
Naomi Segal

3 **Replacement mothers, bedtricks and daughters out of place**   25
Jean Owen

4 **Replacement, renewal and redundancy**   35
James Brown

Part II   Lost children   45

5 **Lost boys in *Little Eyolf***   47
Olivia Noble Gunn

6 *The Sisters Antipodes*: replacement and its ripples of sibling rivalry   57
Jean Owen

7 Artificial intelligence and synthetic humans: loss and replacement   67
Georgia Panteli

Part III Wayward Women   77

8 The metaphysics of replacement in photoplay novels of immigration   79
Marija Dalbello

9 Of ghosts and girls in *Ulysses* 13   91
Patrizia Grimaldi-Pizzorno

10 Medea: founder member of the first wives' club   103
Mary Hamer

11 Replacement and genealogy in *Jane Eyre* and *Wide Sargasso Sea*   113
Nagihan Haliloğlu

Part IV Law and society   123

12 Who is the 'real' mother? Replacement and the politics of surrogacy   125
Samantha Ashenden

13 The ethos of replaceability in European human rights law   137
Sarah Trotter

14	Remembering the disappeared in Lita Stantic's *Un muro de silencio* Alison Ribeiro de Menezes	147

Part V   Replacement films   159

15	Deadness, replacement and the divinely new: *45 Years* Andrew Asibong	161
16	'She was the most beautiful creature I ever saw': visualising replacement in Hitchcock's *Rebecca* Laura Mulvey	169
17	*Married to the Eiffel Tower*: notes on love, loss and replacement Agnieszka Piotrowska	177
18	'That's my son': replacement, jealousy and sacrifice in *Un Secret* Naomi Segal	185

Part VI   The Holocaust   193

19	Replacement as personal haunting in recent postmemory works Susanne Baackmann	195
20	Embodying her ghost: self-replacement in Petzold's *Phoenix* Monika Loewy	207
21	Replacement or ever present: Jerzyk, Irit and Miriam Anthony Rudolf	217

Part VII   Psychoanalysis   229

22   Replacement and reparation in Sarah Polley's *Stories
     we tell*   231
     Agnieszka Piotrowska

23   Replacement, *objet a* and the dynamic of desire/fantasy
     in *Rebecca*   241
     Odeya Kohen Raz and Sandra Meiri

24   Rooms as replacements for people: the consulting room
     as a room object   251
     Deborah Wright

Index   263

NOTES ON CONTRIBUTORS

Samantha Ashenden teaches in the Department of Politics at Birkbeck, University of London. She is the author of *Governing Child Sexual Abuse: Negotiating the Boundaries of Public and Private, Law and Science* (2004), coeditor (with Chris Thornhill, University of Manchester) of *Legality and Legitimacy: Normative and Sociological Approaches* (2010), and (with Andreas Hess, UCD) of Judith Shklar's lectures *On Political Obligation: Lectures in Moral Reasoning* (forthcoming, 2018). Together with Dr James Brown she coedited the 2014 special issue of *Economy and Society* on guilt. They convene the Birkbeck Guilt Group: http://www.bbk.ac.uk/bisr/research/guilt-working-group.

Andrew Asibong is Reader in Film and Cultural Studies at Birkbeck, University of London, cofounder and codirector of the research centre Birkbeck Research in Aesthetics of Kinship and Community, and a psychodynamic psychotherapist trained at the Tavistock Clinic. He is the author of *François Ozon* (2008, reprinted 2016) and *Marie NDiaye: Blankness and Recognition* (2013) and is currently writing a book on the relationship between film-watching and the psychotherapeutic process, *Something to Watch Over Me: Aliveness, Affliction and the Moving Image*, scheduled for publication in 2019.

Susanne Baackmann received her PhD in German Studies at the University of California at Berkeley and teaches at the University of New Mexico. Her current research is concerned with questions of memory, gender and the aesthetic staging of childhood in postmemory work. She has published numerous articles on contemporary authors, filmmakers and artists, most recently on Rachel Seiffert, Cate Shortland and Hans-Ulrich Treichel. She has just coedited a special edition of *Transit: A Journal of Travel, Migration, and Multiculturalism* on 'The Future of the Past'. Her current book-length study on *Performing Memory and Childhood in German Postmemory Work* examines reconfigurations of witnessing in contemporary texts and films.

James Brown used to teach film and literature at Middlesex University, and politics and sociology at Birkbeck, University of London. He is currently an Associate Research Fellow at Birkbeck, while teaching theatre at Richmond University and IES London. Topics on which he has published include Shakespeare, social theory, science fiction, romanticism and literature on film. In 2014, with Sam Ashenden, he coedited an interdisciplinary special issue of *Economy and Society* on guilt. They convene the Guilt Group in the Birkbeck Institute for Social Research: http://www.bbk.ac.uk/bisr/research/guilt-working-group.

Marija Dalbello is an Associate Professor of Information Science at Rutgers University, USA. Her teaching and publications focus on the history of knowledge and history of the book applied to liminal phenomena and visuality. She has published on digital mediation, visual epistemology and immigrant literacies. She coedited *Visible Writings: Cultures, Forms, Readings* (2011) with Mary Shaw, and *A History of Modern Librarianship: Constructing the Heritage of Western Cultures* (2015) with Wayne Wiegand.

Patrizia Grimaldi-Pizzorno holds a PhD in Comparative Literature from Harvard University and teaches at the University of Siena. She has published on Chaucer, Thomas More, Edmund Spenser, Dante, Boccaccio, early modern anti-Judaic carnival plays and Joyce. She focuses on rhetoric (metaphor) and reception theory (intertextuality and classical reception) and is at present revising 'Gerty's hauntology' (her third and last essay on *Ulysses* 13) and 'Gift and Recognition in Boccaccio's Decameron X'. By the end of 2018, she expects to publish a book on the reception of W. Gilbert's theory of magnetism at the London Inns of Court and Shakespeare's *Comedy of errors*. She has received grants from the British Academy and the Accademia dei Lincei, NYU.

Olivia Noble Gunn is Assistant Professor of Scandinavian Studies at the University of Washington. She received her PhD in comparative literature from UC Irvine. Her research interests include comparative literature, queer theory, performance studies and feminism. She has published on topics ranging from Susan Sontag's adaptation of *The Lady from The Sea*, to working-class maternity in Norway's first sound film, to race and empire in the novels of Cora Sandel. Her current book project, *Empty Nurseries, Queer Occupants: Reproduction and the Future in Ibsen's Late Plays*, engages queer theory to reconsider gender, the family and reproductive metaphor in Ibsen's oeuvre.

Nagihan Haliloğlu is an Assistant Professor in the Department of Civilization Studies at Ibn Haldun University. She holds a MSt in Oriental Studies from the University of Oxford and a PhD in English from the University of Heidelberg. Her book on Jean Rhys, *Narrating from the Margins*, came out in 2011. She has published articles on multiculturalism, modernism, travel writing and contemporary Turkish literature. She is currently working on a project on contemporary narratives of melancholy. She writes regularly for the Turkish monthly *Lacivert* and *Daily Sabah*.

Mary Hamer taught at Cambridge for twenty years before taking up fellowships at Harvard and the University of Virginia. Her publications and research interests have extended to both the mapping of Ireland and Shakespeare's Rosalind as cultural icon. She is the author of five books: recently *Incest: A New Perspective* (2002) on child abuse was followed by *Kipling & Trix* (2012), a biofiction account of the lives of Rudyard Kipling and his sister, Trix, which was awarded the Virginia Prize for Fiction.

Odeya Kohen Raz is a Lecturer in the Audio and Visual Arts Division, The Sapir Academic College. She also teaches in the Steve Tisch School for Film and Television at Tel Aviv University and is a teaching coordinator in the Department of Literature, Art and Linguistics, at the Open University of Israel. Her publications deal with questions of ethics in Israeli cinema and Holocaust representations, as well as with historical space and reflexivity in films. Her major theoretical fields of interest are psychoanalysis, aesthetics and intertextuality. She is currently coauthoring a book (with Sandra Meiri) on narrative film and psychoanalysis.

Monika Loewy has completed her PhD in the English and Comparative Literature department at Goldsmiths, University of London. Her thesis focuses on how psychoanalysis, fiction and poststructuralist literary theory can be linked to two physical syndromes: the phantom limb and Body Integrity Identity Disorder. She also teaches English literature, and psychoanalysis and film. Loewy is particularly interested in the ways in which object relations theory and French literary theory can open dialogues about literature and film, and in the relationships between screens, texts and the body.

Sandra Meiri is a Senior Lecturer and Academic Supervisor of Film Studies in the Department of Literature, Linguistics and Art, the Open University of Israel. She is the author of *Any Sex You Can Do I Can Do Better: Gender Crossing and Narrative Cinema* (2011) and coeditor of *Just Images: Ethics and the Cinematic* (2011), and *Identities in Transition in Israeli Culture* (2013). She is coauthor of two books on film theory, has published articles in refereed journals and book chapters on trauma, memory and ethics in Israeli cinema, and is currently coauthoring a book (with Odeya Kohen Raz) on narrative film and psychoanalysis.

Laura Mulvey is Professor of Film and Media Studies at Birkbeck, University of London. She is the author of *Visual and Other Pleasures* (1989; second edition 2009), *Fetishism and Curiosity* (1996; second edition 2013), *Citizen Kane* (1992; second edition 2012) and *Death Twenty-four Times a Second: Stillness and the Moving Image* (2006). She made six films in collaboration with Peter Wollen, including *Riddles of the Sphinx* (1977; DVD publication 2013) and *Frida Kahlo and Tina Modotti* (1980). With artist/filmmaker Mark Lewis, she has made *Disgraced Monuments* (1994) and *23 August 2008* (2013).

Jean Owen obtained her PhD in 2013. Since then, she has been an independent researcher and writer based in London. Jean's interests lie in feminist theory, incest studies, psychoanalysis, anthropology, neobiblical studies, narrative traditions and first-person writing. She has published articles on Anaïs Nin, Kathryn Harrison and Krys Lee and is currently writing a monograph on daughter-led incest narratives. She is also writing a novel based on an ancient biblical story.

Georgia Panteli has recently completed her PhD on 'Posthuman and postmodern retellings of the Pinocchio myth' at University College London. She holds a BA in English and Greek Literature and a MA in Comparative Literature. Her research interests include fairytale retellings, cyborg and cyberpunk literature, graphic novels, posthumanism and metafiction. She is currently working on her monograph *From Puppet to Cyborg: Pinocchio's Posthuman Journey*, forthcoming in 2018.

Agnieszka Piotrowska is an award-winning filmmaker, writer and theorist. She has published extensively on film and, amongst others, is the author of the monograph *Psychoanalysis and Ethics in Documentary Film* (2014) and editor of *Embodied Encounters: New Approaches to Cinema* *and Psychoanalysis* (2015) and *Representing the Unrepresentable* (2016). Her new monograph *Black and White: Cinema, Politics and the Arts in Zimbabwe* (2017) deals with gender and ethnicity in postcolonial encounter. Piotrowska set up collaborative partnerships in Zimbabwe and through them completed her first feature film *Escape*. She is Reader in Film Practice and Theory at the School of Media and Performance, the University of Bedfordshire, UK.

Alison Ribeiro de Menezes is Professor of Hispanic Studies at the University of Warwick. Her research focuses on issues of cultural memory in Hispanic and Lusophone contexts. Her most recent monograph is *Embodying Memory in Contemporary Spain* (Palgrave Macmillan, 2014). She is currently writing a book on cultural representations of the disappeared in transnational perspective.

Anthony Rudolf has published many books touching on the Second World War, in addition to *Jerzyk*, which include *At an Uncertain Hour: Primo Levi's War Against Oblivion* (1990); *Wine from Two Glasses: Poetry and Politics* (1991); *Rescue Work: Memory and Text* (2004); and *Engraved in Flesh: Piotr Rawicz* and his novel *Blood from the Sky* (new edition 2007). Born in 1942, and educated at Cambridge, Anthony Rudolf lives in London. He is a writer, translator, publisher and occasional broadcaster. He is a Fellow of the Royal Society of Literature; his collected poems and his translations of the poetry of Miriam Neiger-Fleischmann were published in 2017.

Naomi Segal is a Visiting Professor at Birkbeck, researching in comparative literature, gender, psychoanalysis and the body. She is the author of ninety-three articles and eighteen books; her most recent monographs are *Consensuality: Didier Anzieu, Gender and the sense of touch* (2009), *André Gide: Pederasty and Pedagogy* (1998) and *The Adulteress's Child* (1992), and she recently translated Didier Anzieu's *The Skin-ego* (2016, orig. *Le Moi-peau* 1995). Since 1999, she has served on or chaired numerous inter/national committees including within ESF, HERA and the AHRB/C. She has run the organisation Cultural Literacy in Europe (see http://cleurope.eu/) since its origin in 2007.

Sarah Trotter is a PhD candidate in Law at the London School of Economics and Political Science. Her primary research interests are in human rights law, European Union law and family law, and she is interested in psychoanalytical theory and how its insights can be applied in these areas. Her doctoral thesis examines how European human rights law imagines the human condition.

Deborah Wright has a BA Hons in Visual Communication from Edinburgh College of Art. Her art and academic work focuses on humans' relationships with their environment. Deborah studied Art Psychotherapy Foundation at Goldsmiths and Psychotherapy training at WPF Therapy. She worked as a support worker and manager in residential care with people with learning difficulties and mental health issues. She works as a psychotherapist in private practice and is a member of BPC, BACP and FPC. She is currently doing a professional doctorate at the Centre for Psychoanalytic Studies, University of Essex and teaches on the BA in Therapeutic Care.

List of Figures

Fig. 8.1	(**a, b**) Stills from *Hungry Hearts* silent film (1922) published in Anzia Yezierska's photoplay novel, *Hungry Hearts: Illustrated with Scenes from the Photoplay, A Goldwyn Picture* (New York: Grosset & Dunlap, c1920)	84
Fig. 8.2	(**a–d**) Stills from *Hungry Hearts* silent film (1922). COURTESY THE NATIONAL CENTER FOR JEWISH FILM	85
Fig. 9.1	Umberto Boccioni, *Scomposizione di figura di donna a tavola* (1912), Museo del Novecento, Milano, © Archivi Alinari, Firenze, Italy	92
Fig. 14.1	Bruno discusses Ana's story with Kate, Lita Stantic, *Un muro de silencio*, Lita Stantic Producciones, 1991	154
Fig. 14.2	Kate discusses Ana's story with Bruno, Lita Stantic, *Un muro de silencio*, Lita Stantic Producciones, 1991	155
Fig. 14.3	Silvia seemingly entrapped by urban architecture, Lita Stantic, *Un muro de silencio*, Lita Stantic Producciones, 1991	155
Fig. 14.4	Silvia believes she may have found Jaime, Lita Stantic, *Un muro de silencio*, Lita Stantic Producciones, 1991	156
Fig. 14.5	ESMA Museum, Buenos Aires, photographed by Alison Ribeiro de Menezes, author's own image	157
Fig. 21.1	Sophie and Izydor in the late 1980s, by permission of Anthony Rudolf	219
Fig. 21.2	Jerzyk aged about eight, with initials on his pullover, by permission of Anthony Rudolf	220

Fig. 24.1 Drawing of Freud's room in the Zoologische Station in Trieste, letter from Sigmund Freud to Eduard Silberstein, 5 April, 1876 (Freud 1990 [1876]) 254

Fig. 24.2 Drawing of Freud's room in the General Hospital in Vienna, in letter to Martha Bernays, October 1883 (Freud, Freud and Grubrich-Simitis 1998) 255

Fig. 24.3 An aerial view of Freud's room (by D. Wright) as described in letter from Sigmund Freud to Martha Bernays, 19 June 1882 (Freud 1961a [1882]) 256

CHAPTER 1

Introduction

Naomi Segal and Jean Owen

'We have learnt from psycho-analysis', wrote Freud in 1910, 'that the notion of something irreplaceable, when it is active in the unconscious, frequently appears as broken up into an endless series: endless for the reason that every surrogate nevertheless fails to provide the desired satisfaction' (2001a: 169). Two years later he returns to this pessimistic conclusion, in somewhat different terms:

> as a result of the diphasic onset of object-choice, and the interposition of the barrier against incest, the final object of the sexual instinct is never any longer the original object but only a surrogate for it. Psycho-analysis has shown us that when the original object of a wishful impulse has been lost as a result of repression, it is frequently represented by an endless series of substitutive objects none of which, however, brings full satisfaction. (2001d: 189)

The contemporary media are full of accounts of the pain of replacement. Vanessa Nicolson writes about an impulsive Facebook message she sent, after the sudden death of her nineteen-year-old daughter, to the latter's boyfriend who had started a relationship with another woman: 'I was on

---

N. Segal
Birkbeck, University of London, London, UK

J. Owen (✉)
Independent Researcher, London, UK

© The Author(s) 2018
J. Owen, N. Segal (eds.), *On Replacement*,
https://doi.org/10.1007/978-3-319-76011-7_1

Rosa's Facebook page when I saw a conversation between Adam and Lucie that made it clear they were in a serious, loving relationship. It was six months after Rosa had died. I instantly felt the most unimaginable pain, as if my daughter's life had meant nothing, as if she had already been replaced' (3). When she invites Adam over to apologise eight years later, she explains: '"I think I felt you didn't love Rosa any more because you had transferred your love to someone else".' Compounded by herself ventriloquising her daughter's Facebook voice, this act of anger was a replacement to avenge a replacement, but such reactions always express the same thing: the feeling that a person's value is blotted out if someone else is now in the place where they once were.

The drama of replacement in human relations is both complex and dynamic; it is potentially damaging to all the *dramatis personae*. In the film *45 Years* (2015), a couple about to celebrate forty-five years of marriage learn of the recovery of the body of the husband's long-dead girlfriend – whose name was Katya, almost identical to that of the wife, Kate – preserved in alpine ice. This discovery implicitly affects the two differently: it appears that the man is shocked at reminders of his lost youth, while the woman is affected by the vivid idea of a rival who seems to have a permanent kind of precedence. In 2017 the female lead, Charlotte Rampling, reappeared in *The Sense of an Ending*, in which another ageing man gets a blast from the past when he is left a friend's diary in the will of his ex-girlfriend's mother. Rampling plays the girlfriend, now also in her seventies, suffering as silently as ever – but this time she plays the replacee rather than the replacer. The implication of both films is that moving the pieces around (as life inevitably seems to do) can cause only loss and bitterness.

An interesting, and perhaps not unconnected, gendering of the replacement drama appears in another set of recent fictions, more directly concerned with the dangers of doubling. In March 2017, a BBC TV series named *The Replacement* ran in three episodes, focusing on the disruption to the life of architect Ellen when she becomes pregnant and is 'replaced' at work – only temporarily, she is assured – by Paula, a similarly talented, dedicated and attractive woman a few years older. Like the almost identical plot of another TV fiction, *The Kindness of Strangers* (2006), this hangs on the idea of the threat to a woman's sense of reality when she gets or loses a baby. Indeed, there are echoes in both these series of feature films *The Hand That Rocks the Cradle* (1992) and *Fatal Attraction* (1987), in which, again, the woman who comes to disrupt the apparently smoothly-functioning life of another woman is by definition made mad by the fact that she cannot have or keep a child of her own. Whether male- or female-authored, when this compulsive contemporary legend is focalised on a pair of female protagonists, its crux is maternity and the supposed overweeningness of our 'wanting to have it all'. Even though the male characters commit acts of violence, the danger is only tangentially, it seems, from men; the stake is implied more viscerally as being between women engaged in a divide-and-rule catfight.[1]

Two recent novels named *The Replacement*, one American (Yovanoff 2010) and the other British (Redmond 2014), are both set in the traditional creepy village and centre on a male figure. Like a number of 1990s films (see Segal 2009, chap. 7), they show what happens to one man when he is placed 'inside the skin' of another. In these fictions, replacement is a career move; women in today's replacement fictions, meanwhile, find their own skins invaded by maternity and then recovered by someone else's envy, like a garment that no longer fits after a too-drastic diet.

The fiction *Rebecca* can be seen as part of a replacement chain, positioned between *Jane Eyre* and *Wide Sargasso Sea* (see this volume, Chap. 11), not to mention many less distinguished fantasies of the plain-girl-conquers-dashing-rogue variety. It has given rise not only to the 'classic' Hitchcock adaptation of 1940 but to many small-screen avatars as well. In 1962 a black-and-white version ran in the American TV series 'Theatre '62', slashed to under one hour and starring Joan Hackett, later the doomed Dottie of *The Group*; in 1969 there was an Italian version, *Rebecca, la prima moglie*, followed by another under the same title in 2008, in which the otherwise universally unnamed protagonist is called Jennifer. Two British TV miniseries not only appeared in the echoing years 1979 and 1997 but have mother and daughter in the parallel role of the second Mrs de Winter – Joanna David and Emilia Fox. The 1979 version also stars Jeremy Brett and Anna Massey, seventeen years divorced at the time, who, their son reports, 'ignored each other for the entire filming' (Huggins, n.p.). Another parallel can be found in the subsequent careers of two Mrs Danvers, Judith Anderson and Diana Rigg, both later celebrated for playing Medea. But the differences are as instructive as the parallels – Joanna David wears Caroline de Winter's wig pinned up and hatless, while Emilia Fox faces the wrath of her husband in a splendid bonnet (as our cover image shows). The ending is especially varied. In every version Manderley burns down, but whereas in du Maurier's novel Mrs Danvers has simply 'cleared out' (421), in most other versions we see her raving among the flames like a latter-day Miss Havisham or Bertha Mason. Here and there Maxim and his loyal wife are exculpated: for Hitchcock, whose hands were tied by the Hays Code, he has not actually murdered Rebecca, only knocked her down; and as Charles Dance in 1997 he plunges into the fire to rescue Mrs Danvers, tumbling down the staircase with her in his arms. Just once, startlingly, we get to see Rebecca – in the same production, her eyes, hands and head are glimpsed bewitchingly in the shape of Lucy Cohu.

Her earliest avatar was surely that of du Maurier's short story 'The Doll', written when she was barely twenty-one, published in 1937 and then 'lost' until its rediscovery and republication in 2011. In it an inaugural Rebecca, the desperate narrator's love-object, is much more in line with the traditional vamp as *la belle juive* – a Hungarian violinist herself crazily obsessed with a male sex doll called Julio.

Of course, Daphne du Maurier's *Rebecca* (1938) makes a virtue of the inaccessibility of the first wife, decisively dead and thus ensconced in the attic of other people's certain memories and uncertain desires. A man marries once; a man marries twice. The second wife enters a house dominated by her predecessor and the obsessive enigma surrounding her. Yet her torment is curiously reversible. Mrs Danvers taunts her: 'She's the real Mrs de Winter, not you. It's you that's the shadow and the ghost' (273), but she has already thought herself out of this logic:

> Perhaps I haunted her as she haunted me; she looked down on me from the gallery as Mrs Danvers had said, she sat beside me when I wrote my letters at her desk. That mackintosh I wore, that handkerchief I used. They were hers. Perhaps she knew and had seen me take them. Jasper had been her dog, and he ran at my heels now. The roses were hers and I cut them. Did she resent and fear me as I resented her? (262)

Like the superb Carmen before her, Rebecca is 'smiling' (313) as she is murdered; thus, having it both ways, even as he escapes the law Maxim insists that she has 'won' (316). But of course, it is his current wife who has won – no longer the vaguely androgynous child to her husband, she now leads him around 'the exile we have brought upon ourselves' (8), for it is he, not she now, who seems 'like a child that has been smacked' (16). Thus, for all the fascination of the haunted corridors, the lasting effect of this fiction is the romantic triumph of the plain girl who respectably does away with all the pillars of arrogance, both human and architectural. She may dream of Manderley but only to find it properly razed on waking, and herself able to rebury its occupants in writing. With the closing of this frame, 'Mrs de Winter' joins the ranks of usually male narrators from early Romanticism on, who disinter a misloved woman from the past only to reinter her in a book slyly labelled with her name.

Most commonly nowadays the first and second wives coincide in time if not in space, separated by the choreography of their rivalry. As for their children, they find themselves perforce in reconstituted families of step- and half-siblings, in which they have to learn to rub along. As adults become more absorbed in their marital rights, children are expected to be 'adaptable'. But the requirement of children to adapt has always been the problem.

We all recognise the original trauma of replacement in the life of infants. As Juliet Mitchell notes: a 'threat to our existence as small children [...] is posed by the new baby who stands in our place' (Mitchell: xv). This shock – for the psychologically unweaned child can never be adequately prepared for it – is based on the insult to the first baby's belief in its special lovability: 'the sibling is *par excellence* someone who threatens the subject's uniqueness' (10). Mitchell may well be right that laterality is the poor relation of the mainly intergenerational modes of desire in psychoanalysis, but a smaller-scale verticality conditions intersibling relations too, and it is also true that Freud recognises the importance of sibling replaceability as the shock that triggers the birth of intelligence, imagination and creativity in children, most strikingly in two texts that were both first published in 1909. At the birth of his little sister, whose name is very like his own,[2] the three-year-old 'Little Hans' 'felt a strong aversion to the new-born baby that robbed him of a part of his parents' love' (Freud 2001b: 68); but 'his sister's birth stimulated him to an effort of thought [...] He was faced with the great riddle of where babies come from, which is perhaps the first problem to engage a child's mental powers' (133). In the same year, Freud introduced Otto Rank's *The Myth of the Birth of the Hero* with 'Family romances', a tiny essay on the fantasies of children which replace their real-life mother and father with socially superior and delightful if often adulterous parents. This leap of the imagination, too, derives from the hostility produced by having to share 'the whole of his [*sic*][3] parents' love [with] brothers and sisters' (Freud 2001c: 237–238), as the child achieves the impressive *coup* of diminishing and elevating its parents at a single stroke.

These points clearly refer to any young children, not only to neurotics in the making; and thus the ordeal of jealousy faced by everyone in one form or other is at the root of both curiosity and imagination. If children are driven to the exercise of intelligence by finding themselves replaced, something more extreme happens with the child who occupies the replacer position in relation to a dead predecessor – as Maurice Porot suggests, these people suffer from 'an altogether paradoxical guilt-feeling' (Porot: 12) and are liable to grow up to be mad or geniuses, or perhaps both (27). His examples include Van Gogh, Salvador Dalí, Beethoven, Chateaubriand, Camille Claudel, Rilke, Hesse, James Barrie and Marie Cardinal.

The term 'replacement child' has been used in psychology and psychoanalysis for about fifty years though, as we have seen, the phenomenon it describes is much older. The dead sibling can shadow and affect everything in the newborn's life, causing blind jealousy, hopelessness or a version of survivor's guilt. According to Porot, this may be because the next child is conceived too soon after the earlier one has died and the parents' process of mourning is incomplete – this is the case of the surrealist Salvador Dalí, whose birth followed the death of his elder brother, also named Salvador after their father. Dalí attributes to the touted 'brilliance […] grace and beauty' (12) of this brother his own tendency to provocation and 'a sort of constant aggressiveness'. Barrie crowds his fiction with 'lost boys' in the name of a brother who never grew older than thirteen. Rilke's fictional Malte Laurids Brigge dresses up as his dead sister Sophie to please his mother but then collapses in terror when he gets trapped in the flowing garments found in a box in the attic (94–103). And if Didier Anzieu, a second-generation replacement child, 'became a psychoanalyst to care for my mother […] in myself and other people' (20) – thus achieving genius without madness – the image of the 'threatening and threatened' predecessor is always there.

This book is a study of versions of replacement as they have been identified in cultural, social and psychological phenomena, by researchers in a wide range of disciplines.

Part I, *What is replacement?*, opens with Naomi Segal's '"An eye for an eye" or "a mile to a mile": versions of replacement', in which she considers definitions of the phenomenon of 'replacement'. Is it as wide as its seemingly infinite versions suggest or is it better – and more accurate – to narrow down the focus, to regard replacement as a system of equivalences, for instance? From translation and replacement children to the triangular drama of sexual rivalry, Segal tackles the infidelity, jealousy, hopelessness and other affects that replacement invariably brings.

In 'Replacement mothers, bedtricks and daughters out of place', Jean Owen presents a comparative reading of Jacques Demy's fairy-tale film *Peau d'Âne* (1970), the Genesis account of Lot and his daughters and the Graeco-Roman myth of Myrrha to show how incest can be read as the replacement of one family member with another in what has been called 'a strange confusion of kinship'. Through these narratives, Owen shows how bedtricks can sometimes lead to a daughter taking her absent mother's place as her father's lover.

In 'Replacement, renewal and redundancy', James Brown begins with a discussion of Tocqueville's endorsement of self-replacement by one's heirs in aristocratic societies and goes on to maintain that modern individuals are more likely to see replacement as threatening redundancy. Brown suggests that this shift in attitudes towards replacement is a result of the way the division of labour differentiates us and of the fact that modernity promotes an internalised vulnerability to substitution.

Part II, *Lost children*, opens with Olivia Noble Gunn's 'Lost boys in *Little Eyolf*', in which she considers the seductive function of innocence and two distinct trajectories of 'lost boys' in Ibsen's antepenultimate play – the lame, drowned son who will never grow up, and the 'naughty boys' who will replace him. She shows how guilt-ridden mother Rita Allmers becomes the philanthropic mother to boys who will take her son's place in the nursery, in 'a circle game of replacement' reminiscent of the lost boys in *Peter Pan*.

In '*The Sisters Antipodes*: replacement and its ripples of sibling rivalry', Jean Owen explores the interplay of replacement and rivalry between stepsisters in Jane Alison's memoir, in which two seemingly identical families trade spouses. Via the tropes of father-hunger, twinning and the Double, Owen traces a complicated account of mirroring through the troubling relationship between the 'metamorphic families' and draws attention to the 'wretched human economics of desire and desirability' in this tragic tale of familial rearrangement.

In 'Artificial intelligence and synthetic humans: loss and replacement', Georgia Panteli first draws on Spielberg's *A.I. Artificial Intelligence* (2001) to examine the complications of simultaneous presence when the replacement, in the form of a sentient robot, and the replaced human are expected to coexist in a malfunctioning domestic setting. She then turns to the TV series *Humans* (2015) to show how the robot child functions to replace a dead child as a form of therapy for the grieving parent(s). Both narratives, Panteli argues, reflect technophobic ideologies that oppose transhumanist values.

Part III, *Wayward Women*, opens with Marija Dalbello's 'The metaphysics of replacement in photoplay novels of immigration', in which she shows how photoplay novels of the 1920s created a sensorium for mainstream audiences and established new protocols for seeing, reading and experiencing the self. With a focus on Anzia Yezierska's autobiographical stories and the films they prompted, Dalbello argues that photoplay novels serve as replacement narratives and reveal irreconcilable geographies of the new and the old world and presentations of a gendered immigrant self that paralleled Yezierska's own condition of incomplete 'replacement'.

In 'Of ghosts and girls in *Ulysses* 13', Patrizia Grimaldi-Pizzorno explores the cinematic narrative technique in James Joyce's *Ulysses*, episode 13 ('Nausicaa'), to ask 'who was Gerty?' She posits that, like Derrida's 'hauntological' spectre, and replaced by a plurality of Doppelgänger from literature, theatre, photography, songs, cinema and advertising, Gerty is transformed, interpenetrated and replaced in a *retrogressive progression* by multiple exposures, to appear as a *mirage* that cannot be touched or spoken to.

In 'Medea: founder member of the first wives' club', Mary Hamer recollects how replacing your wife with a younger model is an ancient trope that still reverberates today through the figure of Medea. Hamer focuses on Euripides, the Greek tragedian who first made the connection between Jason's actions in replacing his wife and the death of their sons, by asking how the effects of making women interchangeable as wives undermines the idea of the myth of the hero.

In the final chapter of this Part, Nagihan Haliloğlu presents a comparative reading of Charlotte Brontë and Jean Rhys in 'Replacement and genealogy in *Jane Eyre* and *Wide Sargasso Sea*', to show how the correspondences between the two novels work. If Thornfield and the two women in it are cultural hauntings, they also highlight larger questions of the literary canon to suggest a kind of transference, and to show how replacement itself becomes a function of genealogy.

Part IV, *Law and society*, opens with Samantha Ashenden's exploration of the politics of replacement through the contentious terrain of collaborative conception in the twenty-first century, in 'Who is the "real" mother? Replacement and the politics of surrogacy'. In particular, she examines how the embodied work of gestation is often occluded by legal and other framings of the foetus in terms of property, the intentions of commissioning parents, and arguments about the 'blood tie'.

In 'The ethos of replaceability in European human rights law', Sarah Trotter argues that the drama of replacement highlights the competing logics of two distinct narratives in terms of performativity and authenticity: *presence*, which is about an individual's sense of self in the world, and *presentation*, which is about representation in terms of a role, life-stage or status, for example 'worker' or 'child'.

In 'Remembering the disappeared in Lita Stantic's *Un muro de silencio*', Alison Ribeiro de Menezes examines the poetics of replacement through the motif of the silhouette, a type of Doppelgänger that was utilised by campaigners in Buenos Aires in 1983 to highlight the violations of human rights committed by the military dictatorship in 'disappearing' individuals.

Part V, *Replacement films*, presents four films that were shown at the conference on Replacement in December 2016. In 'Deadness, replacement and the divinely new: *45 Years*', Andrew Asibong analyses the effect of the moment when a wife 'finds herself uncannily replaced by the glittering spectre of her husband's suddenly re-vivified, un-mourned, earlier love-object'. In '"She was the most beautiful creature I ever saw": visualising replacement in Hitchcock's *Rebecca*', Laura Mulvey shows 'how the film weaves the "Rebecca web" around its heroine' through the use of a spectrum of punctuating devices and narrative traps. Agnieszka Piotrowska presents her own film in a chapter titled '*Married to the Eiffel Tower*: notes on love, loss and replacement', in which we enter the worlds of three women who are in love with inanimate objects. Naomi Segal sets Claude Miller's *Un Secret* (2007) alongside the original autobiographical novel by psychoanalyst Philippe Grimbert in '"That's my son": replacement and sacrifice in *Un Secret*', to query the motives of a key character faced by replacement.

Part VI, *The Holocaust*, begins with Susanne Baackmann's chapter 'Replacement as personal haunting in recent postmemory work', in which she explores how a ghost from the past, a brother 'lost' in 1945 during the flight from the Eastern territories, haunts the child narrator – who never met this lost brother – in Hans-Ulrich Treichel's *Lost* (1998). Through the tropes of impossible or refused mourning, the transgenerational effects of trauma and the reductive subject-positions of perpetrator and victim, *Lost* is compared with Art Spiegelman's *Maus* II and Angelika Overath's *Nahe Tage*.

In 'Embodying her ghost: self-replacement in Petzold's *Phoenix*', Monika Loewy utilises Freud's concept of the uncanny and Winnicott's notion of the True and False Self in her reading of Petzold's film. *Phoenix* traces the journey of Auschwitz survivor Nelly who struggles to be replaced by, and simultaneously to replace, her prewar self in postwar Germany when she reunites with a husband who fails to recognise her, due to reconstructive facial surgery.

In 'Replacement or ever-present: Irit, Jerzyk and Miriam', Anthony Rudolf considers the act of suicide in 1943 by 11-year-old Jerzyk while in hiding as 'the tragic action of a child under pressure' and 'a noble and heroic act', just as keeping a diary – which Rudolf, a relative of Jerzyk's, has translated and edited – was a form of defiance. Turning to Irit, Jerzyk's sister, and to Miriam Neiger-Fleischmann, Rudolf posits the idea of the 'ever-present' in relation to replacement by discussing those children born after siblings who perished during the Holocaust.

Part VII, *Psychoanalysis*, opens with 'Replacement and reparation in Sarah Polley's *Stories we tell*', in which Agnieszka Piotrowska considers replacement through the lens of the psychoanalytic notion of sublimation to suggest that film-making of this sort offers a kind of reparative replacement for trauma. She shows how filmmaker Sarah Polley, in the process of making her film, takes up the challenge of repositioning the power balance of her confused parental history by replacing her dead mother in the lives of her two fathers.

In 'Replacement, *objet a* and the dynamic of desire/fantasy in *Rebecca*', Odeya Kohen Raz and Sandra Meiri maintain that while 'bodiless-character-films', such as Hitchcock's *Rebecca* (1940), transgress the rule of filling '*objet a*' with a fantasy object (an actor), thus resisting the spectator's desire to see, they nevertheless keep desire alive by engaging the spectator in the ardent desire of their protagonist to fill this void with substitutes.

In the final chapter, 'Rooms as replacements for people: the consulting room as a room object', Deborah Wright argues that historical tradition relating to the representation of people in spaces can be applied to the therapeutic consulting room. Through a case study, Wright demonstrates that if a room also represents the *replacement room* of an individual who has been lost, this could be thought of as a *good room object* or a *bad room object*, depending on the nature of the transference within the therapeutic process.

The range of treatments of the motif of replacement contained in this volume bears witness not only to the breadth of perspectives it enables but also to the richness of a theme that touches contemporary imagination and experience. The triangular relationship between the replacee (the first wife or dead sibling), the replacer (Mrs de Winter or James Barrie) and the person who unites the two (Freud's seeker of endless surrogates) generates material across the arts, humanities and social sciences. This is surely just the start of the discussions.

Notes

1. Thus the ending of *Fatal Attraction* was changed in response to test audiences, and to the chagrin of Glenn Close, from a *Madame Butterfly* suicide to a wife-on-mistress murder.
2. The real 'Hans' was called Herbert, so in choosing the pseudonym he did Freud brought his name much closer to the real-life name of his sister Hanna.
3. The masculine gender of this possessive is Strachey's rather than Freud's (the latter uses the normal pronoun 'es', for 'Kind'), though this version of oedipal resentment, like others, is of course gendered, and Freud notes sniffily that 'the imagination of girls is apt to show itself much weaker' (238).

References

Ahearne, Joe, dir., 2017, *The Replacement*, BBC-TV
Anzieu, Didier, 1991, *Une Peau pour les pensées, entretiens avec Gilbert Tarrab* (Paris: Apsygée)
Barrie, J. M., 1988 [1911], *Peter Pan & Wendy* (London: Michael Joseph)
Batra, Ritesh, dir., 2017, *The Sense of an Ending*
Dalí, Salvador, 1973, *Comment on devient Dali [sic]*, as told to André Parinaud (Paris: Robert Laffont)
Du Maurier, Daphne, 2003 [1938], *Rebecca* (London: Virago)
Du Maurier, Daphne, 2011 [1937], *The Doll: The Lost Short Stories* (London: Virago)
Freud, Sigmund, 2001a [1910], 'A special type of choice of object made by men' [Über einen besonderen Typus der Objektwahl beim Manne], tr. Alan Tyson, in *Standard Edition of the Complete Psychological Works*, ed. James Strachey et al. (London: Vintage) [henceforth *SE*], vol XI, 163–175
Freud, Sigmund, 2001b [1909], 'Analysis of a phobia in a five-year-old boy' [Analyse der Phobie eines fünfjährigen Knaben], in *SE*, vol X, 1–149
Freud, Sigmund, 2001c [1909], 'Family romances' [Der Familienroman der Neurotiker], in *SE* vol IX, 236–241
Freud, Sigmund, 2001d [1912], 'On the universal tendency to debasement in the sphere of love' [Über die allgemeinste Erniedrigung des Liebeslebens], tr. Alan Tyson, in *SE*, vol XI, 177–190
Haigh, Andrew, dir., 2015, *45 Years*

Hanson, Curtis, dir., 1992, *The Hand that Rocks the Cradle*
Hitchcock, Alfred, dir., 1940, *Rebecca*
Huggins, David, 'At Christmas I dreaded playing charades', *The Guardian* 14 November 2001, https://www.theguardian.com/books/2001/nov/14/shopping.familyandrelationships (last accessed 4 Dec 2017)
Lumet, Sidney, dir., 1966, *The Group*
Lyne, Adrian, dir., 1987, *Fatal Attraction*
Macchi, Eros, dir., 1969, *Rebecca, la prima moglie*
Milani, Riccardo, dir., 2008, *Rebecca, la prima moglie*
Mitchell, Juliet, 2003, *Siblings* (Cambridge: Polity)
Nicolson, Vanessa, 2017, '"About that awful thing I did..."', *The Guardian: Family*, 22 April, 3
O'Brien, Jim, dir., 1997, *Rebecca*
Porot, Maurice, 2014 [1993], *L'enfant de remplacement* (Paris: Frison-Roche)
Redmond, Patrick, 2014, *The Replacement* (London: Sphere)
Rilke, Rainer Maria, 1975 [1910], *Die Aufzeichnungen des Malte Laurids Brigge* (Frankfurt: Insel)
Sagal, Boris, dir., 1962, *Rebecca*
Segal, Naomi, 2009, *Consensuality: Didier Anzieu, gender and the sense of touch* (Amsterdam & New York: Rodopi)
Smith, Tony, dir., 2006, *The Kindness of Strangers*, Granada TV
Yovanoff, Brenna, 2010, *The Replacement* (London: Simon & Schuster)

PART I

What is replacement?

CHAPTER 2

'An eye for an eye' or 'a mile to a mile': versions of replacement

Naomi Segal

Replication, substitution, reproduction, cloning, copies, avatars, equivalences, translation, plagiarism, imitation, mimicry, transubstantiation, transference... How are these notions all versions of replacement? In each case, a new thing appears to be the same as a preceding thing; the question is what happens to each as a result of this parallel. To replace something or someone suggests that the place of the original is so exactly filled that there is no residue or surround. Clearly this is never true in human affairs. A replacement child is likely to carry with it, like a second skin, the remembrance of the dead sibling, even when – as is presumably most often the case – that remembrance is not their own. In the same way the new monarch or president inherits the 'body' of the preceding one, however different their style or politics. How many Mrs de Winters can there be? Many, it seems, although they will not marry the same man.

Unless otherwise stated, all translations from French or German are my own and reference is to the original text. Any quotation without page reference comes from the last-cited page. In the case of poetry, I give both original and translation.

N. Segal (✉)
Birkbeck, University of London, London, UK

© The Author(s) 2018
J. Owen, N. Segal (eds.), *On Replacement*,
https://doi.org/10.1007/978-3-319-76011-7_2

Replication and *substitution* both suggest that the second item precisely fits the dimensions of the first and can stand adequately in its place. We might think of a snake that emerges from its sloughed skin; it looks and should behave exactly like the previous one, which is cast off and no longer a snake; it substitutes for it. Sexual *reproduction*, as distinct from *cloning*, is designed to be something quite other than exact substitution; its product also coincides in time with the originals, at least for a while; and even cloning places an identical-looking creature in different times and circumstances, destined to develop differently from its original.

Copies, like *avatars*, are never closer than *equivalences*; they are surely not meant to be; in this they resemble *translations*, which knowingly balance inevitable gains and losses. With terms like *plagiarism*, *imitation* or *mimicry* we arrive at the field of accusations of illegitimacy – not because the reproductions are poorly achieved but because they seem overweening. Here we enter the moral field of forgery and its cognates – though who is the 'real thing' between the star and their stunt double, or the infertile woman and the 'surrogate' mother? In a sense this attitude proceeds from the same basis as Walter Benjamin's argument about aura – the 'authenticity [of the original located by] its presence in time and space' (1970: 222). However much a reproduction may override that originality by its ability to 'meet the beholder halfway', 'the quality of its presence is always depreciated' (223).[1] It is this loss of value that lies at the root of accusations of plagiarism. In her brilliant *Rapport de police* (2010), Marie Darrieussecq responds to an accusation of having plagiarised a fellow writer's bereavement in her novel *Tom est mort* (2007) by tracing the ubiquity of the accusation of plagiarism, especially in relation to the 'vampiric' (16) genre of first-person fiction, most particularly in relation to representations of personal suffering; she calls this 'the rights of the victim: I suffer, therefore I am, and certainly no one else is'.

My last two epithets, *transubstantiation* and *transference*, point to the replacement rituals of two ceremonial fields, Christianity and psychoanalysis. In each, the idea is to illuminate an original that has absolute precedence but is no longer accessible, by working (in a magical albeit 'secondary' way) with the equivalent that is at hand.

The phrase I cited earlier, translated by Harry Zohn as 'presence in time and space', is in Benjamin simply 'das Hier und Jetzt' [the here and now] (1963 [1936]: 12*ff*). For Benjamin, the 'here-and-now' of a work of art – unlike that of a piece of nature – constitutes its authenticity; it places it within a tradition in which its use-value was associated with ritual (we return to transubstantiation and transference). But what this shows is that there are two different kinds of here-and-now: the lost, auratic original – Jesus or the mother – and the thing we can lay our hand on in its place. What this plethora of versions of replacement reminds us is that both elements of the pair, replacer and replacee, have claims to the priority of presence; it is the pairing of the two that shows everyone that presence is always relative.

Before moving on to some examples, I want to return to the phrases that make up my title. *An eye for an eye* comes, of course, from the Hebrew Bible (Exodus 21: 24). The equivalence set up here is to do with crime and punishment; it has been much taken up in anti-Jewish rhetoric, and Jesus explicitly invites this reading in his Sermon on the Mount, where he replaces it by the idea of turning the other cheek. But this comparison presupposes that the words were meant literally. In fact, despite the poetic parallels in the text, the eyes and teeth were replaced by a monetary fine scaled to represent the level of the injury. 'No case of physical talion is recorded in the Bible, nor was such talion the intention of the biblical law' (Plaut: 571); apart from murder, which – in some places still today – demanded a life for a life, money stands here not simply as an equivalent but as a legal substitute.

And a mile to a mile? Lewis Carroll said it first, in *Sylvie and Bruno Concluded* (1893):

> 'That's another thing we've learned from *your* Nation,' said Mein Herr, 'map-making. But we've carried it much further than you. What do you consider the *largest* map that would be really useful?'
> 'About six inches to the mile.'
> 'Only *six inches*!' exclaimed Mein Herr. 'We very soon got to six *yards* to the mile. Then we tried a *hundred* yards to the mile. And then came the grandest idea of all! We actually made a map of the country, on the scale of *a mile to the mile!*'
> 'Have you used it much?' I enquired.
> 'It has never been spread out, yet,' said Mein Herr: 'the farmers objected: they said it would cover the whole country, and shut out the sunlight! So we now use the country itself, as its own map, and I assure you it does nearly as well'. (556–557)

Jorge Luis Borges copied him in 1946 and was followed by Umberto Eco in 1982. Copy of a copy as they may be, the Borges and the Eco are probably now better known than the Lewis Carroll, whose *Sylvie & Bruno* is not much read. But they all base the humour on the idea that a perfect copy is the most imperfect thing one could invent.

We see thus that no copy can or should be perfect. Yet we replace things and – more pointedly – people. Is this always a way of being new, 'moving on' – or is it, as the outcast original might feel, an act of deliberate infidelity?

This is what Barbara Johnson wrote about translation in 1985 (presciently, for little has changed apart from the trade names):

> While the value of the notion of fidelity is at an all-time high in the audiovisual media, its stocks are considerably lower in the domains of marital mores and theories of translation. It almost seems as though the stereo, the Betamax, and the Xerox have taken over the duty of faithfulness in reproduction, leaving the texts and the sexes with nothing to do but disseminate. [...] For while both translators and spouses were once bound by contracts to love, honour, and obey, and while both inevitably betray, the current questioning of the possibility and desirability of conscious mastery makes that contract seem deluded and exploitative from the start. But what are the alternatives? Is it possible simply to renounce the meaning of promises or the promise of meaning?
>
> Fortunately, I must address translation, not matrimony. Yet the analogy between the two is extremely far-reaching. It might, however, seem that the translator ought, despite or perhaps because of his or her oath of fidelity, to be considered not as a duteous spouse but as a faithful bigamist, with loyalties split between a native language and a foreign tongue. (Johnson cited by Graham: 142–143)

In looking at the first set of examples which follow let us assume that a kind of faithful bigamy, rather than a snake-like substitution, is what the parents of a replacement child are aiming for. Yet it is rare indeed that they achieve this. The dead sibling shadows and affects everything in the newborn's life, causing blind jealousy, hopelessness or a version of survivor's guilt. According to Maurice Porot, this may be because the next child is conceived too soon after the earlier child has died and the process of mourning is incomplete – the surrealist Salvador Dalí (though he dates it differently in his memoir, as we see below) was born exactly nine months and ten days after the death of his elder brother, also named Salvador after their father. He wrote:

> Everything about my brother – his brilliance, his early genius, grace and beauty – had been a thrill to her. His death was a terrible shock. [My mother] never got over it. Not until my birth was my parents' despair somewhat

lightened, but even then their misfortune permeated every cell of their bodies. I could already feel their anguish in my mother's womb. [...] I felt his persisting presence very deeply: both as a trauma – robbing me of affection – and as a passionate wish to outdo him. From then on all my efforts were dedicated to winning back my right to life, first and foremost by provoking the perpetual attention and interest of my family by a sort of constant aggressiveness. (Dalí and Parinaud: 12)

More positively perhaps, Didier Anzieu describes the birth of his mother as a replacement child:

[My mother] was the third child in the family, the third or fourth... That's the problem. Before her, in fact, three daughters were born. [...] It was a feast-day. Marguerite, the youngest of the three daughters, had an organdie dress on, ready to go to church. She'd been left for a moment in the charge of the eldest girl, the one who was to become my godmother. The child was lightly dressed, it was cold, she went up to the fire to warm herself... and was burnt alive. It was a dreadful shock for her parents and her two sisters. So my mother was conceived as a replacement for the dead child. And since she was another girl, they gave her the same name, Marguerite. The living dead, in a way ... It's no coincidence that my mother spent her life finding ways to escape from the flames of hell. (19–20)

This version of the story – a possibly better known one is that of Jacques Lacan, who treated Marguerite in the psychiatric hospital where she spent most of her life – was told by Anzieu in an interview when he was sixty (see Lacan: 174*ff*). He goes on:

I might put it this way – it sounds banal, but in my case it seems true: I became a psychoanalyst to care for my mother. Not so much to care for her in reality, even though I did succeed in helping her, in the last quarter of her life, to find a relatively happy, balanced life. What I mean is, to care for my mother in myself and other people. To care, in other people, for this threatening and threatened mother. (Anzieu: 20)

A third case is that of James Barrie, who was six when his elder brother David died in a skating accident. Their mother never got over the loss and James' childhood seems to have been shaped by the attempt to make it up to her. In this he was both, obviously, trying to be loved for himself and accepting that he could only be the failed substitute for another. He tells how, a few days after the death, his older sister Jane Ann told him to go to his mother and 'say to her that she still had another boy' (Barrie, cited by Birkin: 4). After a silence,

> I heard a listless voice that had never been listless before say, 'Is that you?' I think the tone hurt me, for I made no answer, and then the voice said more anxiously 'Is that you?' again. I thought it was the dead boy she was speaking to, and I said in a little lonely voice, 'No, it's no' him, it's just me.' Then I heard a cry, and my mother turned in bed, and though it was dark I knew that she was holding out her arms.
> After that I sat a great deal in her bed trying to make her forget him. […] At first, they say, I was often jealous, stopping her fond memories with the cry, 'Do you mind nothing about me?' but that did not last; its place was taken by an intense desire […] to become so like him that even my mother should not see the difference, and many and artful were the questions I put to that end. Then I practised in secret, but after a whole week had passed I was still rather like myself. (Barrie, cited Birkin: 4–5)

'Long ago', Peter Pan tells Wendy, 'I thought like you that my mother would always keep the window open for me; so I stayed away for moons and moons and moons, and then flew back; but the window was barred, for mother had forgotten all about me, and there was another little boy sleeping in my bed' (Barrie: 102). The most interesting thing about this fantasy is its doubled revenge: he is telling the story from the viewpoint of the lost elder brother trying to return, while his younger self is the substitute in the mother's arms for whom window bars are put up to exclude any rival, old or new.

Rainer Maria Rilke was also a replacement child. He was born prematurely in 1875 to parents who had lost a daughter the year before, soon after birth. Christened René, he was renamed Rainer only years later by Lou Andreas-Salomé. In fact, it has been noted (by Maurice Porot) that the name René [reborn] is more than averagely common among replacement children: not only Rilke but a series in the families of Chateaubriand and film-maker René Féret. Some children whose sex differs from that of the dead sibling are called by gender-neutral names (in French, Camille or Dominique), others are given equivalents – a Lauro born after his sister Laura died, a Jacques after a Jacqueline, et cetera. And the many famous cases – add in Van Gogh, Beethoven, Stendhal, Hesse, Althusser, Marie Cardinal and the mother of artist Molly Parkin, who was the 'only one of twelve to survive' early childhood (Parkin 2011) – include a penumbra of cases that seem similar enough to merit the term: a daughter expected to 'replace' a war hero uncle; babies conceived while barely older siblings lie dying in hospital, forcing an impossible choice on the pregnant mother; Philip K. Dick who survived his baby twin sister but had to see his small grave waiting beside hers.[2] And what of pregnancies that follow miscarriages or the IVF attempts that precede a final success? Who, in the last analysis, is not a replacement child?

It is often the doctor who advises the mother to get pregnant again 'to take her mind off things' (Cain and Cain: 445), though nurses may be more sensitive to the consequences of this doubling: 'poor child, he's already been replaced' (Porot: 120). But such women are what André Green cruelly calls 'the dead mother' (247*ff*) – a woman so reduced by a personal loss that her child sees her as an unforgivably blank space or empty mirror. One family discussed in an article of 1964 'initially went to adoption agencies after their loss, requesting an eight-year-old, thin, blue-eyed, blond boy to replace their dead eight-year-old, thin, blue-eyed, blond boy' (Cain and Cain: 445) – Haley Joel Osment perhaps?[3]

The story of this painful circuit between loss and new life is told, in the main, by the surviving child, not the dead one, of course, nor the living parents. But when someone forms a new partnership, leaving behind a past love, all of them generally coexist. We have all probably been both in the situation of replacing and in that of being replaced – sometimes in relation to the same beloved. Serial monogamy leaves a lot of buried (if not dead) bodies behind. I want to begin with three fictional examples, which all involve a kind of disinterring. The first is a man who is thought dead but who has in fact survived, beginning by climbing out from under a heap of corpses: Balzac's Colonel Chabert (1832). This is what a character from Javier Marias' *The Infatuations* (2011) says of him: 'For the person who returns, there is no greater misfortune than to discover that he is surplus to requirements, that his presence isn't wanted, that he is disturbing the universe, that he constitutes a hindrance to his loved ones, who don't know what to do with him' (132).

So, in the end, Chabert promises his wife he will go underground again, and effectively ends up doing so; for around this possibility of the return of the presumed-dead there are always unseemly conspiracies, whether on the part of the returnees – consider the recent BBC-TV series *The Missing* or true-story film *The Imposter* (2013) – or that of those who remain. The law is invoked and someone is punished, like the false Martin Guerre who made his wife so much happier than the real one; or Orpheus, who preempts the colonel by going down to Hades to bring his wife back.

We all know what happens to him; but here is Rilke's particularly poignant version.

We are inside the veins of the earth. In front strides the man with the lyre; behind him, he trusts, is the god of messages, and with him the dead beloved. And then:

> Und als plötzlich jäh
> der Gott sie anhielt und mit Schmerz im Ausruf
> die Worte sprach: Er hat sich umgewendet –,
> begriff sie nichts und sagte leise: *Wer?*
>
> Fern aber, dunkel vor dem klaren Ausgang,
> stand irgend jemand, dessen Angesicht
> nicht zu erkennen war. (Rilke: 70)
>
>> [And as suddenly, sharply
>> the god stopped her and with painful voice
>> spoke the words: 'He has turned round' –,
>> she grasped nothing and said softly 'Who?'
>>
>> But far off, dark before the bright way out,
>> stood someone or other, whose countenance
>> could not be recognised.]

Here we see the effect on the one who still loves of being seen blankly (as Green would put it) by the beloved who is no longer of their world. Nothing left for Orpheus but to be torn apart and scattered in his turn.

In 1854, Victor Hugo wrote two poems about undead children: the first, 'Le revenant' [The revenant], written in August, features a newborn replacement child who whispers to its distraught mother: 'C'est moi. Ne le dis pas' [It's me. Don't tell anyone] (180). Hugo, who changed many dates to reflect when the bright or gloomy poems of *Les Contemplations* (1856) 'should have' been written, labelled it 1843, the year his beloved daughter Léopoldine died on her honeymoon. The second poem, written in November 1854 and correctly dated, turns the lost daughter into Persephone, imprisoned for ever in the brain of the poet Hades, where 'elle rêve dans sa nuit' [she dreams in his night] (320) as one of his lines of poetry. Like Virgil's Eurydice – and many another unfortunate beloved of male Romantic writers – she is preserved forever in literary aspic and, to cite a title of Gide's, 'et nunc manet in te' [and now she remains only in you'] (Virgil: 87).[4]

The first love may remain preserved and interred in his head or heart, like the Katya of *45 Years*. Or, like Maxim de Winter, he may have hated and done away with her, or wished to. The second wife resents having to be friends with the children of the first wife; the latter blames her own inability to replace on the ease with which he has. Are these two the real *dramatis personae* in what appears to be his knight's move to a new start? According to René Girard, what appears to be a *corps-à-corps* between an embracing couple is really something more visceral between the rivals fighting over her.[5] All we can be sure of is the baleful persistence of memory in the shock of betrayal and survival.

Notes

1. Benjamin's term was not 'reproduction', of course, but 'Reproduzierbarkeit' [reproducability], since the issue is the potential rather than the actualisation.
2. I am indebted to Roger Luckhurst for this piece of information, and to Katia Pizzi for the 'Lauro' story.
3. I refer to Spielberg's *A. I.* (2001) in which a couple whose son lies in a coma hire a child robot programmed to love them; half-Pinocchio half-Oedipus, little David ends up abandoned in a forest when the 'real boy' wakes up.
4. Gide's 'Et nunc manet in te' is a tribute to his late wife, written simultaneously with a cruising diary during a trip to Egypt in 1939.
5. Girard: 15–67; Girard's theory of triangular desire is taken up by Sedgwick: 21–25; and both are critiqued in Segal 1986: xi–xii, Segal 1988: 205 and Segal 1992: 59, in which I argue that Freud's Oedipus complex and theory of smut clearly show that the woman is the shared target of the men's murderous passion after all.

References

Balzac, Honoré de, 1964 [1832], *Le Colonel Chabert* (Paris: Livre de Poche)
Benjamin, Walter, 1963 [1936], 'Das Kunstwerk im Zeitalter seiner technischen Reproduzierbarkeit' (Frankfurt am Main: Suhrkamp)
Benjamin, Walter, 1970, 'The work of art in the age of mechanical reproduction', tr. Harry Zohn (London & Glasgow: Jonathan Cape)
Borges, Jorge Luis, 1975 [1946], 'Of Exactitude in Science' in *A Universal History of Infamy*, tr. Norman Thomas de Giovanni (Harmondsworth: Penguin), 131
Cain, Albert C. and Barbara S. Cain, 1964, 'On replacing a child', in *Journal of the American Academy of Child & Adolescent Psychiatry* vol 3: 3, 443–456

Carroll, Lewis, 1939 [1893], *The Complete Works* (London: Nonesuch)
Chanan, Ben, dir., 2016, *The Missing* (BBC TV)
Darrieussecq, Marie, 2010, *Rapport de police* (Paris: P. O. L.)
Dalí, Salvador, 1973, *Comment on devient Dali* [sic], as told to André Parinaud (Paris: Robert Laffont)
Du Maurier, Daphne, 2003 [1938], *Rebecca* (London: Virago)
Eco, Umberto, 1998 [1982], 'On the impossibility of drawing a map of the empire on a scale of 1 to 1', in *'How to travel with a salmon' & other essays*, tr. William Weaver (London: Vintage), 84–94
Gide, André, 2001 [1954], 'Et nunc manet in te', repr. in *Souvenirs et voyages*, ed. Pierre Masson *et al.*, 935–977
Girard, René, 1961, *Mensonge romantique et vérité romanesque* (Paris: Grasset)
Graham, Joseph F., ed., 1985, *Difference in Translation* (Cornell University Press, Ithaca and London)
Green, André, 2007 [1983], 'La mère morte', in *Narcissisme de vie, narcissisme de mort* (Paris: Minuit)
Hugo, Victor, 1969 [1856], *Les Contemplations*, ed. Léon Cellier (Paris: Garnier)
Lacan, Jacques, 1975 [1932], *De la psychose paranoïaque dans ses rapports avec la personnalité* (Paris: Seuil)
Layton, Bart, dir., 2013, *The Imposter*
Lejeune, Philippe, 1996 [1975], *Le Pacte autobiographique* (Paris: Seuil)
Marías, Javier, 2014 [2011], *The Infatuations*, tr. Margaret Jull Costa (Harmondsworth: Penguin)
Plaut, W. Gunther, 1981, *The Torah: A Modern Commentary* (New York: Union of Hebrew Congregations)
Porot, Maurice, 2014 [1993], *L'enfant de remplacement* (Paris: Frison-Roche)
Rilke, Rainer Maria, 1907, 'Orpheus. Eurydike. Hermes', *Neue Gedichte* (Frankfurt am Main: Insel), 67–71
Sabbadini, Andrea, 1988, 'The replacement child', *Contemporary Psychoanalysis* vol 24, 528–547
Sedgwick, Eve Kosofsky, 1985, *Between Men* (New York: Columbia University Press)
Segal, Naomi, 1986, *The Unintended Reader: feminism and Manon Lescaut* (Cambridge: Cambridge University Press)
Segal, Naomi, 1988, *Narcissus and Echo: women in the French récit* (Manchester: Manchester University Press)
Segal, Naomi, 1992, *The Adulteress's Child: authorship & desire in the nineteenth-century novel* (Cambridge: Polity Press)
Spielberg, Steven, dir., 2001, *A. I. Artificial Intelligence*
Virgil, 1916, *Culex*, in 'The Minor poems of Vergil' (Birmingham: Cornish Bros.), 79–92

CHAPTER 3

Replacement mothers, bedtricks and daughters out of place

Jean Owen

Incest is always a riddle of replacement as one family member replaces another in what theologian Hector Davies Morgan referred to in 1826 as 'a strange confusion of kinship' (201). In vertical paradigms of incest, one parent has to be removed so that the child can replace her or him as spouse to the remaining parent. For instance, in the ancient story Freud used as a model for son–mother incest, Oedipus unwittingly replaces his father as his mother's husband via an act of parricide. Similarly, in incest narratives concerning daughters and their fathers, the mother is rendered absent so that the daughter, in taking her place as wife to the father, becomes – to borrow from Mary Douglas – 'matter out of place'.[1] In this chapter, I present three daughter figures from folktale, biblical narrative and Graeco-Roman myth who are of marriageable age, however that is defined historically, and who become bound up in incestuous ties with their fathers following the absence of their mothers.

In Jacques Demy's musical fairytale film *Peau d'Âne* (1970), the only female that can possibly replace the dead wife for the grieving king is their daughter, who happens to be a replica of her mother. This doubling of

J. Owen (✉)
Independent Researcher, London, UK

© The Author(s) 2018
J. Owen, N. Segal (eds.), *On Replacement*,
https://doi.org/10.1007/978-3-319-76011-7_3

mother and daughter is, for Otto Rank, 'typical of the whole father–daughter [incest] complex' (311) and is something Demy exploits to the full, since Catherine Deneuve plays both mother and daughter. In this film, there really is no way of knowing where the mother ends and the daughter begins; there is no difference, no separation of identity. Demy's film is based on 'Donkeyskin'-type folktales dealing with father-led incest, of which there are many variants, each differing only by the kind of animal skin the daughter is compelled to wear and is thus named after.[2] The plot is as follows.

A king promises his dying wife that after her death he will marry only a woman as beautiful as she. In order to fulfil his promise, he searches far and wide for a new wife, only to conclude that the true bride is right under his nose. Following instructions from her godmother, and in an attempt to thwart her father's incestuous attempts, the horrified princess requests a series of ostensibly impossible wedding gifts: three dresses and the skin of a magic donkey that excretes gold, the source of his kingdom's wealth. The king has the donkey killed and presents its skin to the princess, which provides her with a temporary disguise and a new name – Peau d'âne [Donkey skin] – as she takes flight. She finds menial work in a neighbouring kingdom. The prince of that kingdom espies her and falls in love with her. The rest follows the pattern of the familiar Cinderella plot, ending with a wedding at which daughter and father are reconciled.

Peau d'âne's mother dies of a mysterious illness while still in her prime and very beautiful, but not before condemning father and daughter to potential incest in a typical spousal deathbed scene – a deathbed trick, if you will – that marks transgressive tales of this type. The conversation focuses on the queen's dying wish that the distraught king should remarry after her death. While the daughter is the unspoken element during the exchange between her parents, the mother nonetheless condemns her through the caveat: 'you must marry someone as beautiful as me'. As Marina Warner comments: 'The dying queen's demand that her husband should never marry anyone who is not like her in beauty and goodness itself constitutes a riddle: this Other he can marry must be like her. The only figure who can collapse this contradiction is the forbidden daughter, [a] solution [that] cannot be proposed' (331–332). Yet this is precisely what the mother is proposing in *Peau d'âne*. The spousal deathbed trick is the event that incites a father's incestuous desire. The mother's death also signals her daughter's sexual awakening. The mother must be displaced from the bed the daughter will go on to occupy – as wife to the widowed king – if these parents get their way.

In this tale of a mother's instigation of what I categorise as father-led incest, the mother and daughter are never placed together. In fact, the queen is never positioned in the role of mother. Instead, Peau d'âne spends much of her time with that staple of fairytale mother replacements, the godmother. In Demy's film, this is the Lilac Fairy (Delphine Seyrig). As Warner and others have commented, mother figures are often split into two types: 'bad' and 'good', or idealised (see also Gilbert and Gubar 1979). Peau d'âne's dead mother is 'bad' for dying and 'bad' for condemning her daughter to incest, while the 'good' mother is a confidante, who advises the daughter on how she might escape the dead mother's incestuous curse. In seeing in his daughter a replica of his wife, the king becomes a blocking figure, temporarily thwarting what Jack Zipes would call the daughter's 'saga of maturation' (204). Fortunately, Peau d'âne scuppers her father's incestuous plans as she takes flight from his palace in a donkey-skin disguise and ends up as a scullion in what will become her replacement kingdom. At the end of these tale types, we are left with a nasty feeling that the cycle of replacement is about to begin again.

In father-led incest narratives, the daughter does not want to take her mother's place as wife to the father; it is the parents who are putting her in this precarious position since the king must keep his deathbed promise. In Demy's film, there is a comic Freudian moment when the King's scholarly advisor (Georges Adet) tells the lovestruck king that it is normal for daughters to want to marry their fathers, even though it is clear in this case that Peau d'âne does not want to marry hers. However, what of those narrative instances when the advisor is right?

Consider the following situations:

1. Supposing three humans, two sisters and their father, believe themselves to be the only survivors of a divinely inspired catastrophe that has destroyed their city. They take the imperative: 'Thou shalt not commit incest' seriously. Eventually they die. There are no more humans. The imperative, it appears, was a mistake.[3]
2. Supposing three humans, two sisters and their father, believe themselves to be the only survivors of a divinely inspired catastrophe that has destroyed their city. They take the imperative: 'Go forth and multiply' seriously. The human race continues. The imperative, it appears, was a success.

The second hypothesis refers to the story of Lot and his daughters, one of the earliest narratives of daughter-led incest, as told in Genesis 18.
Now consider another situation:

3. A daughter initiates a sexual relationship with her father, but he is ignorant of her true identity. After many nights, he discovers who she is and tries to kill her, but the girl runs away. The gods transform her into a tree, from whom a son is born.

The third hypothesis is based on a myth from ancient Paphos and concerns Myrrha, mother of Adonis, and their father Cinyras. While there are extant fragments of this transgressive tale, it is to be found most fully rendered in Book X of *Metamorphoses* by the Roman poet Ovid (Book X, ll. 298–518). Like *Peau d'âne*, the story of Lot and his daughters and the story of Myrrha also consider incest between daughters of marriageable age and their fathers, but with a very different emphasis: while Peau d'âne is subject to father-led incest, Lot's daughters and Myrrha initiate a trajectory that is distinctly daughter-led, given that the daughter is the perpetrator. Unlike in *Peau d'âne*, it is not made clear from either of these narratives whether the daughters resemble their mothers (although family resemblances may be assumed). While these daughters do not go on to marry their fathers in the traditional sense, each replaces her mother as wife to the father via the bedtrick, which, as one would suppose, involves having sex with someone you mistake for someone else, either by design or accident.[4]

The brief and fragmented story of Lot and his family interweaves the larger genealogy of Abraham and his descendants, where Lot – Abraham's nephew – is seen only in relation to the heroic uncle until the destruction of Sodom, when he comes centre stage in a narrative marked by several transgressive episodes. The first is the attempted rape by the men of Sodom of Lot's guests, angels sent from the Lord to warn them of the impending destruction of the cities of the plain. Lot tries to appease the mob by offering up his daughters in lieu of the guests. This startling moment of replacement suggests that Lot's daughters are being treated as extensions of male bodies, just as later in the cave, they reverse the scenario to become extensions of their mother's body.

The second transgression in the Lot saga concerns the fate of Lot's wife. The angels have told Lot and his family not to look back at Sodom until they reach the mountains. Lot's wife disobeys the instruction and so, as 'bad wife and mother', she is turned into a pillar of salt. The third transgression in this complicated narrative is the incest scene. Lot has taken his daughters to Zoar, the only town left after the destruction of the cities. Unable to settle there, the trio heads for a cave in the mountains. Here is the episode from Genesis:

> And the older one said to the younger, 'Our father is old, and there is not a man on earth to consort with us in the way of all the world. Come, let us make our father drink wine, and let us lie with him, that we may maintain life through our father.' That night they made their father drink wine, and the older one went in and lay with her father; he did not know when she lay down or when she rose. The next day the older one said to the younger, 'See, I lay with Father last night; let us make him drink wine tonight also, and you go and lie with him, that we may maintain life through our father.' That night also they made their father drink wine, and the younger one went and lay with him; he did not know when she lay down or when she rose. (Berlin and Brettler: 39)

During this brief episode, Lot ceases to be 'Lot' and becomes, instead, 'father' – a term that is used eight times. This appellative shift serves to intensify the incestuous transgression against the father. The women, of course, are referred to by their assigned roles – wife and daughters. The elder daughter organises two bedtricks – of which, the narrative is clear, Lot remains ignorant – and the trio embarks on a riddle of replacement that violates all familial arrangements: the elder daughter replaces her mother with the father, then the younger daughter enacts a double replacement by standing in for both wife and first daughter until all family roles collapse into an incestuous heap. In this post-apocalyptic cave, where daughters and father are at once incestuous and pseudo-polygamous, what Arundhati Roy's narrator of *The God of Small Things* (1997) calls 'the love laws, that determine who we can love, and how' (33) simply do not apply. Equally, if proper names provide boundaries, these daughters, without names of their own, become extensions of each other as much as their bodies are extensions of the absent mother-wife's body. They are interchangeable, distinguished only slightly by a marker in age, the elder, as expected, calling the shots. Recognising that she must replace Lot's wife in order to become a mother, she is the only one with a speech-act that, on the one hand, puts her in the role of 'mother' to her younger sister and, on the other, ensures sisterly collusion. It is telling that they are never called sisters: they are only ever Lot's daughters, duty bound to carry on the bloodline after the destruction of their city, and thus properly patriarchal or what Sandra M. Gilbert would call 'instruments of culture' (1989: 262), but with the terms of exogamous exchange turned on their head. In other words, their incest-acts are motivated by a sense of duty and not by desire and the pursuit of pleasure, as Myrrha's is.

The episode ends with two pregnancies and the subsequent birth of two sons. While Lot's paternalism and masculinity have been undermined by his daughters' incestuous initiative, it is reestablished in part when he is restored to his proper name to become the father (and grandfather) of sons who go on to be founders of two nations, the Moabites and Ammonites. This strange story is about Lot's lineage, his generational succession. As for his wife and daughters, they do not need names: they simply turn up, seemingly out of nowhere, when required. What the Lot narrative does not tell us is what happens to the daughters after the cave. This is because it does not matter; with their duty done, they simply disappear as quickly as they appeared, while Lot's Wife is remembered as a feature of the landscape hovering above the Dead Sea.

Significantly, it is the incest-fuelled Myrrha who spells out the riddle of replacement in Ovid's rendering of the myth:

> But can you, impious girl, hope for something further,
> and not understand how many rights and names you are confounding?
> Will you be both the supplanter of your mother and an adulteress with your father?
> Will you be called the sister of your son and mother of your brother?
> (ll. 345–348)

As with many of his heroines, Ovid shows Myrrha to be a clever if confused daughter who, in these few lines, points to the thin boundary between adultery and incest in these riddles of replacement.

Here is an outline of the Ovidian narrative: Myrrha is the only daughter of the king of Paphos and is supposed to be finding a husband. She has the choice of any man among the nobles milling about the palace; instead she falls for her father, Cinyras. Unable to deal with her unlawful passion, Myrrha attempts suicide by hanging but is rescued by her old nurse, who coaxes the secret from her and promises to help.

It is the annual festival of Ceres and married women, including Myrrha's mother Cenchreis, are required to be away from the conjugal bed for nine nights. This gives the nurse an opportunity to approach an inebriated Cinyras and inform him of a girl in the palace who is enamoured of him. When Cinyras discovers the mysterious girl is Myrrha's age, he tells the nurse to bring her to his bedroom that night. The nurse guides Myrrha, who is disguised as a concubine, to her father. They have sex for nine consecutive nights until the curious king uses a lamp to discover the identity of his secret lover. He is shocked and appalled to learn that the stranger is none other than his own daughter. Drawing a sword, he tries to kill her. But Myrrha escapes. For nine months she is on the run until, utterly exhausted, she begs the gods to release her from her shame. The gods oblige and transform her into a myrrh tree. Soon after, the bark cracks open and Adonis is born. The resin that drips perpetually from the bark of the tree is said to be Myrrha's tears.

As in *Peau d'âne*, there is never a scene with mother and daughter together. In fact, we never get to meet Myrrha's mother, who is safely absent at a religious festival. Instead, Myrrha, too, has a replacement mother – her erstwhile wet-nurse. In some ways, Peau d'âne's godmother and Myrrha's nurse are mirror images, acting as confidantes in lieu of the real mother, a situation which has not been unusual historically. Yet in Myrrha's case, it is the absent mother who represents the good, while the replacement mother – the nurse – comes to represent the bad: though she saves Myrrha from suicide and comforts her, when she hears how much Myrrha envies her real mother's choice of husband, in spite of her horror, she is intent on helping fulfil the incestuous fantasy.

I have already referred to the deathbed trick the mother plays on Peau d'âne and her father. Wendy Doniger draws attention to the motif of drunkenness as a stock prop for the incestuous bedtrick (391). Like Lot, Myrrha's father is drunk – inebriation, of course, absolving both fathers of incestuous guilt. In Myrrha's story, the incest-as-bedtrick motif also involves impersonation and deception in order to effect replacement. The indulgent nurse brings Myrrha to her father's bed, not as daughter, or even wife, but under a replacement name and a replacement identity: she is now a courtesan, not a princess, which brings to mind Peau d'âne's temporary and downgraded disguise as an animal-girl.

Unlike the cave in the Lot episode, it can be assumed that the conjugal bed in Ovid's rendering of 'Myrrha' is also the bed where the daughter was conceived (and probably born). In other words, the site of incest is also the site of her origins. Here is the incest scene from Ovid:

> The father takes his own flesh in his lewd bed
> and relieves her maiden's fright and urges her fears away.
> Perhaps too he said 'Daughter', a word to suit her age,
> and she said 'Father', so that the words would not be missing from the crime.
> Full of her father, she withdrew from his bed bearing his impious
> seed in her dread womb, and carrying the wickedness she had conceived. (ll. 465–470)

As in the biblical narrative, the motif of nomenclature dominates this episode: Myrrha and Cinyras address each other by their allotted family titles, one of them knowingly, which, Ovid's narrator implies, adds to her thrill. Again, the textual effect creates a doubling that confounds and collapses all familial roles, as language itself becomes complicit in the incest-act. Moreover, while their desire is sharpened by the use of family names, the usual Ovidian shudder of dread is intensified by Cinyras' apparent unawareness of the congruity between the incest-act and the choice of words the narrator assigns to him. Interestingly, Myrrha has avoided using the term father until this most telling moment, instead favouring his given name, Cinyras, which actually serves to distance him as her father, and thus enables her to look upon him as her mother might.

While Lot's daughters fall pregnant after one night – which is quite a feat for an old and inebriated man – Myrrha returns to the site of incest for nine consecutive nights before the recognition scene, which coincides with the end of the festival, when Myrrha's mother is due to return to her rightful place in the nuptial bed. We can only guess at her reaction to this homecoming!

As these examples show, the absent mother is a prerequisite for vertical incest between daughters and their fathers. In Demy's *Peau d'Âne*, as in the more folkloric versions of 'Donkeyskin', even though the heroine escapes her mother's curse and her father's clutches (and indeed separates from him), there is no real sense that the daughter ever truly separates from the mother. Instead, she becomes an extension, continuing where the dead mother left off, albeit in another – that is, a replacement – kingdom. In daughter-led incest narratives, the daughter has to (in the case of Lot's daughters) or wants to (as with Myrrha) take the mother's place, not 'as mother', but as wife to her mother's husband in the nuptial bed. In Lot's saga, the daughters go on to replace their mother as mothers in order to ensure the continuity of Lot's lineage, though it is here that their tale ends. Myrrha's fate is to be transformed into a tree. Lucina, goddess of childbirth, aids in the delivery of Adonis and then quickly places the baby with Aphrodite, the replacement mother-goddess (who will later become his lover).

In some respects Myrrha is akin to Lot's wife, when she becomes a feature of the landscape and is remembered through the tree that bears her name. And, according to Ovid, she has a lineage – Cinyras is the grandson of Pygmalion, famous for sculpting his own wife-replacement. On the other hand, and this is one of the major differences between the biblical and mythic narrative types, in Myrrha incestuous replacement causes the family lineage to die out, as Myrrha's son and brother Adonis also comes to an abrupt and metamorphic end.

NOTES

1. In fact, Mary Douglas does not claim to have originated this phrase. In *Purity and Danger*, she refers to 'the old idea of dirt as matter out of place' (44). I am grateful to Naomi Segal for informing me of Freud's earlier mention of this idea; in 'Character and anal erotism' (1908) he cites in English: 'Dirt is matter in the wrong place' (Freud 2001: 172–173).
2. Marian Roalfe Cox endeavours to classify the folktale Cinderella by comparing the narrative across a range of cultures and categorising similarities to end up with three groups, as the title of the book emphasises. *Peau d'Âne* [Donkeyskin] belongs to the 'Catskin' category.
3. I have borrowed the first situation from Fox 1983: 3. The other scenarios (2 and 3) are my own.
4. Doniger (2000) posits two scenarios for the bedtrick: impersonation, in which someone pretends to be another in order to copulate, which is Myrrha's situation; and substitution, in which a replacement takes the place of the expected bedfellow, as in the biblical story of sisters Leah and Rachel, the daughters of Laban and wives of Jacob.

REFERENCES

Berlin, Adele & Marc Zvi Brettler, eds, 2014 [2004], *The Jewish Study Bible: Torah Nevi'im Kethuvim* (Oxford: Oxford University Press)

Cox, Marian Roalfe, 1893, *Cinderella: Three Hundred and Forty-Five Variants of Cinderella, Catskin, and Cap O'Rushes* (London: David Nutt)

Demy, Jacques, dir., 1970, *Peau d'Âne*

Doniger, Wendy, 2000, *The Bedtrick: Tales of Sex and Masquerade* (Chicago and London: University of Chicago Press)

Douglas, Mary, 2006 [1966], *Purity and Danger: An Analysis of the Concepts of Pollution and Taboo* (London and New York: Routledge)

Fox, Robin, 1983, *The Red Lamp of Incest: an Inquiry into the Origins of Mind and Society* (Notre Dame, Indiana: University of Notre Dame Press)

Freud, Sigmund, 2001 [1959], 'Character and anal erotism' (1908), in *Complete Psychological Works of Sigmund Freud, Jensen's 'Gradiva' and Other Works*, ed. & tr. James Strachey, vol IX (London: Vintage)

Gilbert, Sandra M. & Susan Gubar, 1979, *The Madwoman in the Attic: The Women Writer and the Nineteenth-Century Literary Imagination* (New Haven: Yale University Press)

Gilbert, Sandra M., 1989, 'Life's Empty Pack: Notes toward a Literary Daughteronomy', in *Daughters and Fathers*, ed. Lynda E. Boose and Betty S. Flowers (Baltimore & London: Johns Hopkins University Press)

Morgan, Hector Davies, 1826, *The doctrine of law and marriage, adultery, and divorce: exhibiting a theological and practical view* (Oxford, England: J. Parker et al)

Ovid, 1999, *Metamorphoses IX-XII*, tr. D. E. Hill (Warminster: Aris & Phillips)

Rank, Otto, 1992, *The Incest Theme in Literature and Legend: Fundamentals of a Psychology of Literary Creation*[*Das Inzest-Motiv in Dichtung und Sage: Grundzüge einer Psychologie des dichterischen Schaffens*, 1912], tr. Gregory C. Richter (Baltimore & London: Johns Hopkins University Press)

Roy, Arundhati, 1997, *The God of Small Things* (London: Flamingo)

Warner, Marina, 1995, *From the Beast to the Blonde: On Fairy Tales and their Tellers* (London: Vintage)

Zipes, Jack, 1989, *Don't Bet on the Prince* (New York: Routledge)

CHAPTER 4

Replacement, renewal and redundancy

James Brown

Sailing into New York in 1831, Alexis de Tocqueville glanced up at the houses overlooking the estuary, and the aristocrat in him was pleased to note marble buildings conforming to the principles of classical architecture:

> When I arrived for the first time at New York, by that part of the Atlantic Ocean which is called the East River, I was surprised to perceive along the shore, at some distance from the city, a number of little palaces of white marble, several of which were of classic architecture. When I went the next day to inspect more closely one which had particularly attracted my notice, I found that its walls were of whitewashed brick, and its columns of painted wood. All the edifices that I had admired the night before were of the same kind. (II: 52)

Such haste to create immediate effect rather than to leave a legacy struck Tocqueville as indicative of something that came to trouble him about America. In many respects he admired what he found there. If

---

My thanks to Naomi Segal for painstaking editing and criticism, and to Sam Ashenden for invaluable comments and discussion at every stage of the chapter's evolution: pp. 37–41 are particularly indebted to her.

J. Brown (✉)
Birkbeck, University of London, London, UK

© The Author(s) 2018
J. Owen, N. Segal (eds.), *On Replacement*,
https://doi.org/10.1007/978-3-319-76011-7_4

'democracy' with its relentless drive to equalise had to come, arguably the Americans had found a better way of dealing with it than the French. However, he remained troubled by the way in which the Americans seemed prey to 'strange melancholy [...] in the midst of their abundance' (II: 139), by the racist and genocidal impulses of the still young republic, and by a short-termism which he associated with democratic individualism. Everyone was in a hurry to get what they wanted, because everything they wanted to achieve had to be accomplished and enjoyed in the span of a single lifetime, or, as Tocqueville put it, 'a native of the United States clings to this world's goods as if he were certain never to die; and he is so hasty in grasping at all within his reach that one would suppose he was constantly afraid of not living long enough to enjoy them' (II: 136). Not for these individualists the aristocratic willingness to plant trees for the enjoyment of great-grandchildren as yet unborn and unknown. The individualism of the Americans went along with an inner resistance to the possibility of being replaced. For the (male) aristocrat, by comparison, being replaced by one's children was the natural condition. No matter how egotistical, the aristocrat attached such importance to family that the idea of his own replacement immediately brought the consoling thought that this was the means by which the family renewed itself. In 'aristocratic nations',

> A man almost always knows his forefathers and respects them; he thinks he already sees his remote descendants and he loves them. He willingly imposes duties on himself towards the former and the latter, and he will frequently sacrifice his personal gratifications to those who went before and to those who will come after him. (II: 98)

The terms in which Tocqueville defines individualism have a bearing on people's vulnerability to replacement in democratic nations. He distinguishes it from mere selfishness or egotism. Egotism is, according to Tocqueville, an exorbitant and vicious feeling. Individualism, by comparison, 'is a mature and calm feeling, which disposes each member of the community to sever himself from the mass of his fellows and to draw apart with his family and friends' (II: 98). As Pierre Manent glosses it, Tocqueville's version of individualism 'is the characteristic of a society where each individual perceives himself as the basic unit of society, similar and equal to all other basic units' (Manent: 54). Individuals may be jealous of their independence, but they are also in certain respects more similar to each other (and therefore more readily replaceable by each other) than are people in aristocratic societies. Or, to be more precise, in Ernest Gellner's terms, modern individualism gives rise to what he calls 'modular man'. Gellner explains why and how 'modular man' is replaceable, starting by drawing a comparison between individuals in simple premodern societies, who are replaceable by each other because they are similar to each other:

> But modern modular man is not replaceable simply because he is so stubbornly similar, because he will only be a shepherd or peasant or whatever constitutes the normative calling of his culture. On the contrary, he is highly variable, not to say volatile, in his activities. He is modular because he is capable of performing highly diverse tasks in the same general cultural idiom, if necessary reading up manuals of specific jobs in the general standard style of the culture in question. (Gellner: 102)

Such individuals can be combined and recombined into complex organisations, not because they are the same as each other, but because they share a style of interaction. A common form for that shared style is a national culture, though one might also see some kinds of software giving rise to a generic literacy capable of application to divers specialist tasks. That shared cultural style has sometimes more pejoratively been regarded as an effect of commercially produced mass culture, which has been seen as tending to render people passive and conformist (see, for example, Adorno and Horkheimer: 94–136). But one needs to register that this enabling cultural uniformity goes along with high levels of division of labour. In Durkheimian parlance, we have to do here with societies of organic rather than mechanical solidarity – that is, ones in which people have different skills and abilities and therefore need one another, as opposed to ones in which people are bound together by their essential similarity (Durkheim: 31–87). To a significant degree, we *are* differentiated from each other (in specialised skills and knowledge, for example), and yet we are so fashioned that we are culturally and psychologically capable of slotting in and out of different organisations and contexts. Thus, we combine individual differentiation with replaceability.

The drive to certain kinds of normative equality, which Tocqueville sees as intrinsic to democracy, ensures that modern individuals are at once more disconnected from each other than individuals in aristocratic societies and yet more apt to gravitate towards commonly held opinions. In aristocratic societies people are likely to form bonds of personal loyalty with their immediate superiors and inferiors. By contrast, modern individuals are more likely to think of themselves as existing in a state of abstract formal equality in relation to each other, and this renders them liable to 'passive social levelling' (Hirst: 72). Ultimately, this modern individualism lands one in an existential plight. In Sheldon Wolin's words, it is 'a product of the disconnectedness inherent in a society of equals' and 'the institutionalization of Cartesian solitude as "each is forever being thrown back upon himself alone and is threatened with being shut up completely in the solitude of his own heart." The remaining link is interest' (Wolin: 216, citing Tocqueville II: 99). To the extent that people come to be linked, however tenuously, by interest, the terms on which they engage with each other will tend to be dominated by calculation, especially in economic affairs in which, in Georg Simmel's phrase, money 'becomes the common denominator of all values' (178). People may manifest their individualism in their manner of calculating their interests in their dealings with each other, but, to the extent that they become the *objects* of such calculation, they risk being caught up in a system in which they figure as substitutable means to the ends of others.

The idea of replacement promises renewal or threatens redundancy. Which of those options seems likelier is partly a matter of identity and partly a matter of individualism. If one's individualism is such that the replacement of oneself can only be seen as a threat, then redundancy (and American melancholia) is all the process has to offer. But if one identifies with something beyond oneself – a family, a nation, a tradition – then replacement may have something to recommend it.

Tocqueville uses the terms democracy and aristocracy in a distinctive and complex way. However, the broad move that he makes would become a common one in social theory: playing off the new against the old. The commonest form of this dualism remains tradition vs. modernity. It is a simple idea that has exerted extraordinary influence. Ferdinand Tönnies' 1887 book *Gemeinschaft und Gesellschaft* [*Community and Civil Society*] is, among the founding texts of modern sociology, perhaps the one that most clearly draws this contrast, even if it also complicates it. Tönnies distinguishes two kinds of social order: community, based on traditions, on cultural norms and on people identifying unselfconsciously with the larger community and with inherited norms so that, in effect, over time the normal expectation is that people replace each other in preestablished roles; and society, in which people experience themselves primarily as rationally self-interested individuals. This bold contrast, which dominates the first part of the book, is complicated by the way Tönnies sees these two kinds of social order as correlating to two kinds of capacity for choice, which may be actualised to different degrees in different circumstances (the kind that informs *Gesellschaft*, for example, is, according to Tönnies, more commonly to be found in cities than in villages, in men than in women, in adults than in children, and so on), but which are always possible. Though Tönnies distinguishes in this way two different kinds of psyche, he sees both types as always potentially existing in human beings. So, his model of historical process complicates his clear-cut contrast between modern *Gesellschaft* and traditional *Gemeinschaft*. Similar points might be made of the way in which Marx (on whose work Tönnies draws) contrasts feudalism with capitalism. *Gesellschaft*, like Marx's capitalism, is characterised in certain inevitable ways as depending on a deliberative, calculative and individualist rationality. Subsequent accounts would complicate this opposition of tradition and modernity without transcending or entirely abandoning it.

As Tocqueville implied, modernity is apt to intensify a self-regarding strain in individualism, and thus make it harder for people to see beyond the span of their own lives. The concept of 'career' as currently practised is an index of this. Many used to follow in their parents' footsteps. In an era in which much useful and practical knowledge was transmitted face to face, master to apprentice or parent to child, this was unsurprising. But as soon as there is a normal expectation that each individual should find a distinctive vocation and identity, we have a situation in which people are objectively more liable to be substitutable (this being the condition of a fluid labour market, which operates relatively independently of any need to reproduce and sustain a given set of social relations and norms), and subjectively more certain of their uniqueness and irreplaceability. Changing attitudes and practices regarding the value (monetary and otherwise) to be attached to children registers this sense of irreplaceability and the difficulty of squaring it with market economics as a system for establishing exchange or replacement value. Viviana Zelizer has argued that over the nineteenth and twentieth centuries, and especially the period 1870–1930, the nature of the relation between the economic and other kinds of value to be attached to children was transformed. Starting with middle-class children, in the USA children were increasingly removed from the labour market, with interesting implications for the price attached to them. Insurance for children in the 1870s sought merely to compensate parents for the loss of the child's labour but, as they left the labour market, the rationale for their insurance shifted by trying to attach monetary value to non-economic worth to do with the emotional or other intrinsic value of the child. The ironic result, as Zelizer notes, was that levels of compensation for accidents suffered by insured children rose as their practical *economic* value decreased (113–137). The paradox lies in the way a replacement economic value gets attached to irreplaceability; hence the title of Zelizer's book, *Pricing the Priceless Child*. This paradox also has implications for the way adults are to be valued. Adults, of course, do have a market value, as workers or property-owners, and systems exist to ensure they can be replaced in respect of these economic functions (through the labour market or by inheritance, sale, or other systems for the transfer of property). Yet at the same time we insist that each of us possesses a priceless essence (a notion one might derive from religious doctrines about the value of each soul – a value that might simply exist in quite a different domain from the economic), and increasingly also seek to have this pricelessness recognised in practical social and economic arrangements.

Another index of this situation is the relationship between romance, marriage and divorce, especially as it evolved over the twentieth century. The Second World War impinged on trends in marriage and divorce in the USA and the UK: in both countries divorce rates rose slowly until about the 1940s. Around 1945 they spiked, and then after the war they resumed their former steady upwards trend, but more rapidly than before. In the UK, since the early 1970s divorce rates have fallen, but that is because the marriage rate itself has diminished (Office of National Statistics 2016). There is a similar turning point in the USA around 1980 (see the table in Celello: 4). Our readiness to replace spouses or partners remains at historically unprecedented levels. This is partly because of increased life expectancy. It has resulted in a significant change in the normative and legal position regarding marriage and separation. The normative notion of marriage as permanent unto death, which was sufficient to taint divorce with shame until well into the twentieth century, has lost much of its force. Our romantic partners are legally more replaceable than they were a century ago. And yet many (perhaps most) of us still hope to offer and find fulfilment in a mutually faithful and monogamous relationship. The advent of no-fault divorce is one marker of the changing normative value attached to marriage. In the USA, California introduced no-fault divorce in 1969, while in the UK the Matrimonial Causes Act of 1973 in effect did the same. But the demand for individual fulfilment, while capable of getting people into exclusive romantic relationships (albeit less often than formerly into marriage) is just as capable of driving them out again to continue their quest for *the* perfect partner. Thus, interchangeability and a belief in the uniqueness of each individual paradoxically coexist.

There is a sociological reason for the coexistence of these seemingly incompatible things. As we have seen Gellner observe, modern labour markets aspire to a condition in which people are mobile and capable of slotting in and out of organisations as required. This ideal type of labour market attempts to remove people from the sustaining network of kinship and belonging that would otherwise make it difficult to treat them as atomised individuals (see Shoumatoff: 128–129, 136–138). One of the reasons why women's employment status has been anomalous in relation to these liberal ideals is that, even though kinship networks broke down in such a way as to liberate male sellers of labour from their supposed constraints, the nuclear family was often retained as a support system for the male breadwinner. So, a seemingly archaic subordination of the woman persisted within the nuclear family – archaic in that it was a subordination resulting from an *ascribed* status of a kind that ought to be incompatible with modern formal freedom and equality. Until well into the twentieth century a 'marriage bar' operated in many professions and its effect, besides excluding women from many fields of employment, was to enforce a gendered division of labour and power within marriage, and to discourage investment in women's education (see Hakim: 123–125). Beyond the nuclear family, however, people who had to live by selling their labour were increasingly disembedded from the defining contexts that might otherwise have sustained their sense of themselves and their role and meaning. The more these defining contexts break down, the more one needs an inner sense of individual selfhood, relatively immune from circumstance. Certain kinds of religion and then the cults of sensibility and Romanticism were among the things that furnished materials for this project. But it proved nowhere more pervasive and persuasive than in the way in which an ideal of romantic love that had once informed a marginal, elite code of courtly love – and which had remarkably little to do with the practical ways in which people actually married, reproduced, raised children and distributed property – became central to accepted notions of what marriage was all about (Solomon: 54–61).

Objectively, as contributors to modern economies, we should all be capable of resisting replacement. The division of labour ought, in principle, to ensure that each of us has some relatively scarce skill to offer to the market. But, quite apart from technological deskilling or the displacement of jobs from high- to low-wage economies, it could be said that we have absorbed the logic of a kind of substitutability into ourselves. There is a story of the violent encounter between a modern industrial and a preindustrial people that illustrates this. In the wars in which the Sioux confronted the forces of the USA, Chief Sitting Bull was troubled by the way the blue-coat soldiers reacted to the deaths of their fellows: 'When an Indian gets killed, the other Indians feel sorry and cry, and sometimes stop fighting. But when a white soldier gets killed, nobody cries, nobody cares; they go right on shooting and let him lie there' (Vestal: 61). Even though the soldiers came from a world that practised high levels of division of labour – and which might seem therefore objectively to differentiate and individuate its members – so far as behaviour on the battlefield went, what Sitting Bull noticed was that each of his warriors was individually valued, whereas the blue-coat soldiers appeared to be treated by their fellows as disposable. That may not have been how they regarded each other, but Sitting Bull's observation captures something about the form of modern life, which Simmel, thinking about the impact of the metropolis, put like this:

> the division of labour demands from the individual an ever more one-sided accomplishment, and the greatest advance in a one-sided pursuit only too frequently means dearth to the personality of the individual. In any case, he can cope less and less with the overgrowth of objective culture. The individual is reduced to a negligible quantity, perhaps less in his consciousness than in his practice and in the totality of his obscure emotional states that are derived from this practice. The individual has become a mere cog in an enormous organization of things and powers which tear from his hands all progress, spirituality, and value in order to transform them from their subjective form into the form of a purely objective life. (Simmel: 184)

Simmel's account of the impoverishment of the individual personality has been widely echoed by artists and social thinkers, notably in Weber's castigation of modernity as giving rise to 'specialists without spirit, sensualists without heart' (Weber: 182). The sense of being 'a mere cog in an enormous organization of things and powers' in which our collective productive and creative powers are externalised and confront each individual as other is worryingly familiar. That experience lies at the heart of Marx's criticism of the way capitalist production deprives workers of a satisfying creative relation with the objects they produce when those objects become industrial commodities. For Marx there is a double alienation at work:

> (1) The relation of the worker to the *product of labour* as an alien object exercising power over him. This relation is at the same time the relation to the sensuous external world, to the objects of nature, as an alien world inimically opposed to him. (2) The relation of labour to the *act of production* within the *labour* process. This relation is the relation of the worker to his own activity as an alien activity not belonging to him; it is activity as suffering, strength as weakness, begetting as emasculating, the worker's *own* physical and mental energy, his personal life – for what is life but activity? – as an activity which is turned against him, independent of him and not belonging to him. Here we have *self-estrangement*, as previously we had the estrangement of the *thing*. (Marx: 73)

Yet in one respect we continue to practise a different kind of production and, correspondingly, a different kind of (self-)replacement. Since modernity has not abolished death (even if its normative motives are often in denial of it) we still have to reproduce ourselves in order ultimately to replace ourselves. The incoherent attitude to death that Tocqueville noted in the USA is now widespread: we appear simultaneously to act as if in denial of mortality *and* as if suffering an excessive fear of it. Notwithstanding the formal and technical apparatus that now surrounds childbirth and education, the key business of producing new people and inducting them into their first language and into social life remains intensely personal. It is a process in which we do broadly the same things as each other, and yet in which we feel ourselves to be (like Sitting Bull's warriors) at our least replaceable – so much so that we are sometimes tempted to regard our children as extensions of ourselves rather than potentially autonomous beings, even though living in the face of mortality challenges us to identify with something beyond ourselves. The way in which we now attach value to children reflects how exceptional (and voluntary) reproduction has become for us. There is a tension between the spirit in which we approach biological reproduction and the spirit in which we approach other kinds of production necessary for our societies to reproduce themselves. In that tension one can see how difficult if unavoidable our self-replacement has become.

References

Celello, Kristin, 2009, *Making Marriage Work: a history of marriage and divorce in the twentieth-century United States* (Chapel Hill NC: University of North Carolina Press)

Durkheim, Emile, 1984 [1893], *The Division of Labour in Society*, tr. W. D. Halls (London: Macmillan)

Gellner, Ernest, 1996 [1994], *Conditions of Liberty: civil society and its rivals* (London: Penguin)

Hakim, Catherine, 2016 [2004], *Key Issues in Women's Work: female diversity and the polarisation of women's employment*, 2nd edn. (Abingdon: Routledge)

Hirst, Paul, 1997, *From Statism to Pluralism: democracy, civil society and global politics* (London: Routledge)

Manent, Pierre, 1996, *Tocqueville and the Nature of Democracy*, tr. John Waggoner (Lanham MD: Rowman and Littlefield)

Marx, Karl, 2007 [1932], *Economic and Philosophical Manuscripts of 1844* [a.k.a. the *Paris Manuscripts*], tr. Martin Milligan (Mineola NY: Dover Publications)

Office of National Statistics, 2016, 'Marriages in England and Wales: 2013', https://www.ons.gov.uk/peoplepopulationandcommunity/birthsdeathsandmarriages/marriagecohabitationandcivilpartnerships/bulletins/marriagesinenglandandwalesprovisional/2013, last accessed 22 Sep 2017

Shoumatoff, Alex, 1995, *The Mountain of Names: a history of the human family*, rev. edn. (New York: Kodansha)

Simmel, Georg, 1997 [1903], 'The Metropolis and Mental Life' in *Simmel on Culture*, eds. David Frisby and Mike Featherstone (London: Sage), 174–185

Solomon, Robert C, 2006 [1994], *About Love: Reinventing Romance for Our Times* (Indianapolis IN: Hackett)

Tocqueville, Alexis de, 1994 [1835/1840], *Democracy in America*, 2 vols bound as one, tr. Henry Reeve (London: Everyman)

Tönnies, Ferdinand, 2001 [1887, 1912], *Community and Civil Society*, ed. Jose Harris, tr. Jose Harris and Margaret Hollis (Cambridge: Cambridge University Press)

Vestal, Stanley, 1989 [1932], *Sitting Bull: Champion of the Sioux* (Norman OK: University of Oklahoma Press)

Weber, Max, 2003 [1905], *The Protestant Ethic and the Spirit of Capitalism*, tr. Talcott Parsons (Mineola NY: Dover Publications)

Wolin, Sheldon, 2001, *Tocqueville: Between Two Worlds: the making of a political and theoretical life* (Princeton NJ: Princeton University Press)

Zelizer, Viviana, 1985, *Pricing the Priceless Child. The Changing Social Value of Children* (Princeton NJ, Princeton University Press)

PART II

Lost children

CHAPTER 5

Lost boys in *Little Eyolf*

Olivia Noble Gunn

Henrik Ibsen's antepenultimate play, *Little Eyolf* (1894), presents readers with at least two orders of lost boys: the lame and drowned son who is lured by the Ratmaid to the depths; and 'all the naughty boys' who will take his place (Ibsen: 76).[1] Each in his own way, Peter Pan and Henrik Ibsen 'empt[y] the nursery' (Gilead: 286). Ibsen's characters also make plans to fill the nursery up, not by returning children once taken away – generation after generation, as in *Peter Pan* – but instead by offering nursery space to other occupants. After Alfred and Rita Allmers' nine-year-old son wanders off unnoticed and drowns, Rita invents a new identity for herself in an attempt to come to terms with her grief: that of philanthropic mother. Alfred has decided that they should part ways, and he asks Rita to tear down all the shacks by the waterfront, the homes of the poor boys who failed to save little Eyolf (even though, unlike him, they can swim). He conceives of this demolition project as a parting gift to his wife, a mission to fill Rita's life after both son and husband are gone. Rita, however, has another mission in mind. She tells Alfred, '[a]s soon as you have left me, I will go down to the shore and bring all the poor, abused children with me up to ours' (Ibsen: 76). Blamed and pitied, stolen and rescued, these anonymous naughty boys will, according to Rita, occupy the empty nursery rooms in *Little Eyolf.*

O. N. Gunn (✉)
University of Washington, Seattle, WA, USA

© The Author(s) 2018
J. Owen, N. Segal (eds.), *On Replacement*,
https://doi.org/10.1007/978-3-319-76011-7_5

47

This chapter approaches Ibsen's various orders of lost boys through comparison with James Barrie's *Peter Pan*. Like Peter, Eyolf is a neglected boy who will never grow up. Unlike Peter, Eyolf really dies (disappears from the world of the play), making him absent and irrecuperable – except in the stories that the adults tell about him. By means of stories, both boys become repositories for a certain understanding of childhood – innocence experienced as loss, estrangement and deferral. The replacement children and projects of *Little Eyolf* provide an opportunity to think about the seductive function of innocence; about adulteration and the work of mourning; about the perpetuation of neglect that can take place when the singularity of the dead is refused; and about the distinct trajectories of lost boys in the landscape of the play. These trajectories offset Alfred's and Rita's most explicit assertions regarding the direction of meaningful and ethical action. While the drowned son is lured down and dragged out, and Alfred's half-sister Asta – a lost boy of yet another order, a lost boy who never was a boy – leaves, the poor and naughty boys are to be used in a circle game of replacement that resists and reinstates the never in Never Land. *Little Eyolf* contains the vertical idealism and seaside-to-heights landscape common to several of Ibsen's works, in which the main characters search for ever-higher ground and an ever-higher calling; but it is also difficult in this play to tell up from down, surfacing from drowning. Thus, I argue, what Rita proposes is a secondary, figurative drowning in the bourgeois home. Lost boys neither go nor look up; they either go down and out, or round and round.

I shall begin by introducing my reasons for comparing *Little Eyolf* with *Peter Pan* (the 1928 version) and *Peter and Wendy* (1911). I shall then address the major replacement project in *Little Eyolf*. The chapter will conclude with a focus on Alfred's relationship with Asta (a sister who never was a sister, it turns out): although she is very likely a replacement child herself, Asta takes the place of the first lost boy in Ibsen's play.

Like all Ibsen's late plays, *Little Eyolf* asks us to take an interest in the effects of repetition and replacement, or supplementation. Habitual idealisation, however, encourages us to place the child outside or prior to the negative implications of replacement, forgetting that children are not just 'gay and innocent' but also 'heartless' (Barrie 1911: 217). In 'What is queer theory doing with the child?', Karín Lesnik-Oberstein and Stephen Thomson describe the child as a 'theoretical exile' and 'occasion of pathos' that '[drags] the dynamics of [the] narratives' in which it is found to a 'virtual standstill' (35–36). Eyolf is certainly an 'occasion of pathos' and a figure for drag, or the dynamic standstill caused by desire and repression. He is also an assignment, an excuse, a rat (to Peter's bird), a stranger and a dead end. Thus, he should enable us to think against our idealising habits – although this possibility has been largely overlooked in Ibsen criticism so far. Even those who emphasise the 'ironic underside' (Goldman: 105) of Rita's project exile the figure of the child. In 'Petrified Time: Ibsen's Responses to Modernity' (2003), for example, Frode Helland describes the project as a theft, in which the poor children are conceived of as mere placeholders: 'When all is petrified and near-dead, everything at the same [time] becomes fleetingly interchangeable – the one child can be in the other's place, they can all "take turns" at being Eyolf' (142). Despite his critique, Helland uses the project to define the child as 'the future, the new [...] change, transformation' (135). His metaphors imply that a child who does not guarantee a better future is less a child than a sign of adult blindness and failure:

> having children turns things around, negates the given in such a way that "past life" receives new meaning [...] Eyolf's appearance on the stage of life changed nothing. The child stayed invisible as such, the parents never saw its individuality and the legitimate demands for change on their part that the child constituted. (Helland: 140)

The question remains whether Helland himself sees the child's 'individuality', or whether he accepts an alternative form of not-seeing when he defines the child as constituting 'legitimate demands for change'. How might Peter – an exile himself, barred from the nursery, with 'another little boy sleeping in [his] bed' (Barrie 1995: 132) – aid us in bringing the child back into play, not only as an ideal or symbol of innocence, but also as a character strung out between originality and replacement, life and death, innocence and adulteration (like the rest of us)?

Both Ibsen's and Barrie's plays contain scenes of seduction and rely on fantasy. In 'Magic abjured: closure in children's fantasy fiction', Sarah Gilead analyses types of 'return-to-reality closural frame[s]', finding that *Peter and Wendy* 'acts in a tragic mode that reveals, without an assuring sense of mediation, both the seductive force and the dangerous potentiality of fantasy' (278). She defines Peter, 'like the other "lost boys"', as 'a victim of and an escape from adult reality in general and from parental neglect in particular' (Gilead: 286). 'Peter Breaks Through', seducing Wendy and taking all the Darling children away (Barrie 1911: 1): 'There are mermaids,

Wendy, with long tails' (Barrie 1995: 102). He returns them in the end (only to return again for Wendy's daughters), so that the fantasy world and its adventures are framed though not fully contained by a more realistic world. In its most realist aspects, *Little Eyolf* remains a play about fantasies that function as both life raft and undertow. Although it is certainly not a work of children's literature, it is both punctured by a non-realist character – the Pied Piper/werewolf figure of the Ratmaid – and sustained by its characters' fantasies of redemption and replacement. In *The Play of Melancholy* (2000), Helland asserts that the effect of the Ratmaid's entrance in *Little Eyolf* 'lies to be sure in the striking *break* with the reader's expectations of a realist drama' (253). This fantastical figure is summoned by all the characters in the first act; she appears to seduce Eyolf; her stories lure him too close to the water's edge. Significantly, both Eyolf and the Ratmaid belong to the first act of Ibsen's play, while the remaining two acts are dedicated to the early stages of grief and to the adult implications of childhood games. *Peter Pan* is a dramatic fantasy for children, which holds certain questions at bay, even as it evokes them: 'those questions about origins, sexuality and death' (Rose: 36). *Little Eyolf* is a late realist play, which stages its characters' wavering attempts to hold similar questions at bay.

Both *Little Eyolf* and *Peter Pan* are morbid works that recognise death and adulteration as at the heart of childhood. In common with Jacqueline Rose and other scholars invested in critiquing sentimental, hetero-teleological understandings of childhood, my chapter aims 'to make some contribution to the dismantling of [...] the ongoing sexual and political mystification of the child' (11). Moreover, I am interested in a particular form of singularity inaugurated by the death of an individual. Even if childhood is a category that asks us to 'look back', appearing in some cases to demand that we judge (regret and justify) our actions and our adultness, a dead child cannot, in fact, look back or demand redemption. That is, Eyolf can take no part in the work of mourning that his mother suggests is motivated by his 'large, open child's eyes' (Ibsen: 53). The bereavement process depicted in Ibsen's play thus evokes some of the inevitable ethical problems involved in telling stories on behalf of the dead. According to Gilead, with regard to *Peter Pan*, 'Peter's strategy is to short-circuit those species-serving systems that collaborate with nature's indifference toward the individual: socialization, marriage, the family [...] But that means taking the shorter route to the same end and enduring constant hauntings by the returned repressed, nicely imaged in Peter's haunting of the nurseries he has escaped' (286).

Death, too, is a species-serving system indifferent to the individual, but unlike Peter's habitation of the island, it provides an absolute limit to return. In Act Two, Alfred lingers by the fjord. The surface of the water both limits his access to the material evidence of loss (concealing the furious undertow that carries the body out and away) and signals the truth of material inaccessibility. Asta encourages him to turn his back, a necessary reprieve and a sign of unavoidable infidelity in mourning. When the play ends, Alfred joins Rita in the imagined repurposing of Eyolf's nurseries, a project that Helland reads as (inversely) authorising a normative understanding of the child as a figure for a better future. The notion of return or haunting that Alfred expresses in the final lines – his hope that they will receive a 'visitation of the spirits' or glimpses of loved ones 'opad' [above or upward] (Ibsen: 79) – is also a matter of socialisation, of coping with loss through a denial of the absolute limit of death. I propose that Alfred's fantasy of potential accessibility in the sky, as well as Rita's reanimation of Eyolf's eyes, involves a greater infidelity than Alfred's turning away from the fjord.

Ibsen kills *a child* – with the help of that child's parents and the Ratmaid – and allows the current to drag him out, in order to use *the child* as the pivot around which this family drama will continue to turn. Rita's replacement project, introduced in the third and final act of *Little Eyolf*, indicates that the poor children will be the (grateful?) recipients of her sudden philanthropic will. Alfred himself wonders what Rita will do with them, given that she is not temperamentally suited to the task. He is incredulous when she insists,

> RITA: I want to bring them here to me.
> ALFRED: *You* want that!
> RITA: Yes, I want that. From the day you leave, they will be here, all of them, – as if they were my own.
> ALFRED (*upset*): In our little Eyolf's place!
> RITA: Yes, in our little Eyolf's place. They'll get to live in Eyolf's rooms. They'll get to read his books. Get to play with his toys. They'll take turns sitting in his chair at the table. (Ibsen: 77)

These children are replacement children, a group of uncertain number but Rita will 'take' them all. A few lines later, she suggests that they could provide her with the means to self-fulfilment: the project will enable her to fill the empty space inside her with something 'that could resemble a kind of love' (77). Insisting that '[i]t isn't love that drives you to do this', Alfred enquires into Rita's true motivations, which include her desire to ingratiate herself with the (imagined) accusing eyes of her drowned son. Apparently moved or convinced by her honesty, Alfred asks if he can join her. As the play comes to a close, Rita and Alfred clearly view this project as a means of achieving higher ground. They will bring the poor children up and thereby get closer to the treetops and the stars, where glimpses of lost loved ones can perhaps be had. But, as Helland has argued, the text is rather explicit about the way in which these unnamed and unknown children are conceived of as mere placeholders. Although they will have access to more and nicer things than before, they cannot expect possessions or a place of their own. They must 'take turns' at the table, sitting in Eyolf's chair.

Little Eyolf thus contains the same kind of movement that Peter himself suggests: a loss or escape recouped through circularity and repression. Peter haunts the nurseries that he has escaped, returning to seduce Wendy's daughters; Eyolf goes down and his replacements will come up. While the Darling children follow Peter to Never Land 'like a flight of birds' (Barrie 1995: 104) and eventually return home with the lost boys, the poor children will enter Eyolf's empty nurseries like a plague of rats. In Act One, Rita insists that they do not have any need for the Ratmaid's services, ridding the house of 'something that gnaws and nibbles, – and creeps and crawls' (Ibsen: 17). But when the Ratmaid lures Eyolf to the water, he shares the fate of all the creepy crawlies that she has drowned, a task that she describes as a favour to 'the poor little ones, who are hated and hunted so fiercely' (13). Moreover, she suggests that she once played the seduction game with people – 'mostly one' (15–16), a beloved who now lies down in the deep with the rats and their babies. As mentioned, Alfred at first demands revenge on the poor children and their families, a demolition project to punish those who failed to help Eyolf. All the poor people who live by the water, the children as well as their mothers and fathers, 'will have to find some other place' (76). Is Rita's replacement project a gift or another form of revenge? In *When Wendy Grew Up: An Afterthought*, Wendy and her daughter Jane (whom Peter will soon fetch) discuss the fate of the lost boys, who have been sent to school and must now be grown like Wendy's brothers ('John has a beard now' and 'Michael is an engine driver'):

JANE: Did they ever wish they were back in the Never Never Land?
WENDY (*hesitating*): I – I don't know. (Barrie 1995: 158)

The goal of Rita's project is to 'soften – and improve' the 'livsskæbne' [life destinies or fortunes] (Ibsen: 78) of the boys, but Rita and Alfred neither hesitate on their behalf nor consider what they might wish for. It does not occur to them that their journey 'up', in terms of landscape as well as class, might also be a kind of drowning in the ambiguous, circling currents of replacement.

In conclusion, I focus on the first lost boy of Ibsen's play: Asta. Of course, there is not really a first lost boy. At some points a truly singular figure – 'All children, except one, grow up' (Barrie 1911: 1) – even Peter Pan goes on and after, as, for example, a replacement for Barrie's dead brother, David, and as a reproduction in the various literary and theatrical versions of himself. In *Little Eyolf*, innocence is suspended at the end of Act One: the living boy, in dying, becomes an object of regret and compensation in a more painful, fixed and explicit way. We might think that this provides us with an opportunity to get a good look at what it means to be innocent. But we can only get this 'good look' because we ourselves are grown up – not dead. Moreover, in Act Two, Ibsen uses his famed retrospective technique to return us to a scene of (queer) innocence, to a time that Alfred and Asta remember as 'lovely', despite poverty and struggle, when they were alone together, following the deaths of his father and her mother, before Alfred married Rita for her 'gold' and 'green forests' (Ibsen: 38 and 19). These memories, which distract Alfred from his grief, are evoked before we learn that Asta is not, in fact, Alfred's half-sister. She has recently read her mother's letters, which reveal an infidelity. Lost boys like Eyolf and Peter are made by a doubling of loss: first actual death; then loss of their singular indefinite status as *a dead child* in favour of definite recuperation, whereby they become exemplary figures of *the dead child*. How are lost boys like Asta made?

The poor and naughty boys are not the only figures in *Little Eyolf* that Rita and Alfred imagine might take their son's place. Before Rita conceives of and communicates to Alfred her plan for repurposing Eyolf's nurseries, they also ask Asta, a grown but unmarried woman, to stay on: 'Remain here and help us! Stay here in Eyolf's place for us' (68). There are no lost girls in *Peter Pan*, because girls 'are much too clever to fall out of their prams' (Barrie 1995: 101). Rita mentions 'all the poor, abused children', but girls are never specifically mentioned in *Little Eyolf* (Ibsen: 76). Asta's status as a lost boy who was a girl becomes apparent when we learn that she once shared a name with her nephew: Alfred used to call Asta Eyolf, and he calls her by this name multiple times now: 'Where is my little Eyolf now? (*smiles heavily at [Asta]*) Can you tell me that, – you, my big, wise Eyolf?' (44).

We learn of this nickname after we discover that Alfred and Asta's closeness is based on those two, essential ingredients for making lost boys: death and neglect. As she sews a mourning flower on Alfred's hat and sleeve, we hear that she did the same on his student cap after his father died, when she was still too little to remember, and then again for her mother. We also hear that Alfred always felt that he owed Asta extra kindness, to make up for his father's neglect.

> ASTA: [...] It was really a lovely time for us, all things considered, Alfred. The two of us alone.
> ALLMERS: Yes, it turned into one, despite all the struggle.
> ASTA: You struggled.
> ALLMERS: [*more lively*] Oh, you struggled just as much in your way, you too, – (*smiles*) you, my dear, faithful Eyolf.
> ASTA: Uh, – don't remind me of that ridiculous nonsense with the name.
> ALLMERS: Well, if you had been a boy, you would have been called Eyolf.
> ASTA: Yes, *if*. But when you began university –. (*smiles involuntarily*) To think that you could be so childish, all the same.
> ALLMERS: Was I the one who was childish!
> ASTA: Yes, I really think so now, when I remember it. Because you were ashamed not to have a brother. Just a sister.
> ALLMERS: No, it was really you. *You* were ashamed.
> ASTA: Oh yes, a little bit, maybe. And I almost felt sorry for you –
> ALLMERS: Yes, you certainly did. And so you took out my old boy's clothes –
> ASTA: Those nice Sunday clothes, yes. Do you remember the blue blouse and the short trousers?
> ALLMERS (*lets his eyes linger on her*): How well I remember you, when you put them on and walked around in them.
> ASTA: Yes, but I only did that when we were home alone together.
> ALLMERS: And how serious and important we felt. And I only called you Eyolf. (38–39)

This cross-dressing game has often been read either as a suppression of heterosexual desire through disguise or as a sign of latent homosexual desire. But instead of insisting on this veiled, either/or structure of desire, we might take a moment to 'linger on' its rather more complex and queer surface characteristics: that this game involves a young girl dressed as a boy, in a time when they are ostensibly free from the influence of guardians; that shame is shared but perhaps misremembered; that 'childish' display felt 'serious' and 'important' and took place when Alfred was old enough to be a student at university (39).

It is tempting to think of this first lost boy as contained in the past, or perhaps in the future-anterior of queer time. Was Ibsen 'intent on making childhood queerness into a story that will not *be*, but will only *have been*' (Bruhm and Hurley: xix)? In any case, it is clear that he is uninterested in containment, showing instead that Asta-Eyolf came *before* (and so would seem to threaten) the original innocence of the Eyolf who is now being mourned. Asta-Eyolf was already a token of another form of (gendered) mourning. Ibsen is interested in reopening Alfred and Asta's memory and in showing his readers and viewers its primacy:

> ALLMERS: I sat here and lived in my memories. And he [little Eyolf] wasn't there.
> ASTA: Yes, Alfred, – little Eyolf was behind it all.
> ALLMERS: He wasn't. He slid out of my mind. Out of my thoughts. For a moment, I didn't see him before me. (40)

By Act Three, when Rita and Alfred beg her to take Eyolf's place, the circumstances of her birth and Alfred's feelings have been suggestively revealed: he regards her as the true, lost companion of his life. Asta chooses to escape, running downhill to catch the approaching steamship, together with the road engineer and her ambivalent love interest, Borghejm. Joan Templeton reads this escape as 'an attempt to bury her love for Alfred', as the moment in which she 'exchanges ethics [the subject of Alfred's abandoned book project] for engineering, one man for another through which to live' (1997: 286). It is also a refusal of the replacement role and an alternative trajectory. Although Ibsen makes it difficult to believe in any exit but death, it is an exit, for the time being, from the fairy-tale world in which Alfred has been living and working (enabled by Rita's wealth). It is also an exit from the vertical – up and down, deep and high – structures that determine the world of the play, even if no one can escape the circular fantasies of innocence, origins and replacement.

Note

1. All translations from Norwegian are my own.

References

Barrie, J. M., 1911, *Peter and Wendy* (New York: Grosset and Dunlap)
Barrie, J. M., 1995, *Peter Pan and Other Plays* (Oxford and New York: Oxford University Press)

Bruhm, Steven, and Hurley, Natasha, eds, 2004, 'Curiouser: On the Queerness of Children', in *Curiouser: On the Queerness of Children* (Minneapolis: University of Minnesota Press), ix–xxxviii

Gilead, Sarah, 1991, 'Magic Abjured: Closure in Children's Fantasy Fiction', in *PMLA* 106, no. 2, 277–293

Goldman, Michael, 1999, *Ibsen: The Dramaturgy of Fear* (New York: Columbia University Press)

Helland, Frode, 2003, 'Petrified time: Ibsen's response to modernity, with special emphasis on *Little Eyolf*', in *Ibsen Studies* 3.2, 135–144, *ProQuest*, Web. 26 Apr. 2016

Helland, Frode, 2000, *Melankoliens Spill: En Studie I Henrik Ibsens Siste Dramaer* (Oslo: Universitetsforlaget)

Ibsen, Henrik, 1894, *Lille Eyolf*, Henrik Ibsens skrifter, Historisk-kritisk utgave, elektronisk versjon (University of Oslo), Web, September 1, 2016, http://ibsen.uio.no/DRVIT_LE|LEht.xhtml

Lesnik-Oberstein, Karín, and Stephen Thomson, 2016, 'What is queer theory doing with the child?', in *Parallax* 8.1: 354–346, *ProQuest*, Web, 26 Apr. 2016

Rose, Jacqueline, 1993, *The Case of Peter Pan, Or, The Impossibility of Children's Fiction* (Philadelphia: University of Pennsylvania Press)

Templeton, Joan, 1997, *Ibsen's Women* (Cambridge and New York: Cambridge University Press)

CHAPTER 6

The Sisters Antipodes: replacement and its ripples of sibling rivalry

Jean Owen

The front cover of Jane Alison's memoir *The Sisters Antipodes* (2009) depicts the upper bodies of two identical girls. While their features are not visible – as they are lying face down – they have fair hair tied in ponytails, their arms are upstretched and they wear matching clothes. It would be easy to understand them as twin sisters, except that the girls they are meant to represent in the memoir are not related by blood.[1] Still, as Alison reflects on her memoir-self Jane and stepsibling Jenny, 'we looked enough alike to be sisters' (2).

The Sisters Antipodes is a complicated account of mirroring. Two seemingly identical families meet and match, spouse-to-spouse, child-to-child. The Cummins family are Australian and comprise Edward and Rosemary, and their daughters Maggy and Jane; their American counterparts are Paul and Helen Stuart, and their daughters Patricia and Jenny. The parents are in their early thirties, attractive and well educated – the fathers are diplomats in the Foreign Service, and the mothers are described as beautiful. The daughters correspond in age and colouring, the younger two even share a birthday, though there is a gap of one year between them.[2] Meeting

J. Owen (✉)
Independent Researcher, London, UK

© The Author(s) 2018
J. Owen, N. Segal (eds.), *On Replacement*,
https://doi.org/10.1007/978-3-319-76011-7_6

in Canberra (Jane's birthplace), the families become enmeshed through dinner parties and picnics until, nine months later, the adults embark on affairs, which result in what Alison refers to as the 'split'. Thus, through a process of 'sudden replacements' (27), the women have new husbands and the daughters have new fathers. There is a further geographical split when Rosemary and her daughters follow Paul to Washington, while Jane's father remains in Canberra with Helen and her daughters. Two years after the split the mirroring continues when, just four days apart, Nicholas is born to Helen and Edward, and Tommy to Rosemary and Paul: 'two babies that consolidated the new marriages and knotted us tighter together' (35). It will be seven years before the girls see or speak to their respective fathers again. During the estrangement, there are no phone calls, no visits; all communication between the 'metamorphic families' (38) is via letters and the exchange of gifts (though nothing for, or between, Rosemary and Helen).

Families reconstitute themselves all the time, with children having to adapt – often to a new parent and stepsiblings – with the minimum of fuss. For the Cumminses and Stewarts, the 'parallels between the two families were so neat we seemed as designed as nature, twinned markings on the wings of a moth' (35). It would seem that 'everything was even. It was fair that there was a Jenny somewhere who had my birthday and father and grandparents [...] because, after all, I had hers' (37). Yet the excessive symmetry is part of the problem, as well as the fact that the children are not prepared for this sudden change of father or for the transition from one family to the other. Indeed, one of the most disconcerting aspects of the memoir is that the parents seem oblivious to the effects their behaviour might have on the children.

> But surely everyone was stunned. The adults, for having done something so astonishing so fast – in 1966 divorce wasn't common, and these divorces were entwined with the men's professional lives and their roles representing countries. And the four girls were stunned, but the way children are: a quiet, numb shock, like a crack inside a stone, not enough to split it but inside, silently fissuring. (25)

While the replacements ignite an era of competition and jealousy among the girls, for Alison it is the younger two, Jane and Jenny – aged only four and five respectively at the time – who are the most damaged by the father-swap. 'Maggy and Patricia were seven when this new era began', Jane reasons, 'young but maybe formed enough to have their own soft shapes already, a thin bark' (27).[3] For Jane and Jenny, the split triggers an intense rivalry, or a version of 'replacement child syndrome' (Sabbadini: 529). For Andrea Sabbadini, this phrase refers to the child born after an older child has died, but for Jane, '[i]t's how I grew up and how I imagine Jenny did, too, with our parents' split at our core, our tissues growing around it, around the fact that we'd each been replaced' (Alison: 28–29).

We first see Jane and Jenny in a bath, 'little girls with wavy hair and bright staring eyes, our wrinkled pink feet pressed together and pushing' (2).[4] They grow up 'as each other's antipode [...] two bodies pressed together, foot to foot', existing 'in symbiotic complement' (Sabbadini: 529): mirror images with no obvious demarcation between them. Significantly, too, if 'a replacement child is given the same name as the one he or she replaces' (541), Jane and Jenny's names are similar enough to be almost interchangeable. Later, Jane and her sister adopt their stepfather's surname – 'a necessary trade [...] Those girls had my name and father. I'd need theirs' (44).

In *Siblings* (2003), Juliet Mitchell writes, 'the sibling is par excellence someone who threatens the subject's uniqueness' (10); this threat leads to a child's ambivalent reaction to the birth of a sibling and the corresponding battle between hatred and love. The same threat surely exists when a child is confronted with a step-sibling who seems to replicate her in every way. While she is only four when she meets Jenny, and the two are soon swiftly parted, Jane is nevertheless haunted by a double, 'that other girl over there, the one like her who now had him [Jane's father]' (47) in a 'world' that 'felt mirrored, unreal' (31). She imagines that Jenny feels the same: 'growing up like me [...] wondering what to do with the ache, the panic that feels like your insides might slip out, the unvoiced question of whether she'd see her invisible father again' (46–47).

For Sabbadini, one of the problems facing a replacement child is 'how to compete with an absent object' (535) when that 'object' is already dead, thus rendering competition impossible, though nonetheless inevitable. For the child Jane, Jenny is absent by geography, an 'invisible presence' (546), her status as living positioning her as more of a rival than if she were dead. How can Jane be sure of her own unique identity when there is a living double who has replaced her as her father's (Edward's) daughter? Indeed, it is what Jane refers to as the 'situation with the fathers' (140, 150, 168, 196) that fuels the rivalry between them and provides most of the tension within the memoir. Jane's father becomes 'a shadow [...], not even a voice' (38). In consequence, Jane and Maggy become 'invisible and silent' to him: 'we could send him nothing' but letters 'to make him *see* us' – which are 'dead by the time [they] reached him', just as 'his words [to them] were dead [...] A phantom limb, not there but aching' (38–39). Thus, it is Paul's daughters who are the 'real girls' (34, 41, 42) and Edward's new family the 'real family' (58, 92), the ones that could pose for a family portrait.

'A girl is abandoned by her father, so she must steal someone else's,' Alison writes (186), and this is what Jane does. Realising that 'if you can't be with the one you love', you must 'love the one you're with' (41), she turns to her stepfather, Paul, whose 'collusive smile' (265) wins her over. Though it makes her uncomfortable, Jane imagines he sees in her 'a little ally, a small consolation' (46). She wonders 'whether there was a moment between us, a silent agreement: *I will be yours if you will be mine. We will replace, and punish, those others*' (46, italics Alison's). She becomes the best in scholarship, sport, and social skills: 'fastest runner, best skater, funniest girl' (47), showing off her prizes to her stepfather for a pat on the head or a hold of his hand. Even after he and her mother divorce, Jane seeks Paul out, while Maggy becomes indifferent to him – since he only ever has time for winners – just as she copes with her absent father by 'pretending' he is 'a nice uncle' (273). In fact, as Jane views it, Maggy and Patricia would never struggle as she and Jenny do 'because between them was not that problem of Paul' (105).

In 1973, both families find themselves in the United States – Jane's still in Washington, Jenny's in New York. When the girls meet up in Jenny's pink bedroom (Jane is now eleven, Jenny twelve), though they 'could hardly remember each other' (37), they 'see only the girl who'd taken everything', but especially the father(s), in a reunion that sparks an intense and aggressive period of competition, though 'Jenny was just enough bigger to win' (105): '[We] stood hip to hip – hurling darts at a bull's eye until we'd nearly hurled away our arms, to see who was better, more clever, more able, really worth something, really should win, in fact should be the only one there because we could not both exist' (104). Yet, hours after battling it out, 'we were exhausted and collapsed on the twin beds [...] and for a sleepy moment we might have realised that we liked the same things, cartwheels and words and puzzles and insects, we were *alike*, maybe we liked each other' (106).[5] Jane reflects, 'so often [...] we lingered on the verge of being just two girls, not creatures embedded in this doubled family'; but then 'we remembered who we were, and that we could not afford this' (106). Though each one has found a friend, as Mitchell explains, '[t]he ecstasy of loving one who is like oneself is experienced at the same time as a trauma of being annihilated by one who stands in one's place' (10). For Jane, '[t]he only thing to do was slash in the water, find the other girl, and push her down' (Alison: 104). In fact, her annihilation would bring an end to such rivalry, an issue I shall return to later.

The themes of replacement and rivalry in *The Sisters Antipodes* bring to mind Freud's short essay 'Family romances' (1909), which discusses the neurotic's phantasy of replacing her or his parents with better ones, but with the terms reversed: here, the father replaces his daughter with (for Jane) a 'real' one. It is the father's 'faithlessness' (Freud: 224) to his biological daughter(s) that drives the sororal rivalry between Jane and Jenny, in which each feel 'slighted' at 'not receiving the whole of [her father's] love' (221) and 'regrets [...] having to share it with' (222) her sisters. While, for Freud, a child's fantasy of replacing her or his parents by better ones is a necessary stage in the process of separating from the 'real' parents, for Jane and Jenny, separation from the father is both premature and traumatic. It activates a longing for the father, or what Margo Maine termed in her work on eating disorders a 'father-hunger [...] a deep, persistent desire for emotional connection with the father that is experienced by all children' (21). Maine's theory claims that father-hunger is a normal – and universal – craving in contemporary society which pulls two ways, from child to father and father to child. While I am not advocating Maine's universalistic claims, especially given that memoir, by definition, deals with the specific and not the general, Alison's memoir can be read as a case study in father-hunger, a phenomenon which is symptomatic of what I have elsewhere defined as a 'Father Romance'.[6] Originally, my theory focused on a daughter's erotic longing for her father when she is an adult. I have since expanded the concept to include a daughter fixated on her father after the point at which separation should have taken place. Thus, it is father-hunger that prompts Electra's 'complex' in the tragedies of Euripides and Sophocles. It is also an experience Sylvia Plath explores in poems such as 'Electra on Azalea Path' (116), in which the poet identifies directly with Agamemnon's daughter, and 'Daddy', in which the narrator declares:

I was ten when they buried you.
At twenty I tried to die
And get back, back, back to you. (222)[7]

This image of getting back to the father is not dissimilar to Jane's recurring dream 'of flying back to [her] father' (32) during the first year of the split.

While Alison's memoir is set in the 'kingdom of [...] fathers' (Owen: 12), the daughters crave paternal affection. Indeed, Maggy and Jane are 'left twice' (81) after their mother's second divorce, even though, according to Jane's diary, '*Helen's made it as if I've won out as far as fathers go, leaving Jenny with none*' (208, italics Alison's). So, while daughter-father relationships are often contradictory, a 'problematic bond, full of ambivalence and longing' (Owen: 11), for Jane and her rival-double

> [i]t would have been better if we hadn't both wanted what we did, or if we hadn't been so much the same [...] if we hadn't both apparently grown up craving, in secret, the attention of a man very far away and evolving the exact same means to get him; if our tissues hadn't been made of pure jealousy. Because it didn't take long for us to know that neither might ever win her own father. (132)

This, then, is one aspect of the Father Romance, an Electra configuration in which the daughter is in a permanent state of longing – not dissimilar to mourning – for the absent father. For Maine, father-hunger 'is not restricted to female adolescents, nor is its expression limited to eating disorders,' it can be 'expressed in many self-destructive behaviors' (xv). For Jane and Jenny, it provokes a kind of thinness that is not bodily (though Jenny's weight is shown to fluctuate): it causes a psychical thinness, where 'love' itself becomes difficult, if not impossible – or, to use Alison's word, 'ruined' (241). Jane remarks: 'I've studied girls with real fathers since, and seen in those girls' eyes a look of absolute safety, as if they know they can tilt their heads back, close their eyes, and fall, and they'll be caught and nested, unconditionally' (68). Sadly, as Maine explains, '[l]ike physical hunger, unsatisfied emotional hunger does not disappear; instead, it grows and grows. Adults who have not found a way to relate to their fathers or resolve their feelings of loss may continue to suffer this hunger indefinitely' (21). As Alison writes: 'When I was thirty, a woman who read my first fiction leaned across a seminar table [...] and said, "Girls who grow up without fathers are full of longing." I thought: Fuck that. But she was right. Longing, a soft, black cavity deep at your core. And the things buried deep are the deadliest' (151).

When they are in their twenties, Jane's boyfriend says of Jenny, 'she just seemed like a fucked-up little girl' (244), but both remain 'little girls' fixated on their fathers, 'caught in the family net like [two] baffled moth[s]'. They are mirrored opposites, full of a desire to be rescued by the father-prince, or by father-substitutes. And even Rosemary is cast as a desperate woman waiting to be rescued after her second divorce: she dates a series of men, all potential fathers to her children, but these attempts inevitably end in disappointment. When Jane is sixteen and her mother forty-three, they sit in on Saturday nights playing Scrabble, 'both restless' (169), waiting for the phone to ring, anxious for a man to call.

Alison underscores the primacy of the father in relation to a daughter's identity and not – as is often the case – of the mother. But this does not diminish the role Helen and Rosemary play in the split and its aftermath, not least because the question 'who do you think did it first?' (107) – presumably the sex act – haunts Jane and Jenny, though it is the latter who whispers the loaded question during that first reunion. In a way, it is frustrating that neither Jane nor the reader finds out. But what really matters here is the effect it has on the sibling rivals.

> [Jenny] surely needed her mother to have done it first, to have chosen and won what she wanted; otherwise Paul had, and therefore had wanted to leave her mother and be able to leave Jenny, too. And I needed my mother to have done it first, because otherwise my father had and had easily left me. For my mother to have done it first, Jenny's father must have. For one of us to get what she needed, the other had to lose. (108)

It is an issue that determines not only who these stepsisters are but also their sense of worth: 'To be wanted, or not to be wanted' (108) is 'the only measure of value. Just being is not enough – and not even an option, because you can't isolate yourself from the wretched human economics of desire and desirability, the currents of value and valuation that forever stream between bodies and eyes' (264). It is a theme running through the memoir: 'What exactly made the woman in one envelope of skin so valuable, so golden, that she could pull a man from his family, she could become all he saw?' (134). Such an evaluation extends to the potential for rivalry and replacement among the 'many girls out there who roamed the land of desire' (172), as Jenny necessarily proves when she steals the roguish Sutter – the boy who shares a first name with Paul – from Jane, having sex with him 'in the hydrangeas' (189) at their shared birthday party.[8]

Alison traces the longing for fathers throughout Jane and Jenny's teenage years and beyond. Whether they live on the same continent or are oceans apart, the rivalry between the two girls never waivers, though it changes form: general knowledge quizzes and spelling tests are replaced by who can smoke, drink and have more sex. Unrelentingly, they swap fathers and territories, Jenny to Washington, Jane to Canberra, trying to reclaim what each believes is hers, trying to displace the other, 'twenty years after we sat in our bathtub […] two aging, maddened girls' still 'pressed foot to foot' (219).

Juliet Mitchell identifies the trauma of sibling replacement as 'the creation of a black hole where we thought we stood' (43); it is an image Alison uses extensively in her memoir. When Jane is made aware of her self-destructive behaviour – she drinks to oblivion and has no recall of what she gets up to – 'a black hole opened up, panic at having no memory, as if for a time I'd been extinct' (194), but then, 'since I had no memory of what I'd done, I hadn't really been there. So I hadn't really done it; it wasn't me; it was someone else. Which meant I could do it and therefore not do it, again' (195). In this disavowed state, she is 'neoJane', the 'craving thing that climbed from the black hole' (202). Yet, though desperate to obliterate the father-hunger, her efforts to 'fill the awful absent presence of Daddy and Paul' (87) are only a diluted version of her stepsister's. They are 'Snow White' and 'Rose Red' (185, 187, 188), the academic and the dropout, still mirror-images, but Jenny is the 'darker version' (185), 'master of her own abandonments' (204), she 'could slice her wrists and her throat […] get herself beaten up […] raped'. Indeed, as Edward writes to Jane, '*Jenny is a mess and making herself a worse one*' (204, italics Alison's). In fact, Jenny wins favour with neither father; it is Jane who seems to triumph.

In spite of her desperate *cris de cœur*, Jane manages to take a very different, antipodal path from her stepsister, graduating from Princeton and later becoming a writer. Jenny, on the other hand, dies when both women are in their later thirties, following a long battle with heroin. 'I can't shake the feeling', Jane reflects, 'that […] a black hole had run through each of us ever since we'd been pulled from that bathwater long ago and gone our separate ways, and that [Jenny] finally fell into hers' (256).

Jane is asked not to go to the funeral. Indeed, Patricia rages at Paul for ringing Jane while still at Jenny's wake: 'Even now', Jane hears her scream. 'Even now I can't believe you're calling her' (254). Even now, Alison insinuates, the replacement sibling cannot stand in the other's place, it would only reinforce the loss. Yet, and obviously, Jenny was already dead when the memoir was being written: once again, the replacement sister Jane stands in her rival's place, only this time to tell their story. In these terms, memoir itself becomes a site of and for replacement. Yet Alison includes extracts from Jenny's letters and poems 'of velvet and blood' (185), which allow her an 'invisible presence', and acknowledgement too, that these 'sisters antipodes' shared writing in common, 'along with our fathers, brothers, names, birthdays, countries, pasts, and longings: everything but our blood' (248).

Notes

1. While this is a memoir and thus based on real-life facts, I shall be referring to it as one would to fiction, that is, in the present tense. Note, throughout this chapter, 'Alison' refers to the author Jane Alison and 'Jane' refers to her child-self in the book.
2. In fact, the parents' birthdays are also uncannily close: 'My father's birthday came a week before Paul's [...] My mother's birthday fell two weeks before Helen's' (35). Of course, the age gap between the girls is a problem for Jane, because Jenny will always be slightly ahead of the sororal game. Even so, Jane Alison is the storyteller here, so everything told is her version of events.
3. Jane Alison (2014) has translated a selection of poetry by Ovid. In *The Sisters Antipodes*, alongside the numerous beautiful descriptions of landscape and nature which I simply cannot do justice to here, Alison makes extensive use of her Ovidian expertise, particularly in the way she depicts girls in various states of becoming and change, such as here (see also 186, 275).
4. Actually, they have differently coloured eyes: Jane's are blue; Jenny's are brown.
5. Of course, there are material differences between the two sets of girls, especially after Paul and Rosemary's split. Jane and Maggy are two Cinderellas scrubbing the house, having little money for clothes, and attending a school where 'being white was a problem' (120). By contrast, Jenny and Patricia have their own bathrooms in a beautiful apartment, wear fashionable clothes, have their own beauty products, and attend a private school.
6. The notion of the 'Father Romance' was the research topic of my 2013 PhD, which I am now developing into a monograph.
7. Jane's stepmother Helen also regards herself as a rival, positioning Jane as a type of Electra to her Clytemnestra.
8. Aside from Jane and Jenny's names, Alison used replacement names for all other characters in her memoir. So were the real names of the stepfather and the boyfriend also identical? Later, Jenny points out how another of Jane's boyfriends – Anthony – 'is exactly like Father' [Paul] (232).

References

Alison, Jane, 2014, *Change Me: Stories of Sexual Transformation from Ovid* (Oxford & New York: Oxford University Press)

Alison, Jane, 2010 [2009], *The Sisters Antipodes* (Boston & New York: Houghton Mifflin Harcourt)

Freud, Sigmund, 1977 [1909], *On Sexuality: 'Three Essays on the Theory of Sexuality' and Other Works*, The Pelican Freud Library, vol. 7, tr. & ed. James Strachey (Harmondsworth: Penguin)

Maine, Margo, 2004 [1991], *Father-Hunger: Fathers, Daughters and the Pursuit of Thinness* (Carlsbad, CA.,: Gürze Books)

Mitchell, Juliet, 2004, *Siblings: Sex and Violence* (Cambridge: Polity Press)

Owen, Ursula, 1983, ed., *Fathers: Reflections by Daughters* (London: Virago)

Plath, Sylvia 1989 [1981], *Collected Poems*, ed. Ted Hughes (London & Boston: Faber & Faber)

Sabbadini, Andrea, 1988, 'The Replacement Child', in *Contemporary Psychoanalysis* 24: 528–547

CHAPTER 7

Artificial intelligence and synthetic humans: loss and replacement

Georgia Panteli

In this chapter, which examines the concept of replacement in the context of posthuman science fiction, I shall argue that, in most contemporary screen media examples, the idea of replacing a human being with an artificial sentient human is closely linked with reactionary attitudes towards technological progress. Although contemporary literature and film have moved away from the portrayal of the evil sentient robot, artificial intelligence in machines is still considered an uncomfortable topic.

In what follows I shall present the robot child in posthuman science fiction to show how it functions mainly in order to replace a dead or terminally ill child as a form of therapy for the parent, a narrative that reflects technophobic ideologies that oppose transhumanist values. I shall also demonstrate how such tendencies resemble similar reactions to early photography, particularly since the element of the photograph of the dead child appears frequently in these films. The examples used in this essay are Steven Spielberg's film *A.I. Artificial Intelligence* and the Channel 4 TV series *Humans*.[1]

A.I. Artificial Intelligence (*A.I.*) was Stanley Kubrick's seventeen-year project that remained uncompleted on his death, which was taken up by Steven Spielberg: the director Kubrick had assigned to the project. *A.I.* is the story of David (Haley Joel Osment), the first Mecha boy (the name

G. Panteli (✉)
University College London, London, UK

stands for mechanic) in an imagined twenty-second century. David is adopted by Monica and Henry Swinton (Frances O'Connor and Sam Robards) because their own son, Martin (Jake Thomas), is in a coma and expected to die. David is the first robot child to be designed and given emotions – in particular that of love – which are activated by an 'imprinting ritual' that Monica performs. In the process, she becomes his mother, and his love for her is unconditional and unending. This imprinting can only happen with one person, so David cannot develop the same emotions for his new father, whom he regards as a competitor for Monica's love.

The adults in the film – both David's adoptive parents and his creator – are portrayed as egopaths who are absorbed in their own emotions at the expense of the robot boy, even though they know he has feelings. Their narcissism also shows in the fact that they adopt David, a child destined to love them, without actually having lost their own child. In fact, their real son, Martin, gets well and returns home. It is clear that his coexistence with his replacement will not be harmonious: Martin cannot accept David as a brother and the parents do not treat them equally.

When David is first brought into the Swinton family, the camera focuses on a family portrait of Monica and Henry with their son Martin, with David's reflection superimposed over the photograph as he is looking at it. This motif is typical of the genre of posthuman science fiction films: a photograph portraying a lost person who is being replaced by an artificial human. The photographic element functions as an explanation, or revelation, that clarifies the motives of the character suffering the loss. In this particular case, it foreshadows David's own replacement by the one he was supposed to replace. I shall return to this theme in a moment.

At a children's party, Martin's friends hurt David, who reacts by grasping Martin in a tight embrace and asking him for protection; as a result, they both fall into the swimming pool. Martin is saved from drowning at the last minute by horrified adults. Perceiving him as a threat, David's foster-parents decide to return him to the factory. Yet Monica knows that if they send him back he will be destroyed. Instead, to save his life, she abandons him in the forest and this traumatic moment marks the beginning of David's quest to be reunited with her. He knows the story of Pinocchio, having heard it, along with Martin, from Monica. If he becomes a real boy, he believes, then Monica will accept him back and love him. He sets out to find the imaginary Blue Fairy who, he believes, will make this possible.

There are differences, however, between Carlo Collodi's Pinocchio and Kubrick and Spielberg's David: while both are examples of artificial children with emotions, unlike Pinocchio, there is no self-exploration for David – his quest is to return home after the trauma of being abandoned. It is for this reason only that he is obsessed with becoming a real boy: to be accepted and loved by his mother. As Tim Kreider points out, 'it looks more like a scary parody of love, a monomaniacal obsession that renders him oblivious to the ugly realities around him' (36). David is given the chance to understand why he was abandoned and how humans see him when Gigolo Joe (Jude Law) – the Mecha love robot that he meets on the way and who has been helping him all along – tries to tell him the truth, but he is in complete denial and remains so until the end of the film.

David arrives at the place where he thinks the Blue Fairy is, but it is actually the headquarters of the company that made him. In another traumatic encounter with Professor Hobby (William Hurt), the scientist who created him, David finds out that he is not one of a kind, as he had formerly thought. Instead, Professor Hobby tells him: 'My son was one of a kind. You are the first of a kind.'

It turns out that Professor Hobby had lost his son and reproduced his exact image in the prototype robot David. Once more, the deceased child, Professor Hobby's son, is seen in a photograph that has captured a moment of happiness frozen in time. The image of the boy in the photograph functions as the symbol of what is worth reproducing and replicating, not only in the photograph's simulacrum but, as a next technological step, in the form of a humanoid robot. Pierre Bourdieu explains how family photographs 'immortalise high points of family life' (19). By juxtaposing these immortalised moments (as captured in the photographs) with the replacement of the lost child, the effect is more intense, especially as, in most cases, it is obvious to the viewer that the replacement child has failed in its original purpose. While it often succeeds in healing the traumatised parent, it can never replace the lost child.

After the traumatic realisation that he is a robot, originally created to replace a real boy, David jumps in the water of flooded New York (the result of global warming) and sinks. Underwater, in what used to be the fairy-tale attraction at Coney Island amusement park, he finds a statue of the Blue Fairy and asks her repeatedly to turn him into a real boy. The ocean freezes and David sleeps in his own frozen state. Two thousand years later, advanced robots awaken him in a world where humans no longer exist. The robots treat David as their ancestor and try to please him by fulfilling his wish. They replicate his dead mother, Monica, from the DNA of a lock of her hair that David has kept. She can only live for one day, but this is enough for the boy to feel the mother love he had always longed for. She acts as a quite uncanny clone of her former self, full of love for David, who becomes the oedipal son as he takes his father's place beside her in the bed, to sleep/die happily. As Tim Kreider suggests, *A.I.* addresses the issue of replaceability by the constant presentation of simulacra:

> Every character in the film seems as preprogrammed as David, obsessed with the image of a lost loved one, and tries to replace that person with a technological simulacrum. Dr Hobby designed David as an exact duplicate of his own dead child, the original David; Monica used him as a substitute for her comatose son; and, completing the sad cycle two thousand years later, David comforts himself with a cloned copy of Monica. (Kreider: 33–34)

David's desire for a happy ending is resolved in a devastating context. Humanity has been eradicated and advanced intelligence robots treat any remainders of the human past with the same respect and curiosity with which we approach museum exhibits. The sweet fairy-tale tone that signals Spielberg's style makes the ending even more disturbing. It is what is not being said that matters most: David never laments the end of humanity or the death of his mother. If she can be recreated as a clone in order to mouth those long-desired words of love for him, then this is enough; nothing else interests him.

Turning now to my second example, the Channel 4 TV series *Humans* takes place in a science fiction universe similar to that of *A.I.*, where humans use human-like robots called 'synths' (that is, synthetic humans) in their everyday lives in areas ranging from hard manual labour to the sex industry and health care. The series opens with the Hawkins family: Joe (Tom Goodman-Hill) buys synth Anita (Gemma Chan) to help with household chores, as his often-absent wife Laura (Katherine Parkinson) is unable to organise a work–family balance. When their relationship reaches a crisis, and with Laura feeling increasingly threatened by the synthetic woman in her home, Joe reminds her: 'I didn't buy Anita to replace you, I bought her to get you back'. In other words, the presence of the synthetic helper is supposed to give the couple more time. As in *A.I.*, however, the consequences of living with a replacement are not always what was previously desired or expected.

In *Humans*, David Elster (Stephen Boxer), one of the three scientists who creates the synthetic humans, later discovers how to make them sentient. He uses the code to revive his son in the form of a hybrid, after the boy almost drowns in an accident. Elster also creates a replacement for his wife, Beatrice (Ruth Bradley), when she takes her own life. But this results in failure, as the synthetic human who shares her genetic material inherits Beatrice's suicidal urges: although her programming forbids her from destroying herself, the family is never restored to its original state. Elster is yet another scientist who creates artificial humans with emotions in order to recover from his loss. As in the previous example, his original family is shown in a photograph to emphasise the loss of his child and wife, and to give the context of replacement.

The series, which has been very successful, with two complete seasons and a third currently being filmed, has multiple references to *A.I.*[2] Even the casting choices for the actors show this. William Hurt, who plays Professor Hobby in *A.I.*, is Dr George Millican in *Humans*, a widowed former scientist who plays a vital role in the creation of synthetic humans, along with David Elster. Dr Millican is losing his memory and lives with Odi (Will Tudor), his synth caregiver. But Odi is more than this to Dr Millican, he is almost like a son to him – a Pinocchian robot, who has stored all the lost memories Dr Millican once shared with his wife. Odi is the only source of comfort for Dr Millican, since he keeps her memory alive as a real son might do. This example also alludes to the replacement child, even though Odi did not replace a dead son. He did, however, fulfil the function of a son, without having been programmed to do so.

In the second season of *Humans*, a new scientist, Dr Athena Morrow (Carrie-Anne Moss), is introduced. She is working on consciousness transference from human to machine. As with artificial intelligence scientists in previous examples, her scientific interest in such an endeavour is triggered by the need to bring back a dead child, in this case her daughter who has died in an accident. Once more, this need is emphasised by the photograph of mother and daughter on the day of the accident, a photograph that appears several times during the series.

As mentioned earlier, all the mourning scientists experience loss and trauma that they attempt to cure through their scientific work, by creating artificial human replacements – in most cases, artificial replacement children. The order they try to restore is immortalised in the photographs that accompany every such example. In the context of posthumanist science fiction, the image of the robot child is strongly linked with the photograph of the deceased child being replaced, and the combination of these two images is a symbol of Luddite regressive ideology. To provide a context for my argument, I shall explain the connection between science fiction and post/transhumanism, and how this relates to film theory.

Posthumanism is an increasingly popular term used in many different contexts. Posthumanist scholars – such as Rosi Braidotti, Cary Wolfe and Elaine L. Graham – often refer to it by revisiting the components of the term and redefining or referring to the concepts of humanism, humanity and what it is to be humanist. This is understandable, since the word itself implies a reference to something after (post-)humanism. However, as Ivan Callus, Stefan Herbrechter and Manuela Rossini point out, 'the posthuman is arguably so unprecedented and so much a product of its time that it has to be viewed as distinct from its supposed affinities with earlier thought and representations. There is, then, much to unlearn before the posthuman as well as much to reaffirm' (Callus et al.: 105). They add further that 'posthumanism has now become so sufficiently [*sic*] established as an academic discourse that it warrants analysis of its diverse strands and configurations' (106). The examples examined here relate to transhumanism, or what Wolfe calls the 'cyborg' strand of posthumanism (Wolfe: xiii). Transhumanism, as Nick Bostrom emphasises, 'embraces technological progress while strongly defending human rights and individual choice' (203).[3]

Even though robots and androids have appeared in literature since antiquity, it is only since the 1920s, when the term was coined, that they have been classified as 'science fiction' (see Luckhurst: 15). Darko Suvin defines science fiction as the 'literature of cognitive estrangement' (372). Suvin explains how 'the effect of [...] factual reporting of fictions is one of confronting a set normative system – a Ptolemaic-type closed world picture – with a point of view or glance implying a new set of norms' (374). Science fiction often addresses the excitement or fear caused by technological advances – in this case the fear of the robot.

Narratives that include androids or robots have been classified as 'posthuman science fiction'. According to Booker and Thomas, posthuman science fiction 'imagines a future in which technological changes have brought about dramatic physical and intellectual changes in the human species itself – or even rendered that species irrelevant through the rise of superior artificial intelligence (AI) technologies' (11). According to cinema and media theorist Vivian Sobchack, all science fiction films make consistent 'use not of *specific* images, but of *types* of images which function in the same way from film to film to create an imaginatively realized world which is always removed from the world we know or know of' (87). The significance of science fiction film iconography lies in the fact that its references invoke in the viewer's memory all the moral debates that were raised in earlier films regarding technological progress and technophobia. This thus defines their own position in the debate. Katherine Hayles considers 'the locus classicus for reframing transhumanist questions to be science fiction and speculative fiction' (216). In science fiction film, it is precisely through visual references such as aliens, spaceships, robots, androids and so forth that different filmmakers choose how to show their political and ideological tendencies. These visual references stand for the battlefield where the struggles between technophilia and technophobia take place. As Katherine Hayles suggests, posthuman science fiction is the subgenre that offers the ideal ground for the debate on transhumanism. To add to Hayles, one reason why science fiction frequently deals with posthumanist and transhumanist topics is, as Suvin suggests, due to the challenge that science fiction poses to normative values.

In the examples I mentioned earlier, the reference is that of the robot child as a replacement, emphasised visually by the recurring photograph-of-the-deceased theme. As the concept of creating artificial life that has emotions is still a controversial topic, the creators of the film and series allow this in the narrative only under special circumstances, as a response to and possibly a therapy for loss and mourning. A sentient robot child would be perceived as uncanny if presented in a different context.

The concept of the uncanny was first introduced by Ernst Jentsch and then further developed by Sigmund Freud in his seminal essay 'The Uncanny'. Jentsch described the uncanny as the feeling of uneasiness that is caused by a hesitation in distinguishing what is real or unreal. Freud added to this by emphasising the concept of the familiar behaving in an unfamiliar way, causing the same feeling of uneasiness that Jentsch described. Freud connected this with revelation of the repressed and used it as an example for his analysis of the automaton Olympia in E. T. A. Hoffmann's story 'Der Sandmann' [The Sandman]. In more recent studies that refer to robots and cyborgs – that is, the contemporary equivalent of automata – Freud's theory of the uncanny is mostly known in relation to Masahiro Mori's concept of 'the uncanny valley'. Mori refers to the manufacture of robots specifically, emphasising that the closer a robot resembles a human being, the more uncomfortable the feeling we experience when we realise that it is not human.

The motif of the photograph also draws parallels between our time and the nineteenth century, in terms of the reception of technological progress. Photography was received initially with fear and distrust, as something disturbing and uncanny (as the robot child is perceived today):

> to look at any daguerreotype was to look at a figure of death, since it recorded a moment of the past that could not be replicated in the present. […] The shock of seeing oneself in an act of contemplation – an act usually invisible to oneself and not recorded in a portrait – also made the daguerreotype uncanny: it always produced a double of oneself even as one attempted to look at another. (Williams: 165)

Williams explains how daguerreotypes, the precursors of photographs, became a popular topic in literature, as 'these stories demonstrated the haunting ability of the daguerreotype to replace the real thing. On the other hand, they enacted plots that ultimately disenchant these images' (162). Almost a century later, the introduction of cinema provoked similar reactions. Such distrustful reactions towards technology are evoked by the motif of photographs in science fiction films: if we take one step back, we can see the parallels between photography and cinema as they were originally received and artificial intelligence in robots today.

The motif of the photograph portraying a deceased human that is later replaced by an artificial simulacrum functions, therefore, as a cinematic *mise en abyme* loaded with ideological tension. This is clear in the examples here: Professor Hobby does not create out of scientific curiosity; his pioneering robot child comes into existence because of the personal trauma of losing his son. This is repeated in the examples of the two scientists in *Humans*.

A.I. presents parenthood as a need of the adult and *Humans* takes this a step further with the creation of sentient robot children that can grow into adults in order for parents to overcome the trauma of a lost child. In both cases, replacement parenting is presented as therapy for the adult. The allusions and visual references to *A.I.*, as well as to other iconic films of the genre, such as *Blade Runner*, give the impression that *Humans* is continuing the narrative of an open-ended topic: the shared life between humans and sentient humanoid robots. The humanoid or cyborg is an image in science fiction films that exists in a separate, parallel universe in the viewer's imagination, in the sense of Sobchack's theory as explained earlier. As such, it carries its symbolism and ideological context from film to film.

My analysis of these two case studies in relation to replacement shows that, despite the context of rapid technological progress, popular culture is still reluctant to accept a transhumanist, progressive vision of the future. Sentient artificial humans continue to be an uncomfortable topic, which is only conditionally accepted in a popular fiction scenario under the narrative proviso that they replace a deceased loved one and, most frequently, a deceased child.

By bringing together the symbols of the photograph and the sentient robot, I juxtapose two different types of replacement that are narratively linked in many examples of posthuman science-fiction film. This comparison encourages a more transhumanist approach towards robots – sentient or not – as it functions as a reminder of how literature reflected early, fearful, reactions to photography, and how it reflects photography today. Illustrating these two symbols together shows that, within the timeframe of two centuries, the photograph – a technological advancement that originally caused fear and inspired feelings of the uncanny – is now used as something familiar and trusted and, as I mentioned earlier, according to Bourdieu, an essential part of family life. At the same time, another technological device of replacement, this time a humanoid robot, is treated with suspicion, as it is largely associated with feelings of uncanniness and fear of replacement. This direct juxtaposition of the two replacement symbols functions as a reminder that this feeling of uncanniness is bound to change with time and familiarisation, as happened with photography.

Notes

1. *Humans* is based on a Swedish science-fiction drama titled *Real Humans*. The directors and writers of *Humans* varied between episodes.
2. *Humans* has reached larger audiences than the average science fiction fan base. See Fullerton.
3. For a detailed definition of transhumanism, see More.

References

Booker, M. Keith and Anne-Marie Thomas, 2009, *The Science Fiction Handbook* (Chichester, UK; Malden, MA: Wiley-Blackwell)
Bostrom, Nick, 2005, 'In Defense of Posthuman Dignity', in *Bioethics*, 19.3
Bourdieu, Pierre, 1990 [1965], *Photography, a Middle-brow Art*, tr. Shaun Whiteside (Cambridge: Polity Press)

Braidotti, Rosi, 2013, *The Posthuman* (Cambridge: Polity Press)
Callus, Ivan, Stefan Herbrechter, & Manuela Rossini, 2014, 'Introduction: Dis/Locating Posthumanism in European Literary and Critical Traditions', in *European Journal of English Studies*, 18.2
Collodi, Carlo, 1986 [1883], *The Adventures of Pinocchio*, tr. Nicolas Perella (Berkeley and London: University of California Press)
Freud, Sigmund, 1955 [1919], The 'Uncanny', *The Standard Edition of the Complete Psychological Works of Sigmund Freud*, tr. and ed. James Strachey et al., vol 17 (London: Hogarth), 217–256
Fullerton, Huw, 2015, 'Humans series review: "A surprise success – thriving where Utopia drowned"', *Radio Times* (Sunday 2 August)
Graham, Elaine L., 2002, *Representations of the Post/human: Monsters, Aliens and Others in Popular Culture* (Manchester: Manchester University Press)
Hayles, N. Katherine, 2011, 'Wrestling with Transhumanism', in *H+ Transhumanism and its Critics*, ed. Gregory R. Hansell and William Grassie (Philadelphia: Metanexus)
Jentsch, Ernst, 2008 [1906], 'On the Psychology of the Uncanny', in *Uncanny Modernity: Cultural Theories, Modern Anxieties*, tr. and ed. Roy Sellars (Basingstoke: Palgrave Macmillan), 216–228.
Kreider, Tim, 2002, 'A.I. Artificial Intelligence', in *Film Quarterly*, 56.2
Luckhurst, Roger, 2005, *Science Fiction* (Cambridge: Polity Press)
More, Max, Humanity+ webpage: http://hplusmagazine.com/transhumanist-faq/#answer_19, last accessed 24 Oct 2017
Mori, Masahiro, 1970, 'The Uncanny Valley', tr. Karl F. MacDorman and Takashi Minato, *Energy*, 7(4), 33–35
Scott, Ridley, dir., 1982, *Blade Runner*
Sobchack, Vivian, 1997, *Screening Space: The American Science Fiction Film*, 2nd ed. (New Brunswick, N.J. & London: Rutgers University Press)
Spielberg, Steven, dir., 2001, *A. I. Artificial Intelligence*
Suvin, Darko, 1972, 'On the Poetics of the Science Fiction Genre', in *College English*, 34.3
Various directors, *Humans*, 2015 (Channel 4/AMC TV)
Williams, Susan S., 1996, '"The Inconstant Daguerreotype": The Narrative of Early Photography', in *Narrative* Vol. 4, No. 2 (May)
Wolfe, Cary, 2010, *What Is Posthumanism?* (Minneapolis: University of Minnesota Press)

PART III

Wayward Women

CHAPTER 8

The metaphysics of replacement in photoplay novels of immigration

Marija Dalbello

Photoplay novels were a genre of text illustrated with images from silent films that reveal the protocols of seeing and reading that were current in the early period of cinema. They were a boundary space for a mediation of texts and images, in which neither system of representation was complete, but together they formed the site of mutual replacements. Both textual and visual (graphic and photographic), photoplay novels supported the narrativity of early cinema. They were an intermedium, in which the visual realism of the stills counteracted and punctuated the fictional novelistic narratives.

Photoplay novels were also sites for the visual consumption of womanhood in the 1920s. In that context, the hybridisation of early cinema and Anzia Yezierska's immigrant stories offered a representation of gendered immigrant selves, and the interpretation of migration and Americanisation as a replacement process. Yezierska's New Woman stories were based on her own experience as an immigrant and featured women in settings that were distinct from the figures of the feminine known from the melodramatic fiction of that era, in which the archetypal and the sublime were

M. Dalbello (✉)
Rutgers, The State University of New Jersey, New Brunswick, NJ, USA

© The Author(s) 2018
J. Owen, N. Segal (eds.), *On Replacement*,
https://doi.org/10.1007/978-3-319-76011-7_8

staged alongside the threatening aspects of femininity. The presentation of foreignness, by which subjectivity is recrafted in the context of immigration, points to the multiple relocations the immigrant undertakes in the search for an American self as replacement. The film *Hungry Hearts* (1922) was based on Yezierska's collection of short stories that appeared in 1920, the same year as the photoplay novel, and the *Salome of the Tenements* (1925) on her 1923 novel. Through photoplay novels, the films enter the novels. Parts of one medium, constructed with images moved over from another, radically shift the codes of reading, seeing and experiencing the 'new' self.

The photoplay novels blended stills from silent films distributed by the major film studios with novels issued by publishers of reprint editions. The combined media effect of the novel and film stills, neither complete nor extricable from the other, participated in creating a new sensorium for audiences.[1] Historically, this hybrid form of novel was concurrent with sound film experiments from 1924, and all but disappeared as a narrative medium at the introduction of sound in 1927. Their emergence, together with the feature film by the mid-1910s, paralleled an increasing filmic sophistication on the part of the audiences of the late silent film era.[2] The photoplay stories aimed to create an experience of immersion and presence. They reflected a shift in the consumption of film – from moving pictures that attracted working-class men, to a medium that gained cultural legitimacy and respectability for middle-class viewers, and especially female viewers. This acculturation also ran parallel with a shift from the nickelodeon to the movie palace.

Intended for middle-class readers of publishers' trade editions, photoplay novels peaked in the classical period of silent film at the threshold of its transition to sound. They represent an arena of triple mediation: (1) of the technologies of presence; (2) of the contemporary construction of the experiences of viewing and reading; and (3) of the fluidity and ambiguity of the social roles of women and the discourse of the New Woman. Photoplay novels also represent an archive of early film. The stills that illustrated the novels remain visual records of films whose copies may be lost. Therefore, photoplay novels also have a historical significance as a threshold genre documenting the transition from silent to sound cinema: they allow for the reconstruction of an immersive visualisation and picturisation that mediated novel ideas about technology, narrativity and femininity. They appear at the cusp of an expansion of the narrative complexity of film that could match that of the traditional medium of the novel. Photoplay novels are at the heart of the sensorium for the newly constructed 'expert viewers' (Inness 1995: 170).

The texts used in photoplay novels were popular prose narratives adapted into film or texts written with an imminent adaptation in mind, a process referred to as 'picturisation' or 'screen continuity'. The models for experiencing the photoplay novels responded to the audience's desire for an augmentation of their narrative experience and an immersion through stimuli that were internal and external to the texts.[3] An introductory text found in photoplay editions in the 1920s, titled 'Read the Book then See the Picture', outlines the model for picturisation:

> The feature photoplay *presents scenes and action as has never been possible on any stage*. Yet the very best of these fails to satisfy us fully, because it can not, even with the best and most skilful direction, give all of *the character, the interplay of emotion, the subtle inner motives* and the finer bits of humor which go to make up the whole of life. All do indeed appear upon the screen in all of their dramatic power, still we want much more if we are to have the fullest possible understanding of all the beauty and strength of personality which go to make up the deeper background of life as the author makes it plain in his pages. The best proof of the need for supplementing the photoplay with very full text lies in the *picturization* of any great novel. *See the picture, then read the novel and you will find out how one helps the other.* Even if you have reversed the best order of procedure: had you read the novel first, and then seen the picture how much deeper would have been your understanding and appreciation of all the scenes! There can be no doubt in the mind of any thinking person that the Book and the Photoplay belong together. One helps the other infinitely. As you read the book you imagine how the characters must have acted at the critical turns in the drama, and when you see the picture your ideas are broadened and deepened, if the picture has been well done. It is because there is a real *demand* upon the part of many *thousands of those who attend the Photoplay theatres for the books out of which some of the plays have grown* that books are being supplied at a reasonable price to supplement the fine work of the Screen. All around us we hear the cry: *read* the *book* then *see* the *picture*. [emphasis added] (Mooers 1920: advertisement)

The imperative of reading the novel first and then seeing the film points to the dominant role of text, and anchors the activity of reading within a broader context of reception defined by the film industry. The star-marketing system called for the film stars to appear in the wording of the title and on dust jackets. The still facing the title page controlled entry into the text and featured female silent-film stars or a star couple. The inter-media effect that operated through picturisation relied on the dual effect of text and image in the photoplay novel.[4]

The popularity of novelisations and their illustration with stills from silent films called for new types of stories. In 1913, Eustace Hale Ball, a prolific writer of photoplays, noted an 'increasing demand for the scripts' of directors who, having exhausted 'their own ideas' from 'the field of melodrama and slapstick comedies of familiar and ancient vintage', were being 'compelled to reach out for original scenarios from fresher sources than the minds of the over-worked producers' (Ball 1913: 7). Among the storylines belonging to these 'fresher sources' were real-life stories and fictions featuring immigrants. One of Ball's novelisations in this genre was the photoplay novel, *Traffic in Souls: A Novel of Crime and Its Cure* (1914). The film of the same title (1913/1994) was 'founded upon stories of real life', based on the exposé of a crime-ring by a woman. Together with her police-officer boyfriend, the woman uncovers a prostitution ring targeting immigrants – who had kidnapped her sister – and exposes a philanthropist as the ringleader (Ball 1914: 2–3). This film reveals the era's paternalistic attitudes toward immigrants. The arrival of the immigrants via Ellis Island was significant in contemporary public discourse during the peak of migration from Europe to the USA. In its reference to 'traffic in souls' (white slavery), the film points to some of the tensions and dangers of that entry point for immigrant women.[5] Ball's novelisation, and the film, were typical of the repertoire of social programmes directed at immigrants, evaluating their place within a moral and normative order of citizenship. Ellis Island was the landing place at which the state and the immigrants negotiated conditions for the latter to enter the New World. Therefore, the immigrants' arrival and progress involved a series of spatial and social relocations at that threshold of citizenship. Their seamless integration into citizenship and self-realisation in American society depended on their ability to be moulded and to replace the old with the new. Echoing the progressive era's mainstream values, and epitomising them, were John Dewey's ideas of education for life: he 'imagined the poor, immigrants, uneducated masses in need of social engineering'[6] (Ginsberg 2016: 99).

Anzia Yezierska's collection of short stories *Hungry Hearts* (1920) and her novel *Salome of the Tenements* (1923) explore gendered immigrant selves. Both appeared as photoplay editions (Yezierska 1920, 1923) and films (1922/2006, 1925). Yezierska's own experiences as an immigrant conveyed in these narratives were recreated through the conventions of picturisation for a wide audience of filmgoers. For the spectators, the films offered an opportunity for picturisation: a launching pad for naturalist fantasies about immigrant life in the tenements. When made into films, Yezierska's realistic stories become a site for de-ethnicisation and filial 'replacement', especially in the film *Hungry Hearts*. The titular 'hungry heart' is a trope for immigrant sensibility epitomised by a desire to become American. The stories mirror Yezierska's personal quest for a path of escape from her role as daughter, wife and mother, and her foreignness as an immigrant 'mandated by experts and philanthropists' into an Americanness she is seeking but that can never be achieved or even understood (Ginsberg 2016: 78). Her biographer, Alan Robert Ginsberg, notes that the story of Yezierska (as a historical person) is one of willing displacement and a desire for self-ownership that 'reflected a commitment to [...] the politics of non-identity' as a form of defiant individualism characterised by 'deliberately eluding identification and direct affiliation' (115). Her life points to these tensions and her 'self-characterization as an outsider that became a central theme of her fiction' (99). Her striving for rebirth from the 'crushing' experience of 'her first American decade' (73) became the painful remembrances filling her stories and novels, once she started writing. The stories were also a means for her to transcend her social position as an immigrant woman and to become a writer breaking into Hollywood circles.

The *Hungry Hearts* characters were caught between the hopes and the hardships of their immigrant condition. From the perspective of the New York Lower East Side tenements, Yezierska's USA is an unspecifiable place of desire. That desire originates in relocations from the East European *shtetl* to the USA through Ellis Island, and it shapes immigrant subjectivities. Life in the liminal spaces of New York's Lower East Side tenements – with their dark interiors and crowded exteriors, with their stores, chaotic and noisy streets, the sweatshop and the courtroom – is a transition point for the protagonists on their paths into American life.

The photoplay novel *Hungry Hearts* features four stills from the silent film. Reading the stills against the text of the photoplay novel offers insights into the intertextual and intermedia effect of this immigrant-focused cultural text. The synopsis of the film follows the Levin family, emigrating from a village in East Europe (Goluth) to New York's Lower East Side, and their move out of the tenements. The suburban family home delineated by a white picket fence at the end of the film signals the fulfilment of the American dream. The characters include the pious if impractical, learned Abraham as head of the family, his more practical wife

Fig. 8.1 (a, b) Stills from *Hungry Hearts* silent film (1922) published in Anzia Yezierska's photoplay novel, *Hungry Hearts: Illustrated with Scenes from the Photoplay, A Goldwyn Picture* (New York: Grosset & Dunlap, c1920)

Hanneh, who is the protagonist of the key dramatic event in the film, their daughter Sara, and her younger siblings. Sara meets and marries David, a young American lawyer and nephew of Rosenblatt, the mean slumlord who owns the Levins' tenement flat (Fig. 8.1a, b).

The first still facing the title page (Fig. 8.1a), subtitled, 'Bryant Washburn and Helen Ferguson as David and Sara in the Photoplay', is in keeping with the tradition of the star system frontispiece. Other stills in the volume are titled 'A Scene from the Photoplay'. The first still (facing p. 54) is from the beginning of the film and depicts a scene from the village of Goluth in 1910 when Abraham reads the 'America letter' from a former village water-carrier Gedalyah Mindel, now a successful American businessman, to the curious Goluth villagers. The letter triggers the desire of the 'hungry hearts' (hungry for freedom from violence represented by the marauding Cossacks who appear early in the film harassing the Levins) and it influences their decision to emigrate. Another (facing p. 150) shows the arrival of the Levin family at their tenement flat in rustic clothes and led by Gedalyah dressed as a proper American dandy. The contrast is meant to externalize a transformation. A third scene (facing p. 230) depicts David and Sara falling in love. They are reading together, under Abraham and Hanneh's admiring gaze, Sara dressed in 'American' clothes – see Fig. 8.1b.

The central dramatic event of the film depicts Hanneh destroying the kitchen, which she had painted white to brighten the darkness of their tenement flat and to assert symbolically the new life that Sara will have in a new society with David. The cause of her behaviour is the landlord, Rosenblatt, who, in a fit of rage upon learning of David's promise of

Fig. 8.2 (a–d) Stills from *Hungry Hearts* silent film (1922). COURTESY THE NATIONAL CENTER FOR JEWISH FILM

marriage to Sara, doubles the rent and forbids the marriage. In his exploitation of immigrants, Rosenblatt serves as an obstruction to the aspirations of the 'hungry hearts'. He also happens to be David's uncle, who pays for his studies at law school, forces him to collect rent from his tenants and refuses to support and release him to set up his own practice (Fig. 8.2a–d).

The white kitchen that Hanneh paints signals the replacement of the darkness of the tenement flat with the idea that she can replicate her employer's white American kitchen. The last scenes of the film – which serve as an epilogue taking place two years later – depict a house in the American suburbs, a white picket fence, with Hanneh and her kids transformed into Americans (superficially indicated by their change of clothes and appearance), while Abraham remains unchanged, still self-involved and immersed in his bookish pursuits on the porch of their suburban new home, oblivious to the surroundings. Yezierska resented that happy ending, which was absent from her stories.[7]

The image at the start of the photoplay novel allows the reader to reenter the photoplay sensorium and rearranges the timeframes of the film and the *Hungry Hearts* short stories. One of the stories, 'The Lost "Beautifulness"', features Hanneh Hayyeh, a woman waiting for her son to return from the Great War, an ultimate expression of citizenship and of becoming American. Hanneh Hayyeh (in the story) and Hanneh Levin (in the film) are merged through a common storyline – both paint their 'dark' and 'ill-smelling' tenement flats white, an event that is the central visual sensation and dramatic culmination of the *Hungry Hearts* film and the story from the *Hungry Hearts* collection. The silent film retains connections with the published story through the symbolism of recurrent objects – a flat knife that Hanneh uses to demolish her apartment in an act of defiance and the drama of eviction from the windowless tenement flat. Hanneh Hayyeh, the mother of the American hero, is thrown out on the street by her landlord in the original story, unlike Hanneh Levin of the film, who moves to the suburbs. The replacement space for Hanneh Hayyeh is the pavement and for Hanneh Levin a suburban dream house. Yezierska's own relocation out of the tenements and her Americanisation is another not fully realised replacement.

The father of the family, *melamed* [scholar] Abraham Levin, was modelled on Yezierska's demanding father. His characterisation is particularly memorable in the film where he epitomises authority associated with the traditions of the old world. He represents what she resists, a counterpoint to replacement. In the Levins' story, he is depicted as a passive protagonist immersed in his books. At the start of the film set in the village of Goluth, he is introduced via the intertitle as follows: 'Abraham Levin – scholar, gentle, pious, impractical', 'Abraham, the wise one; who, in 1910, solved all problems according to a book written in 1200' (*Hungry Hearts* 1922/2006). The first minutes of the film feature multiple references to written culture associated with Abraham that persist throughout the film. The Levin family's journey starts in the moment of collective reading of the letter in Goluth, leading to their decision to leave for the USA. Abraham is an ineffective agent for the Levin family's transformation in the New World. Even when he acts, his actions are misdirected. He thus spends his family's rent money to buy an 'American' hat for his wife, wrongly believing that she wishes to become more American. Instead, his purchase threatens the family's survival. Similarly, when he attempts to sell his watch to the tenement butcher, a close-up of his watch with Hebrew letters, shown alongside the butcher's American watch (see Fig. 8.2a), is interpreted in the intertitle, 'To tell time with your watch, I would need a dictionary', and points to a mutual incomprehensibility – as if the two watches (the traditional and the modern) could not mark the same time. Several other close-up shots feature objects of literacy associated with Abraham: his books, the 'America' letter, the ancient text 'that he uses to interpret life', and his watch. They are depicted as illegible, irrelevant, resistant, even obstructive, in need of but incapable of effective replacement. By contrast, the culmination of the film is a scene in the courtroom epitomising the state and its model of literacy, which is easily navigated by David when he helps Hanneh Levin state her case against the landlord Rosenblatt. The courtroom symbolises transition and the replacement of one site for another. It is the dramatic end of one and the beginning of another stage in their American life.

Sonya Vrunsky is 'the Salome of New York's tenements' and the heroine of Yezierska's novel of the same name (1923). In this autobiographical novel, she presents the sentiments that accompany replacement: the emotional as well as material character of relocation epitomised in the protagonist. Yezierska describes the feeling as 'the over-emotional Ghetto struggling for its breath in the thin air of Puritan restraint' and Sonya as 'an East Side savage forced suddenly into the straitjacket of American civilization', 'like the dynamite bomb and Manning [the millionaire philanthropist she marries] the walls of tradition constantly menaced by threatening explosions' (Yezierska 1923: blurb). The eight stills in the photoplay novel are from the lost Paramount film of 1925 and its only remaining archive. The women with whom she created *Salome of the Tenements* were the socialist activist Rose Pastor Stokes, screenwriter Sonya Levien and actress Jetta Goudal. They all started out as poor, Jewish and female and 'chose to become Americans in the process of determining what that meant [and] by challenging the status quo they helped advance the rights of women, workers, immigrants and other disadvantaged people' (Ginsberg 2016: xi). They also challenged their era's perspectives about 'a new kind of woman' that included leisure-class women who indulged in conspicuous consumption (Rideout 1954/1992: 75). Alongside these traditional 'good women' philanthropists were radicals such as the New Women of the 'Salome Ensemble', caught within a tension of incomplete and impossible replacement of their origins to become integrated into mainstream society.

In her autobiographical writings, Yezierska depicted the conditions of those who immigrated to the United States around the beginning of the twentieth century and her own identity-forming process. The themes of replacement in her immigrant stories were popularised and enriched through the mediation of photoplay novels that enabled simultaneous experiencing of film and narrative storytelling. Their close reading revealed the themes of incomplete relocations or impossibilities of relocation symbolised by transitional states (an elusive 'American' self or the 'new woman'); transitional sites (the tenements); and, irreconcilable geographies and relocations of the Old and the New World. The photoplay sensorium in photoplay novels supported the transference of desires and emotions of the immigrant condition onto the mainstream audiences through an imagistic presence created through the star system in an intermedial space for narrative eidetic imagination. Yet a complete replacement for the protagonists, *pace* Yezierska, could not be realised within that sensorium because her stories resist and defy the process of replacement and assimilation in terms of the narrative conventions of early cinema, crystallising the tensions of her life story.

Notes

1. The term 'sensorium' refers to the human senses as a grouping and 'our habits of indexicality [that] create correspondences between perceptions of the world and the meanings we give to those perceptions' (Panagia and Richard: n.p.). In media theory, the forms of displacement by which perceptions and meanings are shifted and mediated through techniques (for example, photoplay novels as an intermedium that combines film and novel), offer new possibilities for the human sensorium, reworking of senses, subjectivities, and operations of the self, mind and social experience.
2. Initially, films were one or two reels long and lasted less than seventeen minutes. By the mid-1910s, the length of a film expanded to five or six reels of over-an-hour duration of play, a technological change that affected the ability of film to tell a story, with the emergence of the feature film. Film evolved as a distinct medium with its own narrative modes between 1910 and 1917 when motion pictures became an industry.
3. Intertexts (prefaces, advertisements and blurbs) were combined with descriptions in public epitext (including promotional materials); external to texts but having a liminal presence as 'paratextual element not materially appended to the text' (Genette 2009: 344).
4. On the hybridity of text and image see W. J. T. Mitchell's Picture Theory (1993).
5. The references to contemporary events involve Charles S. Whitman, District Attorney for the Borough of Manhattan and *Whitman's White Slave Report* (Ball 1914: [2]).
6. On how Dewey was also an important authority figure in Anzia Yezierska's life and a protagonist of her own 'Cinderella' story, see Dearborn 1989.
7. Her meddling with the screenplay ended her relationship with the Samuel Goldwyn studio (Ginsberg 2016: 106).

REFERENCES

André Andersen's Lost Film Files, http://www.silentsaregolden.com/arneparamountpictures.html, accessed 15 October 2017

Ball, Eustace Hale, 1913, *The Art of the Photoplay* (New York: G. W. Dillingham)

Ball, Eustace Hale, 1914, *Traffic in Souls: A Novel of Crime and Its Cure* (New York: G. W. Dillingham)

Coté, Marc, 2010, 'Technics and the Human Sensorium: Rethinking Media Theory through the Body', in *Theory & Event* 13 (4), https://muse.jhu.edu/article/407142, accessed 15 October 2017

Dearborn, Mary V., 1989, 'Anzia Yezierska and the Making of an Ethnic American Self', in *The Invention of Ethnicity*, ed. Werner Sollors (New York and Oxford: Oxford University Press), 105–123.

Genette, Gérard, 2009 [1987], *Paratexts: Thresholds of Interpretation*, tr. Jane E. Lewin (Cambridge, UK: Cambridge University Press)

Ginsberg, Alan Robert, 2016, *The Salome Ensemble: Rose Pastor Stokes, Anzia Yezierska, Sonya Levien, and Jetta Goudal* (Syracuse, NY: Syracuse University Press)

Inness, Sherrie A., 1995, 'The Feminine En-gendering of Film Consumption and Film Technology in Popular Girls' Serial Novels, 1914–1931', in *Journal of Popular Culture* 29 (3), 169–182.

Loane Tucker, George, dir., 1913 [1994], *Traffic in Souls* (New York: Kino Video)

Mason Hopper, E., dir., 1922 [2006], *Hungry Hearts* (Waltham, MA: Brandeis University)

Mitchell, W. J. T., 1993, *Picture Theory* (Chicago: The University of Chicago Press)

Mooers, De Sacia, 1920, *The Blonde Vampire* (New York: Moffat, Yard, and Co.).

Performing Arts Encyclopaedia, http://memory.loc.gov/diglib/ihas/loc.mbrs.sfdb.378/default.html, accessed 15 October 2017

Panagia, Davide, and Adrienne Richard, 2010, 'A Return to the Senses: Introduction', in *Theory & Event* 13 (4), https://muse.jhu.edu/article/407140, accessed 15 October 2017.

Rideout, Walter B., 1992 [1956], *The Radical Novel in the United States 1900–1954: Some Interrelations of Literature and Society*, 2nd ed. (New York: Hill & Wang)

Yezierska, Anzia, 1920, *Hungry Hearts: Illustrated with Scenes from the Photoplay, A Goldwyn Picture* (New York: Grosset & Dunlap)

Yezierska, Anzia, 1923, *Salome of the Tenements: Illustrated with Scenes from the Photoplay, A Paramount Picture* (New York: Grosset & Dunlap)

CHAPTER 9

Of ghosts and girls in *Ulysses* 13

Patrizia Grimaldi-Pizzorno

In a recent article on *Ulysses* 13 (Grimaldi-Pizzorno 2017), I argued that the *Nausicaa* episode does not just reenact the mythical Homeric encounter between a foreign man and an unguarded girl on the beach of Phaeacia, but alludes, simultaneously and repeatedly, to other versions of the original erotic-elegiac encounter. Gerty MacDowell, like the ideal fictional *scriptae puellae* [written women] of Augustan elegy, is a textual construct fabricated by the artist-lover. She is Leopold Bloom's (flawed) erotic masterpiece. The discovery and examination of a pun on 'feet' and 'legs', both metric and human, reveals that Gerty's feet function as a semantic node in a set of intertextual relationships. The analysis of the encrypted hypotexts shows that the significance of the episode is metapoetical and that Gerty has no existence outside the protean textual matter that constitutes her. The pursuit of erotic-textual desire, in both monologues, culminates when Gerty's disability is revealed and she is exposed as a defective copy of an irretrievable and lost original. The sight of her deformity, revealed when she gets up and leaves (U.13.731*ff*), marks the return to realism and the demise of Bloom as the lyrical 'I': 'See her as she is spoil all' (U.13.855) (Fig. 9.1).[1]

P. Grimaldi-Pizzorno (✉)
University of Siena, Siena, Italy

Fig. 9.1 Umberto Boccioni, *Scomposizione di figura di donna a tavola* (1912), Museo del Novecento, Milano, © Archivi Alinari, Firenze, Italy

In this chapter, I shall focus on the visual and musical hypotexts encrypted in the *Nausicaa* episode and argue that it represents creative imagination as a metapoetical process of intertextual replacements. Intertextual replacement is achieved, in my view, by means of that narrative 'technique' or 'art' of 'progressione, retrogressiva' [progression, retrogressive] defined by Joyce in the 'Linati Schema' of *Ulysses* (see Ellmann: Appendix). I believe in fact that 'progression, retrogressive' refers to the use in both monologues of flashbacks and flashforwards, two devices characteristic of early film, which alter temporality and replace Gerty with negatively eroticised doubles. Described as 'aloof, apart, in another sphere' (U.13.601) and voiceless, Gerty is a lone figure thinking thoughts she will never communicate to anyone. However, her inner life is penetrated by Bloom's eyes, which, like an optical instrument, go beyond the sentimental *kitsch* of the narrated monologue. Both a camera and a projector, his eyes transcend the 'present' time of the narration and, revealing Gerty's inner life, project a plurality of shadows and ultimately the image of death: 'his eyes burned into her as though they would search her through and through, read her very soul' (U.13.412).

Placed at the live centre of the episode, Gerty MacDowell has no real presence in the present of the narrative. The ambiguity of her narrated monologue, balanced between empathy and parody, casts a 'peculiarly penumbral light on the figural consciousness suspending it on the threshold of verbalization' (Cohn: 103) and suggests that she is an invented presence and a fabrication replaced in Bloom's mind by a 'projected mirage': to Joyce the 'meaning' of the episode. The abrupt question of the diegetic narrator: 'But who *was* Gerty?' (U.13.78) appears to be posited, therefore, not in terms of the traditional 'ontology' that thinks being in terms of self-identical presence, but rather of what Derrida has termed 'hantologie' [hauntology]'. Like the ghost in *Hamlet*, alluded to by Bloom ('For this relief much thanks. In HAMLET, that is' (U.13.940)), she is the 'hauntological' spectre, which cannot be fully present because it has no being in itself: suspended between the past and the present it marks a relation to what is no longer or not yet.

The kinetic technique of 'progression, retrospective' used by Joyce for rendering consciousness is filmic. The important analogy of the *Nausicaa* episode with cinematographic technology, and its hidden references to early cinema and primitive pornographic movies, has been discussed by a number of scholars. However, the relevance of early photographic technique, and specifically of experimental Futurist photography to the disintegration of realism and its replacement by the artificial, has been overlooked. In the first half of the episode, the sentimental portrait of Gerty sitting on the rock by the sea, against the gathering darkness cast in sombre shades of blue, recalls the cyanotype postcards of seaside girls at the origin of photography.[2] Gerty's eyes are 'of the bluest Irish blue' (U.13.108), her blouse is 'electric blue,' the under brim of her hat is 'egg-blue' (U.13.57), her skirt is navy blue and blue is also the colour of her garters. Intrinsically 'blue', this sorrowful girl, ironically, also takes 'iron jelloids' (U.13.84) to treat her anaemia; these are made of the same type of water-soluble iron salts that turn Prussian blue in the cyanotype process. However, in an illusionistic visual 'progression, retrogressive', endowed with its own rhythm, the cinematographic present-continuous tense revises the implicit photographic past tense and the photographic incunabulum of the innocent girl in blue begins to animate. The romantic postcard, blurred and smeared by a plurality of visual hypotexts projected by Bloom's excited state of mind, is eventually replaced by an unstable animation and kinetic montage-string of pornographic stills mounted on the rotary wheel of the mutoscope (U.13.794). Bloom's mental projections culminate in the climactic vision of Gerty as Moulin Rouge dancer: in a 'wondrous revealment half offered like those skirtdancers behaving so immodest before gentlemen looking and he kept on looking, looking'

(U.13.731). Even our coy girl refers to pornographic photography twice: first, when she mentions the sexy pictures of 'skirtdancers and highkickers' used for masturbation by Bertha Supple's indigent boarder (U.13.704); second, when she alludes to a 'silly' postcard, obviously a sexy snapshot, which she received from her presumptive beau (U.13.593*ff*).

The image of Gerty as the virtuous exemplar to her sex is both faked and pretended: like a Futurist *papier collé*, she is an emblem 'of the systematic play of difference, the *mise en question* of representation that is inherent in its verbal-visual structure' (Perloff: 51). There is nothing unique or original about her: Bloom's 'pale Galilean eyes' (U.9.607) scrutinise and fragment her into a plurality of photographically captured rapid images. Her body parts, like her fetishised foot swinging rhythmically, work as a magic wand to prod his imagination and conjure ghosts, copies of a copy of the lost original. Gerty's sentimental portrait in blue has thus become 'photodynamic and polyphysiognomic, antigraceful, deforming, impressionistic, synthetic, dynamic, freewordist'.[3] It resembles the experimental portraits of Anton Giulio Bragaglia (1890–1960), the first of the Futurists to challenge the use of the camera as merely reproducing physical reality. As film-frames of hair, throat, arms, legs, ankles and feet are recalled from primitive pornographic movies and voyeuristic films (*Peeping Tom*, 1901; *As Seen Through a Telescope*, 1900; *The Gay Shoe Clerk*, 1903; *Shoe Salon Pinkus*, 1916), Gerty's body becomes progressively fragmented, her sexuality exposed and the deceptive sentimental realism of the narrated monologue deconstructed. The interpolation 'her crowning glory' (U.13.116, 510), for instance, referring to Gerty's magnificent head of dark brown hair, is not a reference to Gorgon Medusa, but to *Her Crowning Glory*, a 1911 film by Lawrence Trimble about an ugly and hypocritical governess (Flora Finch) with a beautiful head of hair who tries, unsuccessfully, to marry her widowed employer. When the child she has ill-treated cuts her tresses off, her ugliness and hypocrisy are unmasked and she leaves the house with her hair in a bag in a long shot that reminds us of Gerty's bathetic departure.

The narrow focus on legs, ankles and feet, Bloom's scopophilia and Gerty's complicit exhibitionism, establishes an important analogy with the cinematographic gaze and male spectatorship that recalls three voyeuristic films produced by Arturo Ambrosio, the founder of Italian cinematography in Turin. The proto-futurist films *La Storia di Lulú* [*The Story of Lulú as told by her feet*], *Storia di un paio di stivali* [*The Story of a pair of boots*] of 1910 and the 1915 *Amor pedestre* [*Love afoot*], which have gone unnoticed by Anglo-American critics, deserve attention. Unlike *As seen through a telescope*, they are not character centred, but spectator centred and the love story between a man and a woman, just as in *Nausicaa*, is visualised by the movements of feet and legs only, or even by shoes alone. Footage is all about feet. Unknown to the nonspecialist of Italian *cinema muto*, they were most probably known to Joyce, an avid cinefile, who lived in Trieste, the hub of early Futurism. Another reason why he is unlikely to have missed them is because Ambrosio's movies, famous in both Italy and France, had inspired Filippo Tommaso Marinetti's 'microdramma' *Le basi* [*The Bases*], staged in 1915, in which the curtain was raised only as high as the actors' legs. *The Bases* inaugurated the short-lived season of 'Teatro futurista sintetico' [Futurist Synthetic Theatre], which was hailed for the brevity of its 'dramas of objects' and convergence of a variety of alternative performance genres in the *Manifesto del teatro futurista sintetico* (1915) – signed by Marinetti, Emilio Settimelli and Bruno Corra – as the only antidote to cinema.

As the seaside picture in blue recedes into the background and the cyanotype is replaced through a kinetic 'progression, retrospective' of texts, images and music, the uncanny behind the mock familiar and homely is revealed.[4] The hypocritical, realist portrait of Gerty as the sentimental 'sterling good daughter' and 'ministering angel' is replaced with 'marketplace' (Joyce 1981, chap. 5) beauties further down on the aesthetic scale. The replacement of the didactic and sentimental imagery of the first part of the episode with pornography in Bloom's stream of consciousness may be explained by Joyce's theory of aesthetic emotion in which didactic sentimentalism is equated with pornography. Like his younger persona, Stephen Dedalus, Joyce rated drama above all literary forms and made what he called the 'dramatic emotion' the prototype of 'aesthetic emotion' in general. He believed in fact that the didactic novel in its classic phase is an 'improper art', akin to pornography, with the intention to generate desire and loathing and thus urge the possession of the good and the abandonment of the bad (see Trilling). As Dedalus explains to Lynch in *A Portrait of the Artist as a Young Man*:

> The feelings excited by improper art are kinetic, desire and loathing. Desire urges us to possess, to go to something; loathing urges us to abandon, to go from something. The arts which excite them, pornographical or didactic, are therefore improper arts. The aesthetic emotion (I use the general term) is therefore static '[that is dramatic emotion]'. The mind is arrested and raised above desire and loathing. (205)

Like Joyce, Antonio Bragaglia aspired to transcendent forms beyond the boundaries of the real and the visible and urged the destruction of mimesis through entropic dynamism. *Fotodinamismo*, he claimed, would liberate the vital spirit frozen in a rigor mortis by realist photography. The Futurists were inspired, like Joyce, by Henri Bergson's concept of time; they claimed that, unlike film, 'photodynamism' gives access to *durée*, pure duration, or time as a continuous stream to which we best gain access through the consciousness of our inner mental life. With Carlo Carrà, Giacomo Balla and to a certain extent Umberto Boccioni, Bragaglia adopted the argument of Herbert Spencer (1890–1903) that motion, including that of human consciousness, is characterised by 'compound rhythms' (Spencer: 93); he claimed that only 'photodynamism' can reveal and represent the 'complex rhythms' of the invisible vibrations of movement. Moreover, like Joyce, he shared with Boccioni, Marinetti and Luigi Russolo a strong interest in spiritualism, the occult and, not without irony, in the mystery of materialisation through a medium.[5] Well before Jacques Derrida's pronouncements in Ken McMullen's film *Ghost Dance* ('cinema is the art of ghosts'), the early Futurists defined photography in terms of phantoms and produced studio portraits, which simulated ectoplasmic manifestations through animated, photodynamic montages. Boccioni believed that the 'occhi veggenti' [clairvoyant eyes] (Boccioni: 29) of the artist-medium would restore to photography its radiant magnetic polarity or, in the words of the theosophists, its 'aura'.

Undoubtedly, Joyce had remarkable powers of visual imagery, which intensified with his progressive loss of sight. But, as a musician and a singer, he also possessed the power of imagining music, which he used to shape the rhythm of his prose and project epiphanies in both *Ulysses* and *Dubliners*.

In *The Dead*, to reveal the dreariness of bourgeois marriage against the glittering background of the celebration of family life and the empty rituals of good society, Joyce had used two songs, one explicit, the other implicit, to summon the dead. 'The Lass of Aughrim', sung by Bartell d'Arcy, summons the ghost of Michael Furey, Gretta's first love. The other song encrypted in the narrative is 'I Hear You Calling Me' whose speaker is a ghost. When Gabriel Conroy notices his wife standing on the stairs listening to the song, he imagines himself as an artist giving a title to the scene: 'Distant Music he would call the picture if he were a painter' (210). Whereas the first song ushers in the ghost of Michael, the encrypted line 'Distant music' from McCormack's ghost-song, reveals Gretta's unending longing for her dead lover and casts a shadow over her ostensibly perfect marriage to Gabriel (Reilly: 150).

In *Nausicaa* too, replacement involves the use of songs. The chanting of the *Tantum ergo sacramentum* (U.13.498), Thomas Aquinas' 'intricate and soothing hymn' (Joyce 1981 [1916]: 210), and the echoes of Thomas Moore's exilic tunes set the elegiac tone of the amorous encounter by the sea. Yet their deceptiveness is eventually revealed when a discordant tune from 'the land of song' (U.13.658) ushers in a ghostly presence. The song encrypted deeply in the text is 'Unfortunate Miss Bailey' a tragicomic-gothic tale about a servant seduced and abandoned by a bold captain, who hangs herself by her garters and returns to her lover as a ghost. Joyce does not mention this, but he entombs 'Miss Bailey', in the explicit reference '*Love Laughs at Locksmiths*' (U.13.653), the title of an 1803 ballad opera by George Colman the younger (1762–1836), which is triggered by Gerty's desire to run away with Bloom. Its plot, the seduction and elopement of Lydia with a captain, despite locks and latticed windows, is 'the story behind [...] the picture of halcyon days' in the grocer's almanac (U.13.334–337) she dreams about. The 'oldtime chivalry' and elegant manners excite Gerty's sensibility, consistently displayed, like other sentimental heroines of the lower class, through the projection of aristocratic phantasies. Yet these popular opera-ballads, though essentially farcical in tone, contained a potential for tragedy that locates them in the didactic and moral tradition of sentimentalism and 'Unfortunate Miss Bailey', which was sung at regular intervals throughout the opera was meant as a cautionary tale for the likes of Gerty in the audience.

The importance of 'Unfortunate Miss Bailey' to Joyce has been proved by the discovery that the song is in fact the English original of the Latin poem 'Balia', which was found among Joyce's loose papers and subsequently (wrongly) attributed to him (see Davis: 740). The Latin poem – on the tribulations and suicide of *Balia* (Latin 'nursemaid') – was not written by Joyce, but by the classicist and divine G. H. Glasse who, incidentally, also committed suicide (see Davis). Joyce, who at some point copied out 'Balia' on a scrap of paper, is likely to have known its English original. He was in fact intimately acquainted with both British and Irish popular songs.

The twilight scene on Sandymount beach with the hovering bat 'that flies from the ivied belfry through the dusk' (U.13.625) – an unnoticed reference to *Elegy Written in a Country Churchyard*, interlaced with a citation from Flaubert's *La Tentation de saint Antoine* – conjures up the mock-gothic atmosphere of the encounter of 'Captain bold and gay deceiver' with the ghost of the 'unburied', 'betrayed and abandoned most wretched' Balia/Bailey.[6] The similarities between Gerty and Miss Bailey/ Balia are also significant. If one thinks about it, Gerty is at Sandymount with her girlfriends not to do the laundry – like Nausikaa and her handmaidens – but to look after children: they are at the beach therefore as *baliae* [nannies], like the protagonist of *Her Crowning Glory*. Our limping heroine, like *Bailey/Balia*, is a *misera* and *infortunata* [poor/unhappy and unfortunate] servant girl. Yet Gerty is not just 'unhappy' and out of luck, she is also 'unfortunate' in the Italian and Latin sense of *infortunata* (from Latin *infortunium*, accident) because she has suffered physical injury (U.13.651): she is in fact lame. Gerty's pale complexion also recalls the ghostly face of Miss Bailey/*Balia*. Her statue-like beauty, 'slight and graceful [...] inclining even to fragility', with hands 'of finely veined alabaster' is like that of a corpse: 'The waxen pallor of her face was almost spiritual in its ivory like purity' (U.13.87) and evokes *Balia*'s 'corporis pallore' [whiteness of the body] and Miss Bailey's 'white and mealy' face. Like Balia, Gerty is 'infinitely sad and wistful. Gerty MacDowell yearns in vain [...] a strained look on her face! A gnawing sorrow is there all the time' (U.13.188), because the 'daydream of a marriage' (U.13.195) with the 'lighthearted deceiver and fickle' (U.13.584) Reggy Wylie has disintegrated. Yet the foolish daydreamer is ready 'to make the great sacrifice' (U.13.654) and dreams of offering herself as a wife to the stranger who loves her with 'whitehot passion [...] silent as the grave' (U.13.691). In Gerty's fantasies Leopold Bloom is in mourning for an 'old flame' and she can see 'the story of a haunting sorrow [...] written on his face' (U.13.423). Bloom, however, just like the Captain, has mercenary sex on his mind and, after ejaculating, he muses on his encounters with prostitutes. Like the Captain who gives the ghost 'One Pound Note' to 'bribe the Sexton for your grave', he imagines paying Gerty for the 'show', 'Suppose he gave her money. Why not? All a prejudice. She's worth ten, fifteen, more, a pound' (U.13.841).

The arrival on the stage of *Nausicaa* of the tragicomic ghost of Miss Bailey, a prostitute who kills herself by hanging by her garters, acts like the apparition of Hamlet's father, alluded to in U. 13.940, to reveal the tainted state of mind of the protagonists, as well as the hypocrisy of Gerty's sentimentality. Like young Hamlet, Joyce bears the curse of his country and the responsibility of unmasking its corruption, and Gerty, one may argue, like old Hamlet, has been poisoned by a polluted society. That the protagonist of *Ulysses* 13 is the ghost of a lame working-class girl – who ends up selling sex along the walk in Irishtown (U.13.662) and kills herself with prussic acid – is confirmed in *Circe*, where Gerty returns to Bloom as the abominable ghost of a prostitute of the bordello (U.15.372):

> (*Leering*, Gerty MacDowell *limps forward...*' MacDowell appears differently to your spelling throughout the chapter: MacDowell. Please consider checking the spelling and altering one, for consistency.*limps forward. She draws from behind, ogling, and shows coyly her bloodied clout.*) [...]
> GERTY: [...] You did that. I hate you.
> BLOOM: I? When? You're dreaming. I never saw you. [...]
> GERTY: (*To Bloom*) When you saw all the secrets of my bottom drawer. (*She paws his sleeve, slobbering*) Dirty married man! I love you for doing that to me. [...]
> (*She slides away crookedly.*)

It could be argued that Joyce's narrative process of replacement for rendering consciousness, based as it is on his theory of aesthetic emotion, becomes in *Nausicaa* a moral standpoint from which he seeks to establish the drama of womanhood. This is not in the sense of orthodox Christian mythology in which Eve, the first woman, is redeemed by Mary, the second – as the allusions to Marian liturgy in *Nausicaa* would have us believe – but in the social, moral and political sense of the price paid by women for the moral degradation of love and marriage in Dublin, a society corrupted by the hypocritical constraints of Roman Catholicism and the petit-bourgeois sentimental morality of the family. With Mary, the archetypal *virgo intacta*, evoked by the incarnational theology at beginning of the episode, the destiny of all the ghostly girls 'encrypted' in the narrative is determined, consensually or non-consensually, by erotic desire. Some, like Ophelia, follow the fatal trajectory of the abandoned virgin and kill themselves; others, less virtuous virgins, extricate themselves shrewdly, and are rewarded with social ascent and financial gain. The rich and the aristocrats who have had the benefit of a good education can take charge of their own destiny, but not so a Gerty or an Eveline. Theirs is not a story of moral success validated by wealth and social achievement: 'Had kind fate but willed her to be born a gentlewoman of high degree in her own right and had she only received the benefit of a good education Gerty

MacDowell might easily have held her own beside any lady in the land' (U.13.99).

Fate (that is, Joyce) is not kind to her: disabled, uneducated and poor, she remains just one of the many underprivileged women who, having lost their virtue, become prostitutes and kill themselves, to return as ghosts:

> (*Many most attractive and enthusiastic women also commit suicide by stabbing, drowning, <u>drinking prussic acid</u>, aconite, arsenic, opening their veins, refusing food, casting themselves under steamrollers, from the top of Nelson's Pillar, into the great vat of Guinness's brewery, asphyxiating themselves by placing their heads in gas ovens, <u>hanging themselves in stylish garters</u>, leaping from windows of different storeys.*) (U.15.1745, italics Joyce's; underlining mine)

As the allusion to Thomas Gray's *Elegy written in a country churchyard* suggests (U.13.624–627), Sandymount beach, where Bloom comes after Paddy Dignam's funeral, is a graveyard – the graveyard of Joyce's memory (see Derrida 1986). The encounter with the sentimental virgin Gerty MacDowell at Sandymount beach, *a paysage artificiel*, represents an erotic mourning ritual and Bloom, like Odysseus, has come to the 'banks of the River of Ocean' (Homer, Book XI) to resurrect the past and call up in a *nekuia* the 'helpless ghosts of the dead'. Yet, unlike Odysseus, who conjures famous women from the underworld (XI, 225–330), Bloom calls up eroticised female figures, a bevy of girls, from all walks of life. Evoked by analogical memory from religion, literature, photography, painting, theatre, film and music, pornography and advertisements, shadows of girls are projected by Bloom's consciousness. To conclude, we can say with Lionel Trilling that, having exposed Gerty's 'numbered bones' (Heaney 1998: 112) Joyce reveals himself to be like Hamm in *Endgame*, the terrible blind storyteller who 'presiding over the quietus of Nature, himself on the verge of extinction [...] makes nullity prevail' (452).[7]

Notes

1. All references to chapter and lines of *Ulysses* are to Joyce 1986.
2. The color blue recalls both Emma Bovary's dress and the girl Cyane (as in cyan blue) with whom the *Minnesänger* of Novalis (1772–1801) *Henry of Ofterdingen* goes in search of the *Blaue Blume*, a metaphor of romantic *Sehnsucht*.

3. See Bragaglia; on *fotodinamismo* see also Lista. Joyce loaned his copy of Boccioni's *Pittura, Scultura Futurista* to his friend Frank Budgen; see Budgen: 194.
4. Both 'hominess' (U.13.224) and 'homely' (U.13.238) refer to Gerty.
5. In *Cyclops* (12.338–373) Joyce parodies a Theosophist's account of a spiritualist seance.
6. Like Flaubert's *saint Antoine*, Bloom (U.13.751) sees the three girls of lust as a bat flies around and above him: 'chauve-souris fait des cercles dans l'air' [the little bat that flew so softly through the evening]. Odilon Redon's illustrations for the *Tentation de saint Antoine* (1889) and Georges Méliès's film (1898) might also be relevant to Joyce's inspiration.
7. Seamus Heaney, *Punishment*: 112.

References

Bragaglia, Anton Giulio, 1970 [1911], *Fotodinamismo futurista* (Torino: Einaudi)
Boccioni, Umberto, 1997 [1914], *Pittura, Scultura Futurista* (Milano: SE Ediz.)
Boccioni, Umberto, 1972, *Altri inediti e apparati critici* (Milano: Feltrinelli)
Budgen, Frank, 1960 [1937], *James Joyce and the Making of 'Ulysses'* (Bloomington: Indiana University Press)
Cohn, Dorrit, 1978, *Transparent Minds: Narrative Modes for Presenting Consciousness in Fiction* (Princeton: Princeton University Press)
Colman, George, 1803, *Love Laughs at Locksmiths: A Comic Opera: in two acts. As performed at the Theatre-Royal, Hay-Market* (London: T. Woodroof)
Davis, Wes, 1995, '"Balia Inventa": The source of Joyce's Latin Manuscript', in *James Joyce Quarterly*, Vol. 32 3/4, 738–746
Derrida, Jacques, 1986, 'Foreword: Fors: the Anglish words of Abraham and Török' in *The Wolf Man's magic word: A cryptonymy* by Nicolas Abraham and Maria Török, tr. Barbara Johnson (Minneapolis: University of Minnesota Press)
Ellmann, Richard, 1972, *Ulysses on the Liffey* (New York: Oxford University Press)
Flaubert, Gustave, 2006 [1874], *La Tentation de saint Antoine* (Paris: Gallimard)
Grimaldi-Pizzorno, Patrizia, 2014, 'Limping in Edenville', in *James Joyce Quarterly*, vol. 51 no. 2, 493–497
Grimaldi-Pizzorno, Patrizia, 2017, 'The Iambic Muse: Gerty's Metaformations in *Ulysses* 13', in *Classical Receptions Journal* 9 (2), 177–192
Heaney, Séamus, 1975, *North* (London: Faber and Faber) repr. in *Opened Ground* 1998 (New York: Farrar, Strauss and Giroux)
Homer, *Odyssey*, 1995, Classical Library, tr. A.T. Murray Loeb, vol. 104–105 (Cambridge, MA: Harvard University Press)
Joyce, James, 1986 [1922], *Ulysses*, ed. by H. W. Gabler *et al* (New York: Vintage Books)

Joyce, James, 1957, *Letters*, eds. Stuart Gilbert and Richard Ellmann (New York: Viking Press)
Joyce, James and J. C. C. Mays, 1992, *Poems and Exiles* (London: Penguin Books)
Joyce, James, 1981 [1916], *A Portrait of the Artist as a Young man* (New York: Penguin Books)
Joyce, James, 1991 [1914], *Dubliners* (New York: Knopf)
Lista, Giovanni, 2001, *Cinema e fotografia futurista* (Milano: Skira)
Lista, Giovanni, 2015, *Fotografia Futurista* (Milano: Sozzani)
Perloff, Marjorie, 2003, *The Futurist Moment: Avant-garde, Avant Guerre, and the Language of Rupture* (Chicago: University of Chicago Press)
Reilly, Séamus, 1997, 'Rehearing "Distant Music" in "The Dead"', *James Joyce Quarterly*, vol. 35, no. 1, 149–152
Spencer, Herbert, 1867, *First Principles* (London: William and Norgate)
Trilling, Lionel, 2001, *The moral obligation to be intelligent: selected essays* (New York: Farrar, Strauss, Giroux)

CHAPTER 10

Medea: founder member of the first wives' club

Mary Hamer

When a three-part BBC thriller aired in March 2017 under the title *The Replacement*, it cast a spotlight into a dark corner. Both title and storyline nudged viewers to register a conventional practice, one that has gone on under the counter, as it were, unobserved. We are used to the notion of second wives. But in the TV scenario, the replacement occurs in the workplace, not hidden in the home: one woman substitutes for another who is on maternity leave. The impact on the woman replaced is not the only consequence explored. The incomer brings disruption to the entire dynamic system, in this case a team of architects: it is a demonstration, a reminder, of the difference between one living woman and another, a difference it is better not to overlook.

The point is not as obvious as it might seem: the replaceability, the interchangeability of women is a premise in our world. Along with it goes the premise of the exceptional man, the one to whom there is no alternative, seen today in the company chief who must be paid astonishing sums in order to secure his unique abilities. The Greeks, as they say, had a term for it – 'the hero'. There has been a connection between the fantasy of the

M. Hamer (✉)
Independent Researcher, London, UK

© The Author(s) 2018
J. Owen, N. Segal (eds.), *On Replacement*,
https://doi.org/10.1007/978-3-319-76011-7_10

mother who can be sidelined without consequence and the fantasy of the male hero, solitary and bold, for as far back as the record goes.

The story of Medea, the mother abandoned by the hero Jason, was already being told in the days of Homer and Hesiod, four centuries before the playwright Euripides took it up in 431 BCE. The question of who tells the story and what they make of it is crucial in the case of Medea, for there is no historical figure behind that name.

However far back you go, there are fantasies woven around the figure of a woman of developed intellect and the part she might play in the achievements of an exceptional man. None of these fantasies are positive. Though there were many versions of her story, the most famous of which is tied to the figure of Jason and his quest for the Golden Fleece, in none of them does Medea, the woman who helps Jason to succeed, come out well. By presenting her as a woman ready to kill any man who gets in her way, the myths downplay Medea's intelligence and her skills, reducing them to minor details: a distraction.

According to some versions of her myth, she is prepared to kill the men of her own family, her brother and even her father. To us, reading today, those myths simply embody fear: fear of the very notion of a woman who knew something a man might not, even if she uses her knowledge to help him. Such a figure could challenge a whole mindset, for women as well as for men, threatening them with intolerable inner conflict. A hero was meant to stand out alone: what if an able woman might be equally powerful, or worse, be in close relationship with him? To preserve the fiction of the solitary male hero, the support of an entire world order, it is necessary to represent the able woman, his mate, as a monster.

Medea the witch, the poisoner, Medea the woman who killed her own children, that is probably how we think of her first. People recoil, say they cannot understand how a woman could bring herself to that dreadful act. This bewilderment is rather surprising, for in Euripides' tragedy of *Medea* the complex factors compelling her act were laid out a long time ago. Approaching the story of Medea as a playwright meant applying reason and reflection to material he had inherited: it involved selection. He had to decide what would be the trigger of action and to identify an emotional logic behind that action as it developed. Euripides, known for his sympathy towards women, chose to make the trigger of action the moment when Medea finds herself abandoned in favour of a younger wife. His account of the pressures, psychological and social, that being replaced as a wife might bring into play was nuanced, as I shall go on to argue.

The myth he was taking in hand is familiar to most of us: Jason, a Greek hero on a quest, found a woman, a young foreign woman, who agreed to give him all the help her magic powers could offer. She made one condition: when he left he must take her with him and marry her. Together they left her homeland. Some years later he announced that he was taking another wife. A gift of poisoned garments sent by Medea to the new bride caused the death of both the bride and her father, the king of Corinth.

But what about the children, you ask? Wasn't Medea the one who murdered her own children? That was not always part of the story. According to one version, there was an accident and the children died; another claimed that the people of Corinth killed them, in revenge for the death of their king. It was at the time of Euripides, possibly as his own invention and maybe even following his lead, that the story absorbed a new element: from then on Medea's sons died by their mother's hand.

This momentous shift grappled the myth closer to the world of real-life lovers, parents and children, real-life husbands and wives. In his own day, Euripides was seen as an avant-garde playwright, his name linked with that of Socrates, the man who went about Athens upsetting people by asking questions. Medea's story offered Euripides the means of asking questions too, questions about heroes and psychological damage.

He begins by making his Medea more like other women. From the words of the nurse, at the opening, to the steady response of the chorus composed of women, they understand how desperate she is made by being abandoned, along with her children. Euripides plays down the tradition – one that has survived his makeover – of presenting her as a sorceress, tradition's way of expressing that though she might have been useful to Jason, Medea was untrustworthy, a woman dangerous because of what she knew. That is not how Euripides chooses to represent her. We never see this Medea chanting spells: her command of poisons is matter-of-fact, close to that of a pharmacist. She simply makes a decision to use poison when she kills the new bride. It is dealt with in a couple of lines. When he makes Medea swear by Hecate as

the mistress I choose as partner
and revere most of all, Hecate,
who dwells in the innermost circle of my hearth (D395)[1]

it is nothing to do with the black arts. Hecate only became associated with magic *after* this play linked her with Medea. At the time the play was written, following the Greek lyric poets, Hecate was associated with sexual desire as an attendant of Aphrodite (Hall 2014: 7).

By linking Medea so tightly with Hecate, and through her with Aphrodite, the playwright creates a language of respect in which to speak of physical love. It is hardly surprising that the Christian tradition, with its contempt for the body, may have rendered generations of us deaf to this. When Jason seeks to devalue the help Medea once gave him, he may contemptuously write off her love as sexual appetite, but immediately he is offstage the play answers back: the chorus sings in celebration of Aphrodite, the resonance of their words amplified by music and dance. Aphrodite can inspire the sort of unbridled desire – like Jason's – that breaks up marriages, they warn, but by saying 'no-one brings such happiness as Aphrodite' (R630), they remind us that there is another, safer possibility and a gentler, happier version of physical love. Today we might name that form of embodied love as something like tenderness, a love that goes with intimacy.

For Medea, a wife who has been replaced, an abandoned mother, her most intimate relationships have been betrayed. And when the playwright does present her as dangerous, it is not because she knows too much. It is the disintegrating impact on a mother of being abandoned that he is interested in. Medea is dangerous in the psychological sense employed by therapists (see Scott 1977). (I am not being anachronistic here, it is agreed that Euripides was pioneering in his psychological insight and initiated a new post-mythical tradition of representing human behaviour.) A person whom therapists term 'dangerous' is one at risk of causing harm to themselves or others. As the play represents Medea, she is at risk in just this way.

As the play opens, the nurse issues a quite specific set of warnings, rather like a list of symptoms: since Medea heard of Jason's betrayal she has refused all food and comfort, staying locked up in her room weeping. But she is not just a threat to her own health; she loathes having her children near her and cannot bear to look at them. Today we can call on specialised language to name states where the inner life has been disturbed. As a dramatist, Euripides makes use of the language of imagery and suggestion. Before we have seen or heard from Medea herself, the nurse reports that her gaze is like a wild animal's: 'I've watched her watching [her children], her eye like a wild bull's' (V91). In the aftermath of the blow she has received, Medea's previous coherence is lost and she is driven by instinct: an instinct of aggression. But that does not complete the account of her state of mind. Conflicting impulses, compulsions, work in her. A hundred lines later the nurse can see in her a lioness guarding her cubs, alongside that mad bull:

> She glares at us like a mad bull
> Or a lioness guarding her cubs. (V189–190)

As these images present her, Medea oscillates between the instinct to attack and the instinct to protect. In his paper 'Hate in the Counter-Transference', Donald Winnicott (1949) argued that the reality of a mother's love must necessarily encompass hatred, a hatred that is contained when the mother herself feels safe enough. In the figure of Medea, Euripides presents a mother humiliated and abandoned: under that stress her love for her children threatens to split, her powerful instinct to protect them at risk of being overridden by a drive to violence. To present this early on, as the play does, is not to offer a kind of moral justification of the children's murder. Instead it offers what might be called the emotional mechanics of the situation. Today it is agreed that the dominant response to humiliation is violence: as a wife replaced, Medea is experiencing humiliation in its most intimate form.

The action is set in train when Creon, the king of Jason's homeland, where the play is set, declares that Medea and her children must go into exile. She has already announced her intention of killing him and his daughter. When she overcomes Creon's fear to win a day's respite, the ruthless ingenuity at odds with the apparent weakness of her position is plain. It is not the behaviour of a nice woman, but it is definitely the sort of amoral resourcefulness Odysseus was admired for. Medea may be a woman, but she refuses the behaviours assigned to women. She operates like a hero, by the codes that shape the actions of men: desire for success at all costs and for reputation. Medea has already secured reputation: Jason confirms that throughout Greece she is famous for her intelligence.

But heroes and their codes of behaviour are the problem in this play. Warning us at its opening that Medea is dangerous, the nurse invokes the hero's story. This moment of danger would not have occurred, she laments, but for the myth of the hero and his quest. If only the very wood for the Argo's oars had never been felled, she cries. The play suggests that being a hero is no guarantee of intelligence, indeed it is wrapped up in delusion: we hear Jason the oath-breaker tell Medea she is lucky to live now among the Greeks, for they stand for justice. This self-deception is not simply Jason's personal failing, it is implied, but a blindness that comes with the territory. Jason goes on to declare that it is vital to him to be famous, to be known as a hero, not seeing, as Medea remarks, that it is the failure of status that comes with age that he is trying to avoid in making a royal marriage.

In replacing Medea as a wife Jason breaks his word, a matter of the utmost gravity in that world set up by men. It is on gods who protect the sacredness of oaths and punish oath-breakers that Medea calls to witness his treachery: on Zeus, 'who guards the promises men swear' (see Hall 2014: 5) and on Themis, his partner in protecting oaths. For Euripides, however, that does not seem to be the main issue. His play suggests that there are other gods to take account of, from Aphrodite to Medea's grandfather, Helios the sun, who was connected at that early period with growing things – and maybe there is a link here with children and with the cycle of life in the world of nature? It is Helios who startlingly appears to endorse her action in killing her children, for he provides her means of escape at the end of the play.

Aphrodite's power is staged when the play presents the tender physical love of Medea yearning over her sons, soon after she has decided to kill them. The family is reunited on stage: 'take his hand in yours' (R898) she urges them, 'ah the pain of it' (R899), she sobs, seeing them stretch out their arms: she breaks down in tears (RVD922). A hundred lines later, when the children return from delivering the fatal gifts so that one way or the other they are doomed, Medea's physical passion for them predominates. Clinging to them, she says:

> Give me your hand to kiss, dear son; yours too [...]
> What it means to hold you! Your skin is so soft.
> These little kisses; your sweet milky breath [...] my babies. (R1070–1075)

Medea has at last managed to reach him: 'I know that I have split you open/and reached your heart' (R1359–1360). Only then can Jason voice the tenderness he has silenced in the interest of behaving like a hero:

> Let me just touch them once more
> Hold them in my arms and kiss them one last time. (R1399–1403)

Here, for the first time his words do not ring hollow.

I suspect I am not the only person whose education left them resigned to finding Greek tragedy inscrutable, not to say empty of relevance to their own lives. Teachers who spoke of its link with religious festivals and spent time interpreting the interventions of the gods did not help. Yet Richard Buxton's article 'Bafflement in Greek Tragedy' reports that bafflement was a frequent feature of response in both chorus and audience: on that basis I can imagine that Greek dramatists, like Shakespeare, were challenging their audience to *think*. If there was one writer who delighted in baffling his audience, claims Buxton, it was Euripides. Perhaps, he ventures, that is why Euripides was not as successful in the theatre competitions as he might have been.

And perhaps that is why we might dare to look for sense in the strange ending of this play. Euripides had two surprises for his first audience. They had not expected to see Medea kill her children – that had not been part of the story they knew. They were even less prepared for the sight of her flying off in a chariot at the play's end – a chariot lent her by Helios, the sun god. Instead of being left with the image of a guilty woman covered in blood, the audience is presented with a figure who is triumphant, apparently justified, positioned like a god. Or perhaps a new kind of sense is being made, as the playwright wrenches convention and the stage picture to his purpose. While Jason is left standing below, where the action took place, the swinging stage crane is brought into play to present Medea with the bodies of her dead children way above him in her chariot.

From the first, it was found difficult to make sense of this. Aristotle, who was not interested in theology as an explanation, approached tragedy in terms of human ethics and psychology, 'the imitation of character' (Hall: 2). Not surprisingly he dismissed Medea's departure in a god's chariot as 'inorganic' and 'improbable' (Hall: 1). He did not care for the way she spoke either, objecting to her foretelling the manner of Jason's death, as though any human knew what the future held. Let us see what we can make of it today. Standing in the presence of their dead sons, Jason and Medea address each other for the last time. In his agony, Jason abuses Medea for 34 lines, in very much the terms he was using earlier: she is a barbarian, capable of acts that no Greek woman could contemplate and motivated now by mere sexual jealousy. Yet when he curses her in this speech as '*a lioness*' (my italics) we prick up our ears. It is a term we have heard before and it is not one associated with bad mothers, far from it. In contrast Medea's reply is brief, calm and self-possessed:

> I could reply to each of these,
> but Zeus the father knows
> what services I rendered you. (R1351)

More, she picks up that loaded word 'lioness'. She accepts it, with 'Call me what you want – savage, lioness, witch…' (R1358). Her appeal is also addressed to the audience, bringing them up short. In view of Medea's quiet confidence, it is not going to be simple to share Jason's view.

For besides speaking calmly, Medea lays claim, via that chariot from Helios, to a kind of authority, protection and endorsement. She also sets out a plan. The figure now in front of us has a project, which calls for her hearers to make a radical shift. In place of honouring mythical heroes, she models a respect for the human vulnerability most clearly seen in small children. Jason wants his sons' bodies, so that he can bury them, but Medea refuses to allow them to be mourned in the traditional way. Instead she is going to take them to a sanctuary, a real shrine across the Corinthian gulf, which every member of the audience would have known of, a shrine where people came to intercede on behalf of babies and young children:

> Oh no! I will myself convey them to the temple
> Of Hera Akraia. There in the holy precinct I
> Will bury them with my own hand. (V1378–1379)

She intends to set up ritual practices to commemorate what she deliberately names as the crime of their deaths.

> And I will ordain an annual feast and sacrifice
> To be solemnized forever by the people of Corinth
> To expiate this impious murder. (V1381–1382)

This is not the voice of the perpetrator but the voice of a moralist. With those words it is no longer so clear where responsibility lies: maybe not in a single person alone but in a state which maintains power for the few by promoting fatal delusions.

Right from the nurse's opening lament, the hero's story has been framed as a disaster. Thirty lines from the play's close, Medea reminds the audience of something they were all familiar with, the traditional ending to Jason's story: he will be killed by a timber falling from the wreck of the Argo – which is not the way heroes are meant to die, as she points out.

The notion of the exceptional man, the hero, has been held up as a fiction, one that promotes violence and loss. In telling Jason's story, instead of simply showing the process by which Jason is punished for breaking his word, Euripides has something more complicated to present about teaching men to seek isolation and glory. Jason was trying to maintain his status as hero, but he only succeeded in making his wife dangerous when he replaced her with one with better connections.

But Jason is not the only one modelling himself on the hero. The notion of the hero is the only game in town: Medea has no other model. Her culture has no other model, no code that would guide behaviour that was aiming to be simply human, rather than inflected by gender. After refusing the silence and acceptance assigned to women, if Medea is to speak she can only speak like a man. It is the voice of the hero that she is adopting, his language, when she repeats that she was 'born for a life of the greatest glory' (R810), she 'will destroy all who stand against' her (R809) and refuses to be mocked as a loser (V197, D198, R199 and *passim*). In pursuit of this fatal ideal, Medea forces herself to set aside passionate tenderness for the children in order to punish Jason.

To make quite sure that the audience registers what it costs her to stick to this plan of heroic revenge, Euripides draws attention to Medea's outbursts of weeping. At two different moments, different men, Jason and the Tutor, exclaim at her tears (V921, D923, R923 and V1012, D1012, R1006). It is precisely her attempt to behave like a hero that opens the way for Medea to stifle her deepest feelings and kill her children.

Hers is the crime that no one can forgive, no one forget. In boldly linking it to the experience of being replaced as a wife, sidelined by a younger woman who will be the new mother, Euripides tore away a veil. When he exposed the link between Medea's experience of replacement and her action in killing her own children, his work asked questions that challenged the basis of the state and all patriarchal organisation. If women could not safely be replaced, if training boys up to be heroes and to seek out danger led only to the ruin of children, how could citizens continue to submit their lives to this order? It is a question that still resonates today.

NOTE

1. Translations are always provisional, never more so than in the case of Euripides, who wrote his play in the form of poetry. In order to get as clear an understanding as I could of the language used by Euripides, I drew on four different translations, comparing and checking them against each other as I worked: a literal translation plus three recent versions. This variety is reflected in the quotations I chose, in search of language that could stand in isolation and still make a point. The source of quotations is indicated in the text as follows: Vellacott's 1963 version by 'V', Robertson's 2009 version by 'R' and Diane J. Rayor's of 2013 by 'D'.

References

Ahearne, Joe, dir., 2017, *The Replacement*, BBC-TV

Buxton, Richard, 1988, 'Bafflement in Greek Tragedy', in *Métis* 3: 41–51

Euripides, 1963, *Medea and Other Plays*, tr. Philip Vellacott (Harmondsworth: Penguin)

Euripides, 2008, *Medea*, tr. Robin Robertson (London: Vintage Books)

Euripides, 2013, *Euripides' Medea: A New Translation*, tr. Diane J. Rayor (Cambridge: Cambridge University Press)

Green, W. C., 1898, *Euripides' Medea, with English notes and a literal translation* (Cambridge: Cambridge University Press)

Hall, Edith, 2014, 'Divine and Human in Euripides' *Medea*', in *Looking at Medea*, ed. David Stuttard (London: Bloomsbury)

Scott, P. D., 1977, 'Assessing dangerousness in criminals', in *British Journal of Psychiatry* 131: 127–142

Winnicott, Donald, 1949, 'Hate in the Counter-Transference', in *International Journal of Psycho-Analysis*, 30: 69–74

CHAPTER 11

Replacement and genealogy in *Jane Eyre* and *Wide Sargasso Sea*

Nagihan Haliloğlu

Thornfield, the quintessentially English house in Charlotte Brontë's *Jane Eyre* (1847), and the two women representing different types of femininity in it, have haunted novelists and theorists for decades, and given us the typology of the 'madwoman in the attic'. In formulating this typology, Sandra M. Gilbert and Susan Gubar called Antoinette Jane's 'truest and darkest double' (360): how Jean Rhys read *Jane Eyre* has made not only Antoinette Jane's double, but also *Wide Sargasso Sea* the dark double of the novel *Jane Eyre*. Accordingly, this chapter considers the relationship between Charlotte Brontë's *Jane Eyre* and Jean Rhys' *Wide Sargasso Sea* (1966) and formulates a poetics of replacement and genealogy. As one of the most famous haunted houses of British literature, Thornfield is where, at the superficial level, the character of Jane Eyre replaces Antoinette as the female partner of the man of the house. The idea of replacement, in the context of 'writing back',[1] can be seen as a larger question of the literary canon: just as one character can be a replacement for another, so one literary work can act as replacement for another.

This idea allows us to conceptualise replacement as a function of genealogy: replacement can be a mode of reiteration, or even a compulsive

N. Haliloğlu (✉)
Ibn Haldun University, Istanbul, Turkey

© The Author(s) 2018
J. Owen, N. Segal (eds.), *On Replacement*,
https://doi.org/10.1007/978-3-319-76011-7_11

113

repetition.[2] When it comes to the story-line, the central 'replacement' in *Jane Eyre* is Rochester trying to replace Antoinette as *wife*; the replacement in *Wide Sargasso Sea* is the replacement of Jane Eyre with Antoinette as the *protagonist*. Accordingly, this exercise will help us question the hierarchies in the canon: can *Wide Sargasso Sea* replace *Jane Eyre* as the hermeneutic key with which we read the hypertext of Antoinette, Rochester and Jane, who have already become larger than life, archetypes that have transcended their texts? Taken to the extreme, this could suggest, after the death of the author, the death of the text, where – through literary engagement and fan-fiction – the characters, once created, have their own multiple lives outside the original text. Once the grammar of replacement, the movements, scenes and lines that echo through these texts are laid out – with the hierarchy allotted to either text turned upside down – we shall also have a better understanding of how narrative works.

The affinities between the characters of Jane Eyre and Antoinette Cosway are multifaceted: a family with colonial connections, a childhood spent in public institutions, and of course, lastly, falling in love with the same man as some kind of death drive. In order to tease out how the correspondences between the two characters work, what follows is a close comparative reading of a few scenes, or movements. This will allow me to work out a poetics of instances, actions, oscillations, presences and absences that can be found in both novels, a poetics of replacement that connects the two texts. Through these movements, I suggest some kind of transference between characters and between novels, within the framework of replacement – even pointing towards a *collective narrative* in which the experiences of women are related. This chapter thus favours an intersectional reading of female narratives, an intersectionality that is informed by the idea of replacement and genealogy.

Rhys read and reread *Jane Eyre*, trying to come to terms with the image of the Creole presented in Charlotte Brontë's novel. In her letters she famously writes of a 'paper tiger lunatic, the all wrong Creole scenes' (262) leaving her with a sense of unease and injustice which seems to have led her to take on the mantle of genealogist. When it comes to realigning hierarchies, it is also important to note that the character Jane Eyre does not appear in *Wide Sargasso Sea*, while Antoinette Bertha Mason's appearances in *Jane Eyre* are, and remain, central to the plot. However, Rhys does not write off *Jane Eyre* as merely a story of exclusion, a female *Bildungsroman* in which certain female subjectivities are silenced; instead she insists on engaging with it, replacing the 'paper tiger lunatic' Bertha with Antoinette. Rereading *Jane Eyre* after *Wide Sargasso Sea*, one realises what a good and thorough reader of *Jane Eyre* Jean Rhys was. So now, rather than walk through *Wide Sargasso Sea* with *Jane Eyre* as the hermeneutic key, in the spirit of replacement, I shall walk you through a reading of *Jane Eyre* that highlights the uncanny similarities between the characters of Jane and Antoinette.

Both Jane and Antoinette are orphans and they rely as children on the kindness of relatives. Jane being locked in the Red Room in Gateshead as a child is a foretaste of Antoinette's confinement in the attic. This episode already makes the English house uncanny and prepares the reader for what is to come. It is not difficult to imagine a young Rhys reading this episode and forming her ideas about the unhomeliness of English homes. The series of replaced actions and actors starts within the space of *Jane Eyre*, before Jean Rhys' intervention enters the literary scene. Here, Jane reacts to her cousin John Reed telling her she must obey him because she has no money and no right to the books she is reading, and then throwing the book she was reading at her:

> 'Dear! Dear! What a fury to fly at Master John!'
> 'Did ever anybody see such a picture of passion!'
> Then Mrs. Reed subjoined: 'Take her away to the red-room, and lock her in there.' Four hands were immediately laid upon me, and I was borne upstairs. (13)

'Fury' and 'passion' in the child Jane corresponds to the 'madness' and 'hysteria' in Antoinette. The Red Room evokes fire in its colour; it also bears remembering that the room is a homage to the deceased father of the house, containing his painting and/or effigy – the sort of room, in fact, that would be perfect if the Reeds had a colonial secret to lock up. Later, Thornfield Hall becomes a replacement for Gateshead as the hostile English house where the heroine will have to assert her will and identity.[3] Almost to drive the point home, a fire is the first thing that Jane sees when she wakes after losing consciousness in the Red Room: 'The next thing I remember is waking up with a feeling as if I had had a frightful nightmare, and seeing before me a terrible red glare, crossed with thick black bars' (21). In conversation with Mr Lloyd, the apothecary who has come to see if anything can be done about her 'hysteria', when asked if Gateshead is not a beautiful place to live in, Jane says: 'It is not my house, sir; and Abbot [a maid] says I have less right to be here than a servant' (26). The cure for hysteria coupled with ingratitude is institutionalisation – themes that Rhys will pick up in her telling of Antoinette's story – and Mr Lloyd recommends that she be sent to Lowood School. After her conversation with Mr Lloyd, Jane overhears Bessie and Abbot discuss her situation: 'Abbot, I think, gave me credit for being a sort of infantine Guy Fawkes' (28), thus likening her, of all rebels, to the patron saint of burning the house down. Jane, the replacement wife to be, is thus herself associated with fire from a very early age. The parallels that Rhys uses in her own novel with a view to replacing the Creole stereotype are worked into the text systematically.

Bessie, the maid, tries to calm Jane down in a prefiguring of Grace Poole trying to calm/contain Antoinette. Bessie, however, who Jane says had a 'remarkable knack of narrative' (31), also seems to have certain characteristics reminiscent of Christophine, the freed slave in *Wide Sargasso Sea*, who teaches Antoinette about Jamaica. From Bessie Jane learns about the folktales and myths of the English landscape, just as Antoinette learns about the folk-figures and black magic of Jamaica from Christophine. It is important to note that her time with Bessie is an education not only about England, but also on the art of narrative. It is also in the Red Room that the effects of Bessie's story-telling come into their own, when she feels the presence of something: 'I thought it like one of the tiny phantoms, half fairy, half imp, Bessie's evening stories represented as coming out of lone, ferny dells in moors, and appearing before the eyes of belated travellers' (16). This foreshadows the moment in which Jane will first encounter Rochester, how he will accuse *her* of being the imp who frightened his horse: 'As this horse approached, and as I watched for it to appear through the dusk, I remembered certain of Bessie's tales, wherein figured a North-of-England spirit called a "Gytrash" [...] in the form of horse, mule, or large dog' (113). While Rochester replaces the Gytrash of the traditional English narratives in *Jane Eyre*, in *Wide Sargasso Sea*, he is taken for a zombie. As he is walking in the woods he discovers the ruins of a house that used to belong to a white man who committed suicide. A girl sees him and takes him to be the ghost of the house (Rhys: 67). He has replaced the spectre of the white man who the locals expect to be haunting the ruins.

In *Jane Eyre*, it is Bessie who provides Jane and the reader with the indigenous vocabulary to categorise him. It is also through Bessie's companionship that Jane passes her last night at Gateshead calmly: 'That afternoon lapsed in peace and harmony; and in the evening Bessie told me some of her most enchanting stories, and sang me some of her sweetest songs' (Brontë: 42). At the same time, this sense of comfort and enchantment is parallel to the scenes in *Wide Sargasso Sea* in which Christophine is trying to soothe Antoinette and convince her to get out of her relationship with Rochester. In *Jane Eyre*, this 'knack for narrative' appears again in Mary Ann Wilson, the student Jane makes friends with after the death of her close friend Helen: 'she had a turn for narrative, I for analysis; she liked to inform, I to question' (79). In both *Jane Eyre* and *Wide Sargasso Sea* women keep telling stories to one another, and build an archive of types and plots that enables them to read situations and act accordingly. The replacement of Bessie with Christophine as the native informant enhances a sense of female narrative knowledge.

A closer look at *Jane Eyre* reveals that although Jane may have been released from the Red Room, her imprisonment does not really end. She is sent to Lowood School and then to Thornfield Hall, where she spends most of her days cloistered. It is when she flees from Rochester to the Yorkshire moors that she is free for the first time and sees a bit of England and experiences it as 'benign and good' and a loving mother who would 'lodge me without money and without price' (Brontë: 320). Jane's discovery of the landscape is echoed in the section in *Wide Sargasso Sea* when Antoinette flees and 'sees England for the first time'. Antoinette does not believe that the room she is imprisoned in is in England and believes she is in England only when she is taken outside to see the landscape that she recognises from the books she has read: 'That afternoon we went to England. There was grass and olive-green water and tall trees looking into the water. This, I thought, is England. If I could be here I could be well again and the sound in my head would stop. Let me stay a little longer, I said, and she sat down under a tree and went to sleep' (Rhys: 119).

Both Antoinette and Jane find the outdoors more benign than Thornfield – it is human-made structures, physical and discursive, and not nature itself that make England a hostile place for these women to live in. Reading *Jane Eyre* after *Wide Sargasso Sea* as a replacement of the Creole story, one's attention is drawn to the fact that Jane, the angel in the house, who is to replace Bertha/Antoinette, the madwoman, has equally been a stranger to the comforts of an English house. Jane is presented as someone who seeks refuge in her imagination from the cruelty and boredom she faces as a child and a young woman, as an outsider to the English family. In Lowood, her imagination finds expression in painting. She paints almost all 'gothic' scenes and they form the basis of one of the first conversations Jane and Rochester have. Up close, particularly in the first picture, it is as if Jane had already begun to commune with Antoinette when she was in school:

> The first represented clouds low and livid, rolling on the swollen sea [...] there was no land. [...] a cormorant [...], its beak hold[ing] a gold bracelet, set with gems. Sinking below the bird and mast, a drowned corpse glanced through the green water; a fair arm was the only limb clearly visible, whence the bracelet had been washed or torn. (127)

There are other references to Antoinette's sea voyage in Thornfield through Adèle, Rochester's ward. Given her French extraction and manners, as well as her name, Adèle is another sort of double for Antoinette. Her voyage from France is a diminutive version of Antoinette's Atlantic one. She, like Antoinette, seems to have been passed down among several carers and at last ends up with Rochester as her guardian. She reveals: 'he was always kind to me, and gave me pretty dresses and toys; but you see he has not kept his word, for he has brought me to England, and now he has gone back again himself, and I never see him' (104).

At first Rochester remains the distant male head of Thornfield. However, in her fascination with him Jane can see the traces of his travels even in the decor: 'All these relics gave to the third storey of Thornfield Hall the aspect of a home of the past – a shrine of memory [...] wrought English old hangings crusted with thick work, portraying effigies of strange flowers, and stranger birds' (107). After a tour of the house, 'You have no ghost then?' asks Jane, reminding us that she is a good reader of Victorian Gothic and that the novel *Jane Eyre* itself is a new kind of ghost story, with hauntings material rather than other-worldly. Bertha fills in the space traditionally accorded to the spectre in the big English house with unused rooms; she unwittingly replaces the figurative ghost with her own body:

> All the people who had been staying in the house had gone, for the bedroom doors were shut, but it seemed to me that someone was following me, someone was chasing me, laughing. Sometimes I looked to the right or to the left but I never looked behind me for I did not want to see that ghost of a woman who they say haunts this place. (Rhys: 122)

The designated ghost, Antoinette herself, is aware of a presence that haunts Thornfield Hall, and refuses to identify with it. In other words, she refuses to be a spectre and, in the end, reasserts her materiality. Thornfield Hall is a malfunctioning shrine to the Empire – it fails to contain the ghost it is meant to house/bury.

In *Jane Eyre*, Jane descends from the upper floors, hears Bertha's laugh, and retrospectively the reader can picture 'the angel in the house' and 'woman (mad) in the attic' in the same frame. Who is the ghost here, and who the heroine? Rochester wants the madwoman replaced by the angel, without there being any traffic between them. Jane, however, feels so restricted by her situation that she takes to walking along the corridor of the third storey, almost as if magnetised by Bertha. Gilbert and Gubar (see 361) also make a reference to Jane's strolls in the attic, saying they mirror the movements of Bertha in her confined space. As Jane is walking the corridor she seems to be drafting a narrative in which she opens 'my inward ear to a tale that was never ended – a tale my imagination created, and narrated continuously; quickened with all of the incident, life, fire, feeling that I desired and had not in my actual existence' (Brontë: 111), almost suggesting that Bertha might be a figment of Jane's imagination. These strolls in the vicinity of Antoinette also help her formulate her own 'vindication of the rights of women': 'Women are supposed to be very calm generally; but women feel just as men feel; they need exercise for their faculties, and a field for their efforts as much as their brothers do' (111). One can almost imagine her sitting down to exercise her faculties by writing the rest of her own story.

The confinement of Jane and the confinement of Bertha become companion pieces, particularly after Antoinette has stabbed her brother in her cell and Rochester goes to fetch a doctor for him. He leaves Jane with the wounded man, in the antechamber of Antoinette's cell. In a text where the placing of bodies has social and emotional significance, the constellation we have here is a woman locked in an inner room, which opens to another locked room with another woman:

> I experienced a strange feeling as the key grated in the lock, and the sound of his retreating steps ceased to be heard. Here then was I in the third storey, fastened into one of its mystic cells; night around me; a pale and bloody spectacle under my eyes and hands; a murderess hardly separated from me by a single door. (209)

Rochester's two partners living in the same house, and a third, conventional prospective bride in the person of Blanche Ingram, raises the spectre, the taboo of polygamy, which comes up during the strange courtship between Jane and Rochester. To his references to 'oriental' luxury, which he wants to offer her, Jane responds by saying he seems to want a seraglio, and that he is welcome to go to Istanbul and 'lay out in extensive slave purchases some of that spare cash you seem at a loss to spend satisfactorily here' (267).[4]

Rochester has already been away to a land where slavery was recently abolished, and if we consider the way he reports his marriage to Bertha/Antoinette – in *Jane Eyre* to Jane, and in *Wide Sargasso Sea* in a letter to his father – he himself has been the flesh that has been bought. Jane's fears of Rochester becoming an oriental despot are compounded for the reader when he says: 'Jane! will you hear reason or I'll try violence' (300). For the reader who comes back to *Jane Eyre* after reading *Wide Sargasso Sea* the threat becomes very real, because through the replacements and interventions in *Wide Sargasso Sea*, Jane Eyre has become a hypertext. Many conversations in the earlier text now have their dark doubles in the later one and *Jane Eyre* functions as the first layer of the palimpsest we see through the superimposition of *Wide Sargasso Sea*. The reader of this hypertext is now alert to the ways in which Rochester names and renames things. He calls her:

> 'Soon to be Jane Rochester [...] in four weeks, Janet; not a day more [...] You blushed, and now you are white, Jane; what is that for?'
> 'Because you gave me a new name – Jane Rochester; and it seems so strange'. (257)

In *Wide Sargasso Sea*, this is how Rhys imagines the first time Rochester calls Antoinette Bertha:

> 'Bertha,' I said.
> 'Bertha is not my name. You are trying to make me into someone else, calling me by another name. I know, that's obeah too'. (Rhys: 94)

Here, the obeah of the islands is superseded by the English sorcery of naming, of calling people names and making people adjust their bodies and selves to that name. By calling Antoinette by another name, Rochester replaces Antoinette with Bertha, a name that suggests Englishness and domesticity, a name that would be more in keeping with 'the angel in the house'. In his turn, when in *Jane Eyre* Rochester wants affection from Jane, who is very formal with him, he seems to be echoing both women trying to hold on to their names: 'Jane, accept me quickly. Say, Edward – give me my name – Edward – will marry you' (Brontë: 253).

The grammar of replacement that we can observe between the two books under discussion manifests itself in these passages as a grammar of naming, and Antoinette is closest to the mark when she names this naming 'obeah', an act of replacing people by their names. It is the emphasis that Rhys places on this naming that encourages us to go back to *Jane Eyre*, and look for the moments of replacement. The Antoinette-like responses that Jane gives to Rochester's attempts at possession lead us to look further for similarities between the two heroines – or three because Bertha/Antoinette straddles the two novels like a changeling – who haunt each other's narratives, complicating our understanding of genealogy and precedent. In both novels, there are uncanny spaces and discursive roles that the characters seem to step in and out of. The landscapes of both Jamaica and England are haunted, and Jane, Rochester, Bertha/Antoinette all find themselves regarded as spectres that they themselves are afraid of. The two *Bildungsromane* with similar stages of growing up finally intersect at the burning of the English house; the metaphors and foreshadowing in the novels suggest that either Jane or Antoinette could be responsible. Fire prevents Thornfield from becoming its own dark double: a harem for the aspiring bigamist Rochester. While Jane replaces Antoinette as Rochester's wife, Antoinette becomes the ersatz arsonist, acting out the visions of conflagration that seem to lurk beneath the narrative in *Jane Eyre*.

Notes

1. I am referring here to the concept of writing back developed in Ashcroft, Griffiths and Tiffin.
2. According to James Clifford, 'Genealogy makes sense in the present by making sense selectively out of the past. Its conclusions and exclusions, its narrative continuities, its judgments of core and periphery are finally legitimated either by convention or by the authority granted to or arrogated by the genealogist' (267).
3. The genealogy of the English house haunted by former owners, or indeed wives, threatening the identity of the newly arrived young Englishwomen while they are being accused of being *usurpers* continues in Manderley in Daphne du Maurier's *Rebecca* (1938).
4. Rochester replies that he would not exchange her for 'the whole seraglio of the Grand Turk'. She then says: 'I'll be preparing myself to go out as a missionary to preach liberty to them that are enslaved – your harem inmates amongst the rest. I'll get admitted there and stir up mutiny' (267). Perhaps Jane realises that her position in Thornfield with Adèle and all the female maids is not that different.

References

Ashcroft, Bill, Gareth Griffiths and Helen Tiffin, 1989, *The Empire Writes Back: Theory and Practice in Post-colonial Literatures* (London and New York: Routledge)

Brontë, Charlotte, 1994 [1847], *Jane Eyre* (Harmondsworth: Penguin)

Clifford, James, 1988, *The Predicament of Culture: Twentieth-Century Ethnography, Literature, and Art* (Cambridge, Mass.: Harvard University Press)

Gilbert, Sandra M., and Susan Gubar, 2000 [1979], *The Madwoman in the Attic* (New Haven: Yale University Press)

Rhys, Jean, 2000 [1966], *Wide Sargasso Sea* (London: Penguin)

Wyndham, Francis & Diana Melly, eds, 1984, *The Letters of Jean Rhys* (New York: Viking)

PART IV

Law and Society

CHAPTER 12

Who is the 'real' mother? Replacement and the politics of surrogacy

Samantha Ashenden

'There is something so shocking in a child's being taken away from his parents and natural home! [...] To give up one's child! I really never could think well of anybody who proposed such a thing' (Austen 1966 [1815]: 68). Jane Austen's character Isabella Knightley, quoted here, highlights both differences and similarities between the eighteenth century and our present ways of imagining filiation. At the time, it was possible to have more than two parents, and those with money and influence could have this recognised in law. Witness Jane's brother Edward.[1] Edward was adopted as their heir by Thomas and Catherine Knight in 1783, when he was sixteen. Edward's parents were 'on the fringes of the gentry' (Fergus: 5) and, in a world keen to preserve estates and names, heirs were often imported via adoption. In fact, until the mid-nineteenth century, adoptions were mostly undertaken to establish heirs and most of those adopted would already have achieved adulthood (United Nations 2009: 11). Austen's text registers that in the late eighteenth century this was beginning

---

Thanks to Naomi Segal and James Brown for many insightful suggestions on earlier drafts of this paper.

S. Ashenden (✉)
Birkbeck, University of London, London, UK

© The Author(s) 2018
J. Owen, N. Segal (eds.), *On Replacement*,
https://doi.org/10.1007/978-3-319-76011-7_12

to give way to a sentimental and protective attitude to children: Jane was initially horrified that Edward had to take the Knight family name as a condition of his inheritance of the Godmersham Park Estate (see Honan 1987), but such arrangements were a regular occurrence in a world that still had a functioning aristocracy.[2]

Edward Austen's adoption was effected just the other side of a *Sattelzeit* that divides his world from ours.[3] The late eighteenth century was a time of flux. This was especially so with respect to ideas of filiation. Ludmilla Jordanova points out that in the eighteenth century reproduction was in transition, and that 'the middling sort' were active in 'constructing naturalised categories through which social relations could be imagined and managed' (371). It was then that children, previously '"naturally"' associated with their fathers, came to be associated with their mothers (373). In the late twentieth and early twenty-first century kinship is being reconfigured again, with particular implications for the role of mothers.

While people may no longer expect to inherit social standing from their families, 'hereditability of personal attributes has been amplified within the past century' (Finkler: 44). This is a period that has been termed 'the century of the gene' (see Fox Keller 2000). Foucault highlights the late eighteenth century as exactly the moment when the aristocracy's '*symbolics of blood*' gave way to the bourgeoisie's '*analytics of sexuality*' (1979: 147, emphasis in original). In fact, we might say that a key difference between the eighteenth century and ours is that, whereas the former operated through a symbolics of blood, the late twentieth and early twenty-first centuries have seen the emergence of the analytics of the gene. In this, as we will see, 'blood' is still regularly deployed as a metaphor, though one with unstable meanings.

Periods of instability can produce new levels of self-consciousness, but they can also lead to intense pressures to naturalise key concepts and practices. This is perhaps particularly so with respect to reproduction and filiation since the ways we imagine and act on these are regarded as central to social and political order. Kinship has come to be understood as a set of biogenetic ties and this, combined with developments in new reproductive technologies (NRTs), means that, notwithstanding the principle *mater semper certa est* [the mother is always certain], the identity of a child's mother is no longer obvious (fatherhood has always been uncertain, as expressed in the principles *pater semper incertus est* [the father is always uncertain] and *pater est quem nuptiae demonstrant* [the father is he whom the marriage points out]). But the idea that the 'gestational carrier' is not the 'real' mother expresses a particular, biomedical and genetically inflected view of personhood. It is to the problem of motherhood and replacement that this chapter is addressed. In particular, the purpose here is to trace the replacement, displacement, and possible multiplication of mothers in the contemporary politics of surrogacy. I seek to plot the shape of some of the new changes, the role of law in them, and the to-and-fro between new developments and moments when the ghosts of old metaphors are made, often uncomfortably, to do new work.

The Oxford English Dictionary (OED) defines a surrogate as 'a person or thing taking the place of another; a substitute'. The word surrogate entered English from Latin in the seventeenth century, where it was used to denote those deputising for another, especially for a judge or bishop.[4] Since the 1970s the term has been applied to 'a woman who bears a child on behalf of another woman, either from her own egg fertilised by the other woman's partner or from the implantation in her womb of a fertilised egg from the other woman' (OED).[5] While the practice is old, going back at least to Genesis in the Hebrew Bible, in the form of the slave Hagar carrying the child Ishmael for Abraham and Sarah, it has become an issue of intense concern of late, as a result both of technological developments and of the growth of markets in reproductive services.

One way to understand the character of the replacement that occurs in reproductive practices involving surrogacy is to look at its legal regulation.[6] In the UK, this currently occurs under the Surrogacy Arrangements Act 1985 and the Human Fertilisation and Embryology Act 1990 (hereafter HFEA 1990), as amended by the Human Fertilisation and Embryology Act 2008 (hereafter HFEA 2008). This regulatory framework reflects entrenched ambivalence concerning surrogacy. The 1985 Act outlaws commercial surrogacy but allows altruistic surrogacy where no payment takes place, or where only 'reasonable expenses' are paid.[7] In the UK, private surrogacy agreements are legal but not binding; section 26 of the HFEA 1990 specifies that 'no surrogacy arrangement is enforceable by or against any of the persons making it'. Section 27(1) of the 1990 Act (s. 33(1) HFEA 2008) provides that the 'woman who is carrying or has carried a child as a result of the placing in her of an embryo or of sperm and eggs, and no other woman, is to be treated as the mother of the child'. Section 28 of the 1990 Act (s. 35 HFEA 2008) specifies that the surrogate's husband or, after April 2009, civil partner is to be treated as the father as long as he consented to the procedure. Where the surrogate mother is single, the commissioning father can be recognised as the legal father if he is named on the birth-certificate; however, in order to acquire legal parenthood and extinguish the parenthood status of the surrogate (and her husband or partner if she has one) the commissioning parents must apply to court for a parental order (s. 30 HFEA 1990, replaced by s. 54 HFEA 2008). This requires that at least one of the intended parents has a genetic link to the child. The 2008 Act, which came into force in 2010, removed the restriction of parental orders to married couples. Unmarried and same-sex couples (but not single people) may now apply for this faster route to post-birth parenthood (previously those outside marriage seeking parenthood following a birth through surrogacy would have to apply to adopt the child). Notably, despite this element of liberalisation, the 2008 Act continues to assert that a child can have a maximum of two parents and requires at least one of them to prove a genetic connection to the child.

Therefore, while the fragmentation of parenthood brought about by NRTs opens up the possibility of recognising multiple parents, the logic of law is to reduce this multiplicity. This reduction is directed towards the normative ideal of two parents, at least one of whom has a genetic connection to the child. Thus, notwithstanding the variety of ways in which people can be 'parents', legislation surrounding surrogacy (and NRTs in general) espouses a particularly genetic conception of the parent (see Johnson 2003: 93). As we shall see, this has some startling consequences for women's capacity to be recognised as parents of children born as the result of such agreements. We can examine this more closely by looking at how metaphors of 'blood' work to designate parental status in recent legal cases.

The concept of the 'blood-tie' is an interesting feature of both popular discourse and legal judgments concerning parent–child relationships, but conceptions of 'blood' have been reconfigured dramatically in the face of the science of genetics. The 'blood-tie' has long been legally and culturally important in symbolising filiation,[8] but blood offers an unstable metaphoricity. Slightly amending Foucault's discussion of the symbolics of blood, noted at the outset, what we see in recent legal reasoning concerning parenthood in contexts of surrogacy is the continuation of the metaphor of blood, but where the meanings attached to the word 'blood' have been transformed. Before DNA testing the understanding of filiation symbolised by the concept of the blood-tie was one that construed connections more in terms of the inheritance of property than physical and psychological attributes *per se*, though these were important too (see Finkler 2000, chap. 4). In a world of genetics, 'blood' – an archaic word – is now regularly used as a synonym for shared genetic inheritance. Historically, the 'blood-tie' (or what we now know as shared genes) has been, and often still is, ignored by law in determining parenthood. So, for example, until 1840 an illegitimate child was *filius nullius* [a son of nobody], a position that reflected the concern to uphold patrilineal descent regarding property (Smart 1987: 101, also Maclean 1994). Marriage, not blood, continues to confer paternity in the rebuttable presumption[9] that a man married to a woman is the father of her children; in other words, law/custom rather than biology creates the legal relationship between fathers and children. However, with the advent of DNA testing this presumption is now supplemented by claims resting on genetic parentage. For women, the situation is different. The principle *mater semper certa est* continues the assumption that the mother of a child is the woman who bore it. The advent of DNA tests and the possibility of egg donation have not interrupted this; in particular the HFEA 2008 explicitly rules out the possibility that a woman is to be recognised as a parent '*merely* because of egg donation' (HFEA 2008 s.47, italics added). This produces marked differences in the legal implications of NRTs for men and for women, regarding the acquisition of parental status.

A woman with a genetic connection to a child but who has not given birth to it cannot gain legal recognition as a parent other than through a parental order or adoption. A man who has a genetic connection can be on the birth-certificate provided the surrogate is unmarried. Where once fatherhood was a socio-legal 'fact', it has become increasingly predicated on intent and genetic contribution. But for women the principle that the woman who gives birth to the child is its mother interrupts such a reframing. They have no way to assert a genetic tie (other than through a male partner if they have one) since the principle *mater semper certa est* breaks this in a way that it does not for men. Therefore, we can say that NRTs and their legal framings parcel out parenthood differently for men and for women, and more specifically male gametes are recognised as determining parenthood in law more easily than female ones.[10] In arguments in which genetics are increasingly made to be the measure of filiation, a woman's contributions are often occluded even when they are genetic.

The claim to legal authenticity in respect of parenthood is grounded in exclusion, so that some of those contributing to the coming into being of a child are legally effaced, replaced by a normatively prized two-person parenting unit. In this respect it is significant that the HFEA 2008, an Act of Parliament directly addressing the multiplications produced by NRTs, continues to hold that a child can have a maximum of two parents. Whilst this legislation broke with the requirement that this must be one man and one woman, recognising same-sex parents for the first time, it nonetheless held on to what McCandless and Sheldon (2010: 177), following Fineman (1995) describe as the 'sexual family' form (Fineman 1995: 143). This is the model of the two-parent sexual couple. McCandless and Sheldon trace in some detail how, during the passage of the HFEA Act 2008, and in the face of widespread disagreement concerning the grounds on which parents should be recognised, 'acceptance of the fact that we can have two – and only two – "real" parents has proved a unifying article of faith' (2010: 190). Thus whilst it might look at first sight like a major departure, the extension of recognition of parenthood to female civil partners of women who give birth undertaken by the 2008 Act in fact represents the attempted assimilation of civil partnerships to the idea(l) of marriage, it is not a radically new way of recognising parent-child ties (McCandless and Sheldon 2010: 189; see also Diduck 2007). A number of difficulties of language indicate some of the ways in which this legislation strains to encompass new forms of procreation and family formation.

One of the more interesting features of this new provision for the recognition of same-sex parents is the way in which it works via rebuttable presumption, for this legal formulation enables the ghost of old ideas of filiation to structure new family forms. To elaborate, under the terms of the HFEA 2008, where two women are in a registered civil partnership or marriage, the partner of the woman who gives birth will be recognised as the child's 'other parent' unless it can be shown that she did not consent to the treatment or artificial insemination (HFEA 2008 s. 42). This directly mirrors agreed fatherhood conditions under the Act (2008 s. 35), but it also strongly echoes the old common law presumption of paternity. However, in cases involving same sex parents it does so in the face of knowledge of a lack of genetic relationship (unless the other 'female parent' is also the egg donor though, as noted, egg donation in itself carries no rights of recognition); thus in this instance, rather than the attribution of parenthood status following from a presumption of paternity, as with heterosexual marriage, law prescribes a relation in the context of the known absence of any genetic tie. In the provisions of the HFEA 2008, therefore, we can see an attempt to reimagine parental dimorphism in the face of multiplicity and same-sex relations. This is most clearly articulated in the strained language used to describe one mother plus one gender-neutral parent: motherhood remains grounded in gestation and so 'the price to pay for the reward of children becomes conformity to the nuclear family ideal' (Smart 1987: 100). The 'de-gendered "parent" is [still] opaque' (Diduck 2007: 5).

There is inherent substitutability in the 'surrogate's' role. This substitutability of the surrogate as a 'gestational carrier' continues a long line of thinking about reproduction in which the birth-mother is an arbitrary vessel (see Laqueur 1990) and stands in sharp contrast to the pressure toward the importance of those considered to be 'biological' (meaning genetic) and/or intended parents. While there may be no (legal) problem when the surrogate remains a 'substitute', that is hands over the baby after the birth, considerable problems open up when the woman who has carried the child changes her mind and decides she wishes to keep it. In such cases 'surrogate' mothers overstep the surrogate role and make a claim to be the 'real' mother, something they may fail to enforce even when they are also the genetic mother. Such was the case in *Re N*.[11] In this case, a woman had offered herself as a 'surrogate' but told the commissioning couple that she had lost the baby early in the pregnancy, whilst going on to give birth and keep the child as her own. When the case came before the courts the baby, known as N, was eighteen months old, and was settled with the birth mother and her husband. The judge asserted the equivalence of the claim to parenthood of the birth mother and the commissioning father, on the basis of the 'blood-tie', and went on to judge the case on the basis of N's interests, which were deemed best served by residence with the commissioning couple. Thus the 'blood-tie' was reduced by the Court to genetic contribution. This case was decided on the principle of 'best interests', but one cannot help thinking that the 'surrogate' effectively became a scapegoat: a woman who enters a surrogacy agreement deceptively, notwithstanding legislation providing that she is the legal mother of the child at the point of birth, oversteps the line and makes a claim to be the 'real' mother; for this she is punished (for a more detailed discussion see Ashenden 2013).

In recent discussions of surrogacy, the 'biological' is regularly reduced to the 'genetic' (or the 'blood-tie' where this concept is used as a synonym for the genetic tie), thus occluding from view other biological processes that are essential to reproduction. 'Blood' has been used to talk about inheritance and filiation since the middle of the thirteenth century, and to signify 'a person of one's family, race and kindred' since the late fourteenth century (Online Etymology Dictionary). But none of these uses refers to genetic contribution. They cannot, since the science of genetics did not exist before the twentieth century. So, it is worth asking what 'gene talk' is for, and noting that the words we use shape 'landscapes of possibility' (Fox Keller 2000: 138, 139). The use of 'blood' as a synonym for genes lends the genetic claim authority. But it is a very strange synonym, for blood signifies that which is spilt, which 'swells, gushes, spurts' (Online Etymology Dictionary), but also that which pollutes (see Knight 1991).[12] From this perspective, conception in a test-tube looks bloodless, unlike the deeply embedded, embodied physicality of the placenta that feeds the foetus. It is interesting to note that, notwithstanding the attempt to pin the 'blood-tie' to genetics, in one recent case the judge used a different understanding of blood in his summing-up, emphasising that 'the mother's blood does not circulate within the body of the foetus while in the womb'.[13] In this case, the High Court of Ireland found in favour of the genetic mother's claim to be the 'true' mother, but this was overturned by the Supreme Court, which refused to endorse recognition of the genetic mother as legal parent and argued that it was up to the National Parliament to enact legislation that might make this possible. In the absence of such legislation, the 'surrogate' or birth-mother remains the child's legal parent.

Arguably, the examples referred to in this essay make the case for recognising the multiplicity inherent in the idea of collaborative conception (see Wallbank 2002). Yet a child can have a maximum of two parents on its birth-certificate in the UK, notwithstanding the fact that many more people may have been involved in its coming into being. Personhood is always symbolically mediated, and biological facts and normative judgements interwoven. Could Ishmael, born today, be recognised as the son of Hagar, Abraham *and* Sarah? Or would Hagar and Ishmael still be cast out following the birth of Isaac?

Notes

1. Thanks to James Brown for this suggestion.
2. On the transformation of childhood since the eighteenth century see Zelizer 1985, Cunningham 2006.
3. *Sattelzeit,* or 'axial time', is the term coined by Reinhart Koselleck to denote the period of conceptual flux dating from approximately 1750 to 1850, during which many modern constellations of meaning emerged. See Tribe 1985: x.

4. Note that 'vicar' comes from *vicarius*, meaning a deputy or substitute, see www.etymonline.com.
5. Sometimes this involves the woman acting as surrogate using her own eggs combined with artificial insemination, which is known as 'partial surrogacy'; sometimes the woman acts as a 'carrier' of the gametes of the commissioning couple and/or of gametes donated by third parties, often termed 'gestational surrogacy'.
6. Of course, surrogacy arrangements can be, and often are, wholly informal. However, as we will see below, even those informal arrangements in which there is no conflict between the parties involved can produce problems, for example when the state refuses to recognise those who are parenting the child as the legal parents.
7. Recently in the UK *post facto* judgments have licensed increasing sums paid as 'reasonable expenses'.
8. This is so both for individuals and for populations; with respect to the latter the designation of citizenship on the basis of *ius sanguinis* is especially important.
9. A 'rebuttable presumption' is an assumption of fact accepted by a court until disproved. It is otherwise called a disputable presumption.
10. Though see recent discussions of chimerism, used as a term to describe single organisms composed of two distinct zygotes, which complicates the idea that DNA uniformly marks out personhood and filiation.
11. *Re N (A Child)* [2008] FLR 177; *In the matter of N (A Child)* [2007] EWCA Civ 1053; see also *H v S (Surrogacy Agreement)* [2015] EWFC 36.
12. Note the different valences attached to male and female blood: male blood is spilled in battle, but female blood, especially menstrual blood, is often regarded as dirty; see Knight 1991, also Buckley and Gottlieb 1988.
13. *M. R & Anor v. An tArd Chlaraitheoir and Others* [2013] IEHC 91; M.R v. An tArd Chlaraitheoir [2014] IESC 60.

References

Ashenden, Samantha, (2013), 'Reproblematising relations of agency and coercion: surrogacy', in Sumi Madhok, Anne Philips, and Kalpana Wilson, eds, *Gender, Agency and Coercion* (Basingstoke: Palgrave Macmillan), 195–218

Austen, Jane, 1966 [1815], *Emma* (Toronto: Airmont)

Buckley, Thomas and Alma Gottlieb, eds, 1988, *Blood Magic: The Anthropology of Menstruation* (Berkeley: University of California Press)

Cunningham, Hugh, 2006, *The Invention of Childhood* (New York: Random House)

Derrida, Jacques and Elisabeth Roudinesco, 2004, *For what tomorrow? A dialogue* (Stanford California: Stanford University Press)
Diduck, Alison, 2007, "'If only we can find the appropriate terms to use the issue will be solved": Law, Identity and Personhood', in *Child and Family Law Quarterly*, Vol 19, No 4, 1–21
Fergus, Jan, 2005, 'Biography' in Janet Todd, ed, *Jane Austen in context* (Cambridge: Cambridge University Press), 3–11
Fineman, Martha, 1995, *The Neutered Mother, the Sexual Family, and Other Twentieth Century Tragedies* (London: Routledge)
Finkler, Kaja, 2000, *Experiencing the New Genetics: Family and Kinship on the Medical Frontier* (Philadelphia: University of Pennsylvania Press)
Foucault, Michel, 1979 [1976], *The History of Sexuality Volume 1: an introduction*, tr. Robert Hurley (London: Penguin)
Fox Keller, Evelyn, 2000, *The Century of the Gene* (Cambridge MA: Harvard University Press)
Honan, Park, 1987, *Jane Austen: her life* (New York: Fawcett Columbine)
Human Fertilisation and Embryology Act 2008, available at http://www.legislation.gov.uk/ukpga/2008/22/contents, last accessed 28.10.2017
Human Fertilisation and Embryology Authority (2016) Press release: 'HFEA permits cautious use of mitochondrial donation in certain, specific cases', December 15, available at hfeaarchive.uksouth.cloudapp.azure.com/www.hfea/gov.uk/10563html, last accessed 28.10.2017
Johnson, Martin, 2003, 'Surrogacy and the Human Fertilisation and Embryology Act', in Rachel Cook, Shelley Day Sclater and Felicity Kaganas, eds, *Surrogate Motherhood: international perspectives* (Oxford: Hart), 93–97
Jordanova, Ludmilla, 1995, 'Interrogating the Concept of Reproduction in the Eighteenth Century', in Faye Ginsburg and Rayna Rapp, eds, *Conceiving the New World Order: the Global Politics of Reproduction* (Berkeley: University of California Press), 369–386
Knight, Chris, 1991, *Blood Relations: Menstruation and the Origins of Culture* (New Haven: Yale University Press)
Laqueur, Thomas, 1990, *Making Sex* (Cambridge Mass.: Harvard University Press)
Maclean, Marie, 1994, *The Name of the Mother: Writing Illegitimacy* (London: Routledge)
McCandless, Julie and Sheldon, Sally, 2010, 'The Human Fertilisation and Embryology Act (2008) and the Tenacity of the Sexual Family Form', *Modern Law Review* 73 (2), 175–207
Online Etymology Dictionary www.etymonline.com last accessed 28.10.2017
Oxford English Dictionary www.oed.com last accessed 28.10.2017

Smart, Carol, 1987, '"There is of course the distinction dictated by nature": Law and the Problem of Paternity' in Michelle Stanworth, ed, *Reproductive Technologies: Gender, Motherhood and Medicine* (Cambridge: Polity)

Tribe, Keith, 1985, 'Translator's Introduction', in Reinhart Koselleck, *Futures Past: On the Semantics of Historical Time* (Cambridge Massachusetts: MIT Press), vii-xxii

United Nations, 2009, *Child Adoption: Trends and Policies* (New York: United Nations Publication)

Wallbank, Julie, 2002, 'Too Many Mothers? Surrogacy, Kinship and the Welfare of the Child', in *Medical Law Review*, 10, 271–294

Zelizer, Viviana, 1985, *Pricing the Priceless Child: the changing social value of children* (New York: Basic Books)

CHAPTER 13

The ethos of replaceability in European human rights law

Sarah Trotter

European human rights law has, as its central organising principle, 'the individual',[1] and in constructing a vision of order in its terms, law here claims a capacity both to represent human experience and to secure the individuation that its foundational principle expresses. This chapter examines the means by which human rights law seeks to fulfil these claims; and, in particular, it discusses the tensions that are inherent within the idea of 'the individual' in human rights law and the role that is played by the notion of replacement in this context. Drawing on my analysis of the jurisprudence of the European Court of Human Rights (ECtHR) and the national Constitutional Courts of France, Germany, Italy and Spain, I argue here that the idea of 'the individual' in European human rights law is comprised of two doctrines: presence and presentation. The doctrine of

---

I am grateful to Damian Chalmers, Kai Möller, Chetan Bhatt, Emmanuel Melissaris and the participants in the LSE Law lunchtime seminar and the LSE-Essex-Cambridge Doctoral Research Triangle for their comments on an earlier version of this chapter, and to the participants in the Replacement conference and Naomi Segal for their comments on this version.

S. Trotter (✉)
LSE, University of London, London, UK

© The Author(s) 2018
J. Owen, N. Segal (eds.), *On Replacement*,
https://doi.org/10.1007/978-3-319-76011-7_13

presence is about the specificity of the individual, cast in terms of the unique sense of place and identity of an individual. The doctrine of presentation is about the replaceability of this individual, and it is based on a representation of the individual through the terms of an alienable role or status. While these doctrines belong to the same idea of 'the individual', they are wholly at odds with one another, to the point that their mediation instigates a crisis in the individual, whereupon it is revealed that the representation of 'the individual' is, in fact, a representation of replacement.

The doctrine of presence seeks to provide a full account of one's sense of being, accommodating all the roles, statuses, and identities that constitute a particular individual. The focus of this doctrine is a conception of individual security and stability, which is located in the sense of place of an individual – a sense of place that is then cast as generating a sense of orientation.[2] This sense is constituted uniquely by each individual. Considered abstractly, however, we could think of how it may be partly or wholly constituted by, for example: relations with significant others; a state of health; relations to significant activities, work, or interests; memories and the ability to maintain a continuous self-narrative; and the ability to delineate and preserve a sphere of personal space. The key point that human rights law makes is that this unique feeling of orientation is central to a sense of self, and that it is this sense and knowledge of self that is consonant with being.

As part of this, a great deal of emphasis is placed on securing the capacity of the individual to construct and project her own image.[3] This process of projection is deemed important because self-image signifies a social identity – a setting out of a unique self, which is available for interpretation and mutual engagement with the world. The individual must, therefore, be able to control and communicate her own image; and any violation of this capacity, such as by way of humiliation, is cast as entailing a loss of sense of self.[4] It involves the loss of the basis of what it means to be a distinctive self, and, as such, it is the point at which what Julia Kristeva calls 'the abject' – the realisation of the possible 'relation to death, to animality, and to materiality' (Gross: 89) – is experienced. As Kristeva describes it, abjection is experienced as if the self has been replaced by some other – as 'if an Other has settled in place and stead of what will be "me"' (10). This is primarily recounted in human rights law in terms of the elimination of the space and conditions of orientation of the individual. Such an experience of total estrangement, in its interpretation, is torture, in which space is reduced right down to the body and reveals it in its immediate experience, and the mind is driven into submission by the dominance of the experience of this body (see Scarry: 33). The self, in this way, is possessed by pain and terror; and the state of abjection becomes fixed.

In the cases on this, which address instances in which the very possibility of one's sense of orientation has been eliminated, and the self is experienced as an other, the control of the individual over her self-image is violated and so is her capacity to attach and create meaning. This capacity is deemed integral to the constitution of the self in human rights law, as is exemplified by so-called 'disappearance' cases. These involve family members who have disappeared and about whom the authorities have done nothing.[5] European human rights law is particularly concerned here with the uncertainty with which these surviving relatives are made to live. This stems from its recognition that the sense of orientation of these family members might be disrupted by uncertainty and fear as to the fate of their relatives, whose security and wellbeing is, at least partly, constitutive of their own sense of orientation. The focus, therefore, is on how these surviving relatives are to manage the absence of their loved ones – on how they are to incorporate loss into their sense of self, and reorientate themselves accordingly.

This latter point about attachment indicates that – in the disappearance cases, for example – human rights law is especially concerned with the individuals before the Court (the surviving relatives). The attachments themselves, or the objects of these attachments, are not relevant or valued for their own sake. They only matter because of what they mean to the individual in question. The doctrine of presence is, thus, quite thin on considering the individual as a relational being. Its focus is, rather, on the individual psyche, and this is further emphasised by the weight that is placed on the sense of control that the individual has over her self-image, self-organisation and self-attachment.[6] This control is cast in law as being integral to the formation of individual identity. But this raises the question of the scope of this control. What does it entail and enable one to do? This comes to be naturally formulated as a matter of the limits of control. There is a demand for an account of the boundary of the individual, and for a contextualisation of this individual. As we have seen, however, the doctrine of presence is exclusively focused on psychic individuation. It does not elaborate a vision of the community in which the extent or limits of this control can be imagined. In the absence of this imagination, the use of control as a basic unifying principle of the vision of individual presence leads to the theorisation of the community itself as a limit. And so, within the doctrine of presence, we have a driving principle that demands a relation with the community, but a vision of order elaborated only in terms of the individual.

There is, then, an inherent tension within the doctrine of presence and its vision of individuation. What comes in to respond to this tension, and to imagine the collective, is a doctrine of presentation. The idea of presentation originates in the persona (the mask). This is about the face that is presented socially – the roles and statuses that the individual plays (Mauss: 274–277). Human rights law selects among representations and ascriptions in order to present a picture of the individual in this way. It establishes an account through the lens of a role, categorised life-stage or status ('worker', 'infant' or 'marriage', for example); and this account always entails a strong representation of associational ties. Thus each form of presentation contains a referential element that points either to the central activity or to some other co-participant in it. A case about a 'parent' is necessarily a case about a 'child', a case about an 'employer' one about an 'employee' and so on. It follows that forms of presentation only make sense in the context of their broader set and the activity in question. The focus is on participation in a shared activity; and membership of a body is formed around this. Critically, there is no agreement on how to frame the activity, since it necessarily means something different to each participant. For example, what to one person is a question of the freedom of the press and of the publishers to publish is to another a matter of the freedom of the audience to receive the information.

The representation of the persona in law thus always involves a selection among memberships; and – since the articulation of a role or status only reflects the placement of the individual in relation to one activity – the account supplied by the persona is only ever partial. Nevertheless, each account has, in itself, an aura of cohesion (a definitive activity and a definitive vision of a set of participants). This derives not least from the fact that each form of persona is imbued with an ideal status form – a master image – meaning that the individual comes to be oriented, in her capacity *qua* whichever role or status, towards a normative and normalising conception of this. Reference is accordingly made to highly stylised conceptions of categories – to what a 'child' needs,[7] or to the 'appropriate' appearance of a 'teacher',[8] for example – with human rights law revealing itself to labour under a particular vision of various relationships and their accompanying statuses. Moreover, this is not exclusive to individual statuses. It extends to institutions too. In Spanish constitutional law, for instance, an 'institutional guarantee' protects the 'master image' of particular constitutionally recognised institutions, such as marriage.[9] Consequently, when a challenge to the introduction of same-sex marriage came before the Constitutional Court in 2012, the Court had to interpret the 'master image' of marriage, in order to determine whether the amendment to the Civil Code enabling same-sex marriage ran contrary to this. It held that it did not. The law enabling same-sex marriage merely developed the institution of marriage; the institution itself did not, in the process, become unrecognisable from its master image, its status form.[10]

With the institutional 'master image', what we see emerging is not only an account of the normative and normalising orientation of the form of any persona, but also a vision of collective agency, represented in the form that is carried by an institution. The individual is represented as part of the collective, charged with the task of upholding and protecting it. An example of this is the principle of *vivre ensemble* [living together], which has been accepted in European human rights law as a justification for the prohibition on the covering of the face in public in France.[11] The French Government argues that this ban pursues the objective of respect for 'the minimum requirements of life in society', in that it is aimed at a conception of 'living together', in which it is necessary and significant to see the face of the other.[12] If this notion has its history in the writings of Emmanuel Levinas, it entails here a representation of 'the community' as preestablished and maintained on its own terms. The individual is required not only to pursue the master image of whichever role or status she is presenting, but also to uphold and participate in a particular conception of the collective.

Whereas the doctrine of presence is, then, about the delineation of the distinct individual, the doctrine of presentation is about what the individual represents – about the alienable function performed or the contribution made by the individual. Moreover, since presentation hinges, in this way, on an activity, and since the roles and statuses invoked pertain solely to this activity, it follows that the activity could be carried out by whoever qualifies as presenting in the necessary (or better) way. This is the essence of the ethos of replaceability, which underpins the doctrine of presentation. It is particularly familiar in the realm of employment and in other areas in which roles are mostly assumed, as opposed to being assigned. Employees who present in ways that are deemed incompatible with their roles may thus find themselves being dismissed and replaced,[13] or else they may be cast as being 'free to leave' and able to go elsewhere.[14]

Elsewhere, the way in which this ethos manifests itself is not always immediately clear. This is particularly so in the 'replicability' cases, in which individuals are deemed free to leave and able to replicate elsewhere whatever possibility or form of life is thought to conflict with the weightier 'general' interest. This has been applied in a range of cases, including in instances in which individuals or their family members are refused leave to enter or remain in a country, with consequences for their family life (where it might be concluded that this in itself is no bar, as they could replicate this family life elsewhere)[15]; in cases concerning local schooling provision (where parents might be told that in the absence of some public provision – for example, of teaching through the medium of a particular language – they are 'free' to move their child)[16]; and in cases concerning noise pollution (where, in the face of a purportedly greater general economic interest in its source – an airport, for example – families might be told that they are 'free' to move and live elsewhere).[17] The refrain of 'free to leave' in such cases is cast in terms of the capacity of the individuals to replicate the activity in question, and its environment, elsewhere. That, at least, is how it is presented, notwithstanding the reality that the moves in these cases (of families, homes, jobs, and children) are not as straightforward as they are made out to be. But this articulation of the possibility of replication, of reproduction – which is cast as being the choice of these individuals – also communicates their redundancy. Someone else will fill the place that they are 'free' to relinquish; only in rare cases of high specificity, in which there is a drive towards rebuilding or reconstituting a unit with exactly the same members as before, is this any different. Such cases involve, for example, situations in which the maintenance of a child's ties and contact with its family are at stake; and, in such instances, 'everything must be done to preserve personal relations and, if and when appropriate, to "rebuild" the family'.[18]

The ethos of replaceability is, therefore, concerned with what the individual represents in terms of her function or role. This is alienable from the self. The question is whether the alienable performances of the individual are living up to the normative vision asserted in and by law. Thus the individual comes to be controlled by the doctrine of presentation, which takes its form entirely through the ethos of replaceability, and, moreover, demands a widespread reconceptualisation of relations, and the imbuing of these with a sense of detachment. This culminates in cases involving the application of the ethos of replaceability to those claiming to be family members. There are therefore cases of paternity challenges in European human rights law in which the ECtHR has focused on securing and preserving the stability of the 'existing' family unit in the face of the 'threat' of disruption posed by the man claiming to be the legal father of the child in question.[19] To reach this conclusion, the ECtHR has to focus on the performance of the role of 'fathering', and since the social father is presently performing this, he is experienced by the potential biological father – the man contesting his legal paternity – as having replaced him in this role.

It is irrelevant, in this respect, whether the man claiming paternity has ever 'done' any 'fathering' in the first place, which, in any case, is not merely a matter of his display of commitment but also of whether the mother has enabled him to be involved. What is at issue in these cases is, rather, the sense of loss – something that can be experienced even if its object has not been 'held' in the first place. The experience of the ethos of replaceability, and the sense of having been replaced, may be just as deep where the chance to perform the role or status was not even had – where the opportunity did not even arise, therefore, to be in a position to be properly replaced.

The trouble with the ethos of replaceability is that it is damaging in its disregard of the individual identity that is so emphasised by the doctrine of presence. Its interest lies only in the function served or the activity performed by the individual, and this generates a frailty and competitive quality in every role and status. It introduces a temporal logic of insecurity, because the possibility of being replaced is instigated by taking up the role or status at hand. It also introduces a disciplinary logic. It adds to the normative aspect of the master image – an aspect which already orientates the individual in some direction – a capacity to test and replace this same individual.

But more than this, the conceptualisation of human experience in these terms also renders the singular individual anonymous. The sole interest is in the replaceable function that is performed by the individual, and this stands in direct contrast with the logic of authenticity and individuality that underpins the doctrine of presence. For whereas the doctrine of presence is about the formation of individual identity, the doctrine of presentation is about its suppression.

It could be said, of course, that human rights law needs rules and categories like the ones it sets out through the doctrine of presentation, on the grounds that it needs to be able to generalise and classify. But what is striking about the way in which this classification takes place is that it demands an alienation of actions from individual selves, at the same time as 'the individual' is posited as the basic principle. This generates a fragmented vision of the individual, not least because the doctrine of presentation, which is the backdrop against which the doctrine of presence has to realise itself, splits the individual, between her self (represented in the vision of presence) and her role in the construction of the collective (represented in the vision of presentation). She is split between constitution and representation. The possibility opens up for the individual, who was articulated in terms of a unity by the doctrine of presence, to be sacrificed by the terms of an order founded upon the very idea of 'the individual'. Thus the moment of naming – of presenting – the individual in law also becomes the moment that renders the individual anonymous.

The resulting vision of the community is also fragmented. This is because the doctrine of presentation, in representing separable spheres of activity and in interpreting an individual only in relation to these, creates communities and oppositions. It delegates the imagination of these to political choice, which is what we see in conceptions like 'living together'. The account of such principles, by dint of their construction in terms of presentation as opposed to presence, establishes a demand for incorporations and exclusions. This is exactly what European human rights law was intended to counter; and its significance here lies in the possibility that any breakdown or division in the real experience of the lived community might be unintentionally supported by the original attempts of human rights to generate this community. In other words, its relentless refrain of opposed categories, roles and statuses, which are formulated in terms of 'the other', might not be unrelated to any lived experience of opposition and division.

We are left with a situation in which the order of individuation formed in European human rights law – an order based entirely on the principle of 'the individual' – is constituted upon a crisis. This is the crisis generated by the tension between the two parts of the same idea of 'the individual': the doctrine of presence, which elaborates a vision of the individual in terms of her individuality; and the doctrine of presentation, which casts out the individual and focuses instead on her replaceability.

My suggestion in this chapter has been that the articulation of individual presence, because it is done against the backdrop of individual presentation, is at the same time the articulation of absence, such that the representation of 'the individual' in European human rights law is essentially a representation of replacement. In other words, such is the effect of the ethos of replaceability that in the attempt to articulate presence in the face of presentation, the possibility opens up for the former to be submerged by the latter – for the singular individual to be lost within the terms of the order of individuation. The mechanism for articulating the individual is also, then, the source of its loss, its absence: it is the source of a crisis in and of the individual, and one which leaves the order of individuation constituted upon the potential sacrifice of its foundational principle.

NOTES

1. This has its origins in the systematisation of human rights in the mid-twentieth century, at which point the individual was envisaged as the end source of value and elevated accordingly within legal and political orders. The underpinning theory of the European Convention on Human Rights was, therefore, that of 'restoring the primacy of the individual against the over powerful state' (Simpson: 157). Post-war national constitutions took on a similar emphasis, focusing on individual freedom (e.g., Article 66 of the French Constitution), individual value (e.g., Judgment 118/1996, Italian Constitutional Court, para.5), and the core rights of the individual (e.g., Judgment 1 BvR 253/56 [1957], German Constitutional Court).
2. E.g., 60333/00, *Slyusarev v Russia* (2010, ECtHR).
3. E.g., 27473/02, Erdoğan Yağiz v Turkey (2007, ECtHR); Judgment 170/2014 (Italian Constitutional Court).
4. E.g., 23380/09, Bouyid v Belgium (2015, ECtHR), para.104.
5. E.g., 16064/90 et al., *Varnava and Others v Turkey* (2009, ECtHR).
6. See e.g., 1 BvR 921/85 (1989) (German Constitutional Court), Part I, para.2.
7. E.g., in visions of a child's 'best interests': 41615/07, *Neulinger and Shuruk v Switzerland* (2010, ECtHR).
8. E.g., 42393/98, *Dahlab v Switzerland* (2001, ECtHR).
9. Judgment 198/2012 (Spanish Constitutional Court), para.7.
10. Ibid., para.9.
11. 43835/11, *S.A.S. v France* (2014, ECtHR).
12. Ibid., paras.81–85.
13. E.g., 18136/02, *Siebenhaar v Germany* (2011, ECtHR); 56030/07, *Fernández Martínez v Spain* (2014, ECtHR).
14. E.g., 29107/95, *Stedman v UK* (1997, ECtHR); 8160/78, *Ahmad v UK* (1981, ECtHR). Cf. 48420/10 et al., *Eweida and Others v UK* (2013, ECtHR), para.83.
15. E.g., 9214/80 et al., *Abdulaziz, Cabales and Balkandali v UK* (1985, ECtHR), para.68.
16. E.g., 1474/62 et al., *Case 'Relating to Certain Aspects on the Use of Languages in Education in Belgium' v Belgium* (1968, ECtHR), para.7.
17. E.g., 36022/97, *Hatton and Others v UK* (2003, ECtHR), para.127 *et seq*.

18. 40031/98, *Gnahoré v France* (2000, ECtHR), para.59.
19. E.g., 45071/09, *Ahrens v Germany* (2012, ECtHR); 23338/09, *Kautzor v Germany* (2012, ECtHR).

REFERENCES

Gross, Elizabeth, 1990, 'The Body of Signification', in *Abjection, Melancholia and Love: The Work of Julia Kristeva*, eds. John Fletcher and Andrew Benjamin (London: Routledge)

Kristeva, Julia, 1982 [1980], *Powers of Horror: An Essay on Abjection*, tr. Leon S. Roudiez (New York: Columbia University Press)

Levinas, Emmanuel, 1969 [1961], *Totality and Infinity: An Essay on Exteriority*, tr. Alphonso Lingis (Pittsburgh: Duquesne University Press)

Mauss, Marcel, 1938, 'Une Catégorie de l'esprit humain: La notion de personne, celle de "moi"', in *The Journal of the Royal Anthropological Institute of Great Britain and Ireland* 68 (Jul–Dec), 263–281

Scarry, Elaine, 1985, *The Body in Pain: The Making and Unmaking of the World* (Oxford and New York: Oxford University Press)

Simpson, A. W. Brian, 2001, *Human Rights and the End of Empire: Britain and the Genesis of the European Convention* (Oxford: Oxford University Press)

CHAPTER 14

Remembering the disappeared in Lita Stantic's *Un muro de silencio*

Alison Ribeiro de Menezes

In line with the broader direction of Cultural Studies, Memory Studies have recently taken an affective turn. This can be seen as representing a desire to reenchant the past as a means of accessing it, and it goes right to the heart of embodied approaches to memory (see Ribeiro de Menezes 2015). These latter I understand in two senses: first, as a focus on bodies and individual victims, whether living, suffering, or deceased; and second, as a process of remembrance that stresses, utilises and plays upon embodied practices and affective resonances (Ribeiro de Menezes 2014: 2). Analyses of affect in contemporary cultural explorations of memory often privilege art-works that are, in Jill Bennett's terms, 'transactive' rather than 'communicative', in their demand for an emotional response from the viewer (7). In contrast, in this chapter I examine strategies for exploring the legacies of traumatic memory in Lita Stantic's 1993 film *Un muro de silencio* [*A Wall of Silence*], which predates this new direction and is transactive in a different manner, one that downplays affective appeals in favour of a more distanced, structural and architectural approach. This is particularly evident in the use of character pairings and substitutions, metafilmic references and an emphasis on recursion in the *mise-en-scène*.

A. Ribeiro de Menezes (✉)
University of Warwick, Coventry, UK

Together, these strategies evoke the notion of replacement as a means of both signalling the absence of the disappeared and conjuring up their spectres as a challenge to present and future generations.

Lita Stantic, who is best known as a film producer, made a major contribution not only to the *nuevo cine argentino* [new Argentine cinema], which came to international prominence in the late 1990s and the 2000s, but also to the field of Argentine cinema before that. Having trained with Argentina's 'new wave' movement of the 1960s (see Burucúa 2016), she began a collaboration with María Luisa Bemberg that would see her produce Bemberg's earliest – and some of her most important – films, including *Camila* (1984), *Miss Mary* (1986) and *Yo, la peor de todas* [I, the worst of all] (1990). After this, Stantic and Bemberg's paths diverged, with Stantic turning to the topic of the disappeared in her first and, to date, only directing role. Eschewing the melodrama of films such as *La historia oficial* (Luis Puenzo 1985), she opted in *Un muro de silencio* for an approach that would 'hacer pensar, no pegar el estómago' [make one think, rather than feel like a punch in the stomach] (cited by King: 50).

Muro is set in 1990, in the Argentina of Carlos Menem's first presidency, which saw reversals of the transitional justice measures introduced by Menem's predecessor, President Raúl Alfonsín. These had included the establishment in 1984 of a commission on the disappeared, or CONADEP, and trials of former leaders of the military regime, who faced sentence in 1985. By 1987, unrest among the military and fears of a coup had led Alfonsín to limit justice measures by enacting two controversial laws, the Ley de Punto Final [Full Stop Law] and Ley de Obediencia Debida [Law of Due Obedience]. In 1990, supposedly in the name of reconciliation, Menem sealed off the route to justice by declaring an amnesty that impeded further prosecutions against both the military and guerrilla groups from the late 1960s and early 1970s.

Against this background, Stantic tells the complex story of an English film director named Kate Benson (Vanessa Redgrave) who travels to Argentina to make a film about the haunting memories of an Argentine woman, Silvia Cassini (Ofelia Medina). Silvia had been abducted by the military regime along with her partner, Jaime (Tony Lestingi), and their baby daughter. Jaime was tortured and subsequently disappeared, leaving Silvia to raise their child, María Elisa (played in the film's present by Marina Fondeville). Benson is guided in her investigations into Silvia's story, and thus into recent Argentine history, by Bruno (Lautaro Murúa), an embittered left-wing intellectual. As her former teacher, Bruno believes that

Silvia has rebuilt her life on the basis of wrongfully forgetting Jaime and the traumas of the past. Silvia remarries early in the film and her status as 'viuda' [widow] in her wedding ceremony would seem to point to such forgetfulness. Nevertheless, Silvia is clearly conflicted and her story opens up multiple temporalities within Stantic's film, which draws on a cinematic aesthetic for representing the disappeared that is not based on affective appeal, but rather is structured in terms of doubles, replacements, and surrogate figures, and is thus haunted by a sense of the uncanny.

In their study of the representation of genocide and massacres throughout Western art José Emilio Burucúa and Nicolás Kwiatkowski argue that it is from moments of perceived representational impossibility that new paradigms to assist in the understanding of such events emerge. With the horrors of the twentieth century a new paradigm arose, they propose, which stresses 'el quiebre de la cadena de causas y efectos y el derrumbe de la continuidad histórica' [a break in the chain of cause and effect and thus a rupture in historical continuity] (Burucúa and Kwiatkowski 2014: 180). Based on ideas of doubling, replicas, Doppelgänger, ghosts and – specifically in the Argentine case – silhouettes, this new paradigm uniquely uses the notion of replacement to stress a radical rupture both in the social fabric and in the individual. Burucúa and Kwiatkowski cite Gabriel Gatti, for whom 'the disappeared person' is 'a figure that embodies the destructuring and rupture of the most prototypical product of modern subjectivity, the individual-as-citizen' (Gatti 2011: n.p.). This rupture is also reflected in cultural representations. As Burucúa and Kwiatowski note: 'la única forma en que el pasado se hace presente es por medio del doble y la repetición' [the only form in which the past makes itself felt in the present is by means of doubling and repetition] (195). The 'chronic dualism' (194) suggested by this focus on doubles and Doppelgänger, on replacements and divided selves, points to a pathologically divided subjectivity and therefore to a spectral 'otherness' within the self that evokes the uncanny. It also points to formal artistic techniques of doubling and recursion, *mise-en-abyme*, intertextuality, and citation. The polysemy of the figures of the Doppelgänger – replica and ghost – as well as the relational networks of images and meanings that these figures evoke, opens up a radical gap that the spectator is called upon to fill, at least temporarily. The act of replacement thus facilitates a transactive art in Bennett's sense, in which an imaginative investment in healing can occur, if only provisionally.

Argentine recourse to the silhouette as a means to represent the disappeared illustrates Burucúa and Kwiatkowski's point. Silhouettes were first deployed on 21 May 1983 in an action organised by artists Rodolfo Aguerreberry, Guillermo Kexel and Julio Flores in conjunction with human rights organisations such as the Mothers and Grandmothers of the Plaza de Mayo (see Longoni and Bruzzone 2008: 7). Derived from a poster by Polish artist Jerzy Skapski, published in the *Unesco Courier* in October 1978, the Argentine silhouettes are intended to *aparecer* [make visible] uncomfortable questions about those who had been disappeared, touching directly on issues of absence and presence, individual and collective identity, and underlining the sheer numbers of the absent (Burucúa and Kwiatkowski: 183; Masoletti Costa: 227). As Ana Longoni and Gustavo Bruzzone note, the 1983 *siluetazo* (which translates roughly as 'campaign of silhouettes') marked an exceptional moment of coincidence between an artistic venture and public need: 'En medio de una cuidad hostil y represiva, se liberó un espacio (temporal) de creación colectiva que se puede pensar como una redefinición tanto de la práctica artística como de la práctica política' [In the midst of a hostile and repressive city, there appeared for a time a space of collective creativity that altered both artistic and political practice] (2008: 8).

The silhouette is a flexible marker of disappearance and of familial protest at state actions. Janus-faced, it has a double function as an accusation and a gesture of reparation: it evokes both the individual and the collective – or rather, *an* individual and *a* collective – yet it remains a formula transposable to other contexts. Akin to the narrative templates that James Wertsch (see 139) has identified as constructive forces within collective memory, the silhouette simultaneously denotes uniqueness and universality. A surrogate for the disappeared, each silhouette can be taken to embody the circumstances and mythologies of victimhood in every context in which it appears. It is precisely the means by which such abstraction is provisionally filled with contextual specificities that reveals the processes of the formation of memory. The silhouette, emptied of its specificities, stands as an accusation in the face of a lack of knowledge – that is, the assertion of a 'right to know' the fate of the missing – and as a potentially melancholic gesture of restoration and reparation that can only ever be partial and insufficient. Developing the argument by Burucúa and Kwiatkowski, I suggest that the figure of the silhouette can prompt us not only to fill in details of the 'individualised truths' of instances of disappearance – what, for instance, the underground rooms of the Holocaust memorial in Berlin seek to do – but also to balance this with the generalities of the particular situation of violence that may have led to those enforced disappearances.

How exactly might the figure of the double, acting as a replacement or as the ghostly shadow of a disappeared person, achieve this effect in cultural works? Recent performance theory has approached the reenacting of memories of violence though the figures of the effigy and the surrogate. For Joseph Roach, for example, the effigy 'fills by means of surrogation a vacancy created by the absence of the original' (1996: 36). For Rebecca Schneider, the live actor is a surrogate for a 'prior figure', and the performance a surrogate for the prior text or script (2011: 62, 89). These are important approaches, and I link them here to Burucúa and Kwiatkowski's idea of the silhouette as Doppelgänger or replacement which foregrounds the fractured subjectivity that Gatti argues is the result of enforced disappearance. Andrew J. Webber defines the Doppelgänger as a figure of 'visual compulsion [...], an autoscopic, or self-seeing, subject [who] beholds its other self as another' (1996: 3). For Webber, the Doppelgänger manifests a repetitive speech disorder that 'operates divisively on language'; hence, it 'echoes, reiterates, distorts, parodies, dictates, impedes, and dumbfounds the subjective faculty of free speech' (1996: 3). This leads to an inherently performative identity, always 'caught up in exchange'. The Doppelgänger is a 'figure of displacement', characteristically appearing 'out of place, in order to displace its host' (1996: 4). The link to performativity is strong and encompasses issues not only of embodiment but also of aesthetic form. As Webber notes, the Doppelgänger 'troubles the temporal schemes of narrative development and literary history', leading to a compulsive return in the form of intertextual invasions of host texts: 'Its performances repeat both its host subject and its own previous appearances. It therefore plays a constitutive role in the structuring of its texts, by doubling them back upon themselves. This function of return will be read as "unheimlich" – uncanny – in the Freudian sense' (1996: 4). Aesthetic features such as character surrogates and the doubling of plots, narrative and cinematic recursion, intertextual and intermedial citations, temporal shifts and multiple temporalities, displacements and replications, the use of the uncanny, and the disruption of kinship ties (which functions as a metaphor for rupture and trauma), are not only relevant here but are also key elements of Stantic's film.

Un muro de silencio establishes a duality between the present and the past through dual plots and character surrogates in Schneider's sense of the term. Benson, an outsider figure, has travelled to Buenos Aires in order to understand not only the Argentina of the early 1990s but the Argentina of the 1960s and 1970s, in order to probe what might have made young people militant and what might have led to the military coup in 1976. In her reenactment of the past, which takes the form of a film titled *La historia de Ana*, Silvia is played by a character named Ana Laura (played by actress Soledad Villamil), Jaime is played by Julio (Julio Chávez) and María Elisa by Inés (Ximena Rodríguez). Flaunted as doubles for the main characters' earlier selves, this series of pairings serves to underline Jaime's absence. But my listing of the actors who play actors in Benson's film underlines the relevance of Schneider's notion of the theatrical surrogate or replacement, which Stantic multiplies through the structural *mise-en-abyme* of a self-reflexive film that contains a self-reflexive film: Jaime is represented only by a surrogate actor, and is missing in the filmic present. Further metafictional layers are added by the fact that Silvia's story, transformed into that of Ana, is scripted not by Benson but Bruno, who is unsympathetic to the youthful dreams of Silvia and Jaime's generation.

Muro is strongly intertextual and intermedial. Fragments of Benson's finished film, its script written by Bruno, are inserted into *Muro*, and the viewer also encounters recovered footage of key events in contemporary Argentine history, including the *Cordobazo* or worker's uprising in May 1969, the return of Perón in 1973, and a protest march by the Mothers of the Plaza de Mayo in 1985. While the recovered newsreel images are clearly identifiable as visual citations that provide important historical context, the fragments of Benson's film have a more ambiguous status: on the one hand, scenes of her directing her actors stress the performativity and imaginative investment involved in recreating someone else's story at some historical distance; on the other hand, the completed takes from Benson's film seem to meld into Silvia's memories. This somewhat ambiguous ontological status, which is resolved in the film as the viewer gradually disentangles the plotlines, extends to the images with which *Muro* opens: the sight and sounds of a couple and their small child on a bike. This spectacle of a happy family stands as an impossible dream for the generation of Argentinians affected by the human rights abuses of the military regime.

Stantic is careful to avoid an over-emotional montage in *Muro*. Thus, the first of Benson's takes, a scene between Ana and Julio in bed, is followed by newsreel footage of the *Cordobazo*, providing the historical context for Julio's political activism and Ana's fears for his safety. Nevertheless, the take is preceded by a shot in which Silvia stares out of a window, an anguished expression on her face, her discomfort seemingly intensified by the fact that her daughter is embracing her. The ensuing clip seems more like a memory than a filmic reconstruction, although it will ultimately be María Elisa whose gaze offers a more hopeful future, based on an acknowledgement of and accommodation with the past (Burucúa 2009: 150). Thus, behind the outsider Benson's quest to understand Argentina in 1990, and Silvia's reawakening memory, lies María Elisa's coming to awareness of her own parents' history and of the fact that, as Silvia says at the end, 'todos sabían' [everyone knew].

There are nine takes from Benson's film in *Muro*, but the second is perhaps the most visually shocking, the abduction of Julio, Ana and Inés. It is followed by an intratextual citation – a filmic interplay of memories and temporalities – as Stantic cuts to Benson discussing Menem's *indulto* [pardon], only for her to be interrupted by childish giggling as the actress who plays Ana tickles the toddler playing Inés. This laughter echoes that of the child in the basket of a bike from the opening credits. The scene then switches to Ana in prison with her daughter as Julio is dragged away groaning. Julio is permitted to phone Ana intermittently, a technique used by the regime to unsettle families, increase fear and even extort money. We later learn that it is believed that 'lo trasladaron' [he was transferred], shorthand for Julio's having been secretly murdered. The legacy of his uncertain fate casts a ghostly shadow over Silvia's life, and she feels an uncanny sense that he is not dead at all.

If the uncanny, in psychoanalytical terms, signals the return of the repressed, this is both individual and national in *Muro*. Stantic's work suggests a collective yet fragmented subjectivity through the use of replacements or Doppelgänger, and the structural *mise-en-abyme* of a film within a film. She reinforces this visually with the use of mirrors to suggest excessive recursion, most clearly in the montage of a discussion between Benson and Bruno in the director's dressing room. This is a conversation that focuses on Bruno, and his imaginative investment in writing Silvia's story, rather than on Silvia herself. Both Benson and Bruno refer to Silvia as Ana, the name of her surrogate, and Bruno observes that Benson's film character is as true to life as the real Ana – that is, Silvia – who refuses to be interviewed by Benson. We are lost here in the labyrinthine doublings of the plot, and Stantic stresses the point through a series of mirror reflections that suggest infinite regression and replication. Benson and Bruno are both reflected in several mirrors, projecting a series of image/reverse-image pairs back and forth in an illustration of the multiplication of the

Doppelgänger (Figs. 14.1 and 14.2, cinematography Félix Monti, static photography Graciela Portela).

This scene occurs at *Muro*'s midpoint, and is preceded and followed by images of Silvia set against a form of architectural regression (Figs. 14.3 and 14.4, director of cinematography Félix Monti). Having followed the person she suspects of being Jaime, she ends up in a high-rise development, itself a product of the replication of the same apartment design over and over again. Its decaying state suggests the melancholy of ruins. The result is both a literal allusion to the neoliberal economic policies of the military regime, and a metaphorical evocation of the multiplier effect of replicas and replacements that lies at the heart of the use of the silhouette to designate both a single disappeared person and the many disappeared as a collective.

The *mise-en-scène* of *Muro* repeatedly stresses architectural form, not only in its visual emphasis on uprights, doorways and windows, but also through the backlighting that highlights such features. These repetitive visual motifs suggest a rigidity of social memory and the entrapment of the characters in an unresolved trauma. Yet, doorways and windows are boundary zones, liminal points between spaces. For Walter Benjamin, ruins are allegories of thinking itself, a space of ambivalence (177–178). With Silvia in the foreground and a run-down urban high-rise behind

Fig. 14.1 Bruno discusses Ana's story with Kate, Lita Stantic, *Un muro de silencio*, Lita Stantic Producciones, 1991

Fig. 14.2 Kate discusses Ana's story with Bruno, Lita Stantic, *Un muro de silencio*, Lita Stantic Producciones, 1991

Fig. 14.3 Silvia seemingly entrapped by urban architecture, Lita Stantic, *Un muro de silencio*, Lita Stantic Producciones, 1991

Fig. 14.4 Silvia believes she may have found Jaime, Lita Stantic, *Un muro de silencio*, Lita Stantic Producciones, 1991

(Fig. 14.4), Stantic seems to pose a question rather than articulate a direct protest. At this point in the film, Silvia is watching and waiting for her spectral Jaime, and deliberating on how to begin again to confront her traumatic past.

In the Romantic tradition, ruins stood as markers of a lost past; with respect to the disappeared, however, the ruined body is precisely what is missing, precisely that trace of the past that Argentines cannot contemplate. Something else must replace it, something capable of being at once specific and universal, finite and infinite, limited and excessive, present and absent. The silhouette, spectre, ghost, surrogate, Doppelgänger, replacement is precisely that – indeed, the recursion of its multiple names indicates its inherent suitability as a means to give meaning and representation to (bodily) ruins that we need to mourn yet do not even possess. As John King notes of *Muro*, 'it is an elliptical film, whose long sequence shots provide spaces for thought and debate' (45). It is precisely in the film's metaphorical spaces that we find the formula which Burucúa and Kwiatkowski label the multiplication of the Doppelgänger. This is the same recursive technique that is used to memorialise the disappeared in the recent remodelling of the infamous Navy Mechanics School, or ESMA, detention centre (Fig. 14.5, photograph by the author), which appears in many other memory museums, including those in Santiago, Chile, with its wall of faces of the disappeared, and Medellín, Colombia, with its

Fig. 14.5 ESMA Museum, Buenos Aires, photographed by Alison Ribeiro de Menezes, author's own image

photographs of the missing that are alternately illuminated and obscured to reveal the rent in families and societies that enforced disappearance creates. This trope of visual repetition and recursion finds an architectural parallel in the urban fabric of *Un muro de silencio*. If, stretching back to classical times, memory was conceived of in architectural terms (Purdy: 147), then in *Muro* architecture – along with doubles, surrogates, Doppelgänger, silhouettes, and uncanny spectres of the past – comes to signal a rupture of the social fabric and of individual subjectivity caused by enforced disappearance. This is a quite different approach from the contemporary affective turn, but it is an equally effective means of evoking the absent, ruined bodies of the disappeared and the emotional fractures that their absence creates within families and in Argentine society as a whole.

References

Benjamin, Walter, 1977 [1928], *The Origin of German Tragic Drama*, tr. John Osborne (London: New Left Books)

Bennett, Jill, 2005, *Empathic Vision: Affect, Trauma, and Contemporary Art* (Stanford: Stanford University Press)

Burucúa, Constanza, 2009, *Confronting the 'Dirty War' in Argentine Cinema* (Woodbridge: Boydell & Brewer)

Burucúa, Constanza, 2016, 'Lita Stantic: Auteur Producer/Producer of Auteurs', in *Beyond the Bottom Line: The Producer in Film and Television Studies*, ed. Andrew Spicer, Anthony McKenna and Christopher Meir (London: Bloomsbury), 215–227

Burucúa, José Emilio, and Nicolás Kwiatkowski, 2014, *'Cómo sucedieron estas cosas': Representar masacres y genocidios* (Buenos Aires: Katz)

Gatti, Gabriel, 2011, 'The Detained-Disappeared: Civilizational Catastrophe, the Collapse of Identity and Language', tr. Sheena Caldwell, in *RCCS Annual Review*, 3, n. p.

Longoni, Ana and Gustavo Bruzzone, eds, 2008, *El siluetazo* (Buenos Aires: Adriana Hidalgo)

King, John, 1995, 'Breaching the Walls of Silence: Lita Stantic's *Un muro de silencio*', *Revista Canadiense de Estudios Hispánicos*, 20/1, 43–53

Masoletti Costa, Laura, 2014, 'Memory Work in Argentina 1976–2006', in *Concentrationary Memories: Totalitarian Resistance and Cultural Memories*, ed. Griselda Pollock and Max Silverman (London: I. B. Tauris), 223–240

Purdy, Daniel, 2011, *On The Ruins of Babel: Architectural Metaphor in German Thought* (Ithaca and London: Cornell University Press)

Ribeiro de Menezes, Alison, 2014, *Embodying Memory in Contemporary Spain* (New York: Palgrave Macmillan)

Ribeiro de Menezes, Alison, 2015, 'The Enchantment and Disenchantment of the Archival Image: Politics and Affect in Portuguese Cultural Memories of the Salazar Dictatorship and Carnation Revolution', in *Film, History and Memory*, ed. Jennie M. Carlsten and Fearghal McGarry, (Houndmills: Palgrave Macmillan), 65–82

Roach, Joseph R., 1996, *Cities of the Dead: Circum-Atlantic Performance* (New York: Colombia University Press)

Schneider, Rebecca, 2011, *Performing Remains: Art and War in Times of Theatrical Reenactment* (London and New York: Routledge)

Webber, Andrew J., 1996, *The Doppelgänger: Double Visions in German Literature* (Oxford: Oxford University Press)

Wertsch, James V., 2008, 'Collective Memory and Narrative Templates', in *Social Research*, 75/1, 133–156

PART V

Replacement films

CHAPTER 15

Deadness, replacement and the divinely new: *45 Years*

Andrew Asibong

For me, it is in the film's first ten minutes, when Geoff (Tom Courtenay) utters the words '*my* Katya' just after he has read a letter telling him in German that his dead girlfriend of 1962 has been found, preserved in a frozen glacier on a Swiss mountain, that the horror of *45 Years* begins. This is the moment when Kate (Charlotte Rampling), after forty-five years of marriage to Geoff, finds herself uncannily replaced by the glittering spectre of her husband's suddenly revivified, unmourned, earlier love-object. The film goes on to show us Kate's mind collapsing in on itself, her sense of being a real, knowable, unloveable person evaporating at an alarming rate. What if this is no temporary aberration in Geoff's mind? If Katya really *was* Geoff's one true love, then what does that make Kate? Can we really become 'nothing', the film needlingly asks, just because we have been 'replaced' – or fear we have been – in the mind of the one we love?

Andrew Haigh's cinema has always been preoccupied by the kind of envy that is provoked when one is terrified of being replaced by a more desirable version of oneself, a version of oneself that is both more powerful and more dead. The little-seen 'mockumentary' *Greek Pete* (2009) trailed pornographic

A. Asibong (✉)
Birkbeck, University of London, London, UK

© The Author(s) 2018
J. Owen, N. Segal (eds.), *On Replacement*,
https://doi.org/10.1007/978-3-319-76011-7_15

model, actor and escort Peter Pittaros, who was constantly in danger of having his soul eclipsed by his glamorous, Covent Garden-dwelling, sexual fantasy-based alter ego 'Greek Pete'. The film effortlessly captured the complex phenomenon of 'self-envy' (*cf.* López-Corvo: 1995), wherein an individual finds themselves in competition with aspects of themselves from which they feel traumatically dissociated. The more mainstream *Weekend* (2011), Haigh's breakthrough film, on the surface told the story of two men falling in love after picking each other up in a Nottingham nightclub on a Friday night; but it is simultaneously a film which documents the envious loneliness of watching others either pairing off or disappearing into their own narcissistic sunset while one feels oneself to be unloveable. Perhaps unsurprisingly, the film's own impossibly romantic miracle of love between Russell (Tom Cullen) and Glen (Chris New) seems to be often experienced by gay male spectators with a strong degree of wistful identification, melancholia and projection.[1] Both *Greek Pete* and *Weekend* leave me strangely affected by their provocative representations of splitting, abandonment and longing. Their characters seem to lack the 'alive' core which reassures the viewer that emotional meaning and psychical stability exist. I find myself almost embarrassingly moved at the end of both these films to 'check in' with myself, to find proof that I truly exist, that my thoughts are real and tangible, that (to paraphrase the late pop singer George Michael – a lyricist obsessed with addictive romantic replacement, if ever there was one) I, the voyeuristic spectator, have, in 'real life', been loved.

In *45 Years*, Kate must struggle to convince both herself and her husband that she is more alive, more desirable, more 'real' than the frozen Katya-object which she imagines to be internalised, perfectly preserved, in Geoff's psyche. The situation is oddly reminiscent of the challenge incumbent upon the analyst whose patient suffers from what André Green (2005) would have described as a 'dead mother complex' – that form of post-traumatic psychopathology wherein the developing infant internalises a maternal imago which, for complex intra-psychical and environmental reasons, s/he comes to experience as lifeless, zombified, spectral. This deathly internalisation swells up monstrously to choke the infant's unconscious mind and libido, which is consequently riddled with psychical 'holes'. One result of such a complex is a severely damaged capacity to love, and accept love, from the living. As Green puts it, 'the subject's objects remain constantly at the limit of the ego, not wholly within, and not quite without. And with good reason, for the place is occupied, in its centre, by the dead mother' (154). Katya may not be Geoff's 'dead mother', but Geoff is nevertheless depicted as a man whose psychical structure as an adult appears to be organised around an archaic need to serve, preserve and somehow *animate* a lifeless woman upon whom he continues to project a thwarted desire, rather than to engage with the living woman who loves him. How can Kate possibly hope to triumph over this corpse-bride of Geoff's nostalgia? How can she reassert herself as a subject in her own right, rather than as a bland replacement for the deathless, irreplaceable Katya? Moreover, the film insists with unnerving cruelty on Kate's lifelong collusion with her own retroactive annihilation. She speaks of a time 'before *we* existed'; sighs that she doesn't want '*us* to start smoking again'. We get a clear sense of *Geoff's* political values (he is a Tory-baiting socialist); *Geoff's* interests (bird-watching; Kierkegaard; climate change); *Geoff's* various quirks and idiosyncrasies (secret smoking; beating his chest like a geriatric Tarzan) – but Kate's loves and pet hates (other than two shared pets: 'Max' and the late 'Tessa'), are hard to discern. Who *is* this woman, outside the ideologically sustained, normative identity of 'Geoff and Kate'? In her friendship with the bossy Lena (Geraldine James), a 'fascist', in Geoff's view, Kate is oddly passive and subtly bullied. She snipes at the unctuous organiser of the anniversary party, using 'anti-bourgeois' taunts that appear lamely borrowed from Geoff. Kate is trapped in a veritable nightmare of self-eradicating isolation, a lonely echo-chamber, neatly exemplified when she phones an absent and nonresponsive Geoff from Norwich city centre, only to be confronted with the answering message she herself has recorded on his behalf.

It seems to me that what Haigh's film demands of both Kate *and* the spectator is that she – we – move beyond a self-annihilating envy of dead and tantalising objects to locate something within herself – ourselves – that might be called alive, connected, real. Fairbairn writes brilliantly and movingly of our internal battles with dissociated, post-traumatic, rivalrous 'sub-egos', suggesting that psychical splitting tends to occur along early phantasmatic fault-lines, which organise internalised others as alternately 'exciting' and 'rejecting'. When the living-dead Katya is reawakened in Geoff's mind as his object of desire, emerging as simultaneously unattainable and impossibly lovely, it is significant that his character seems to develop markedly regressed and schizoid tendencies: he starts to suck furiously and privately on cigarettes, retreating to the masturbatory attic of nostalgia where Katya's ghost resides. This suddenly howling, haunted attic functions in the film as the psychical retreat where a suddenly fragmented and secretive Geoff can hide both physically and emotionally, tantalising the living characters who seek connection with him in this important anniversary week, whilst he himself is unbearably tantalised by the undead Katya. He is not altogether unlike Jack Nicholson's character (also named Jack) in Kubrick's *The Shining* (1980),[2] taken over by glamorous ghosts from the past while his long-suffering wife Wendy (Shelley Duvall) looks helplessly on. Another cinematic precursor is Bernard (Jean-Baptiste Thiérrée) in Resnais' *Muriel ou le temps d'un retour* (1963), obsessively watching slides and old film footage[3]; in *Muriel* these evoke the Algerian torture victim (raped and murdered by him and fellow French soldiers) whom he enigmatically names 'Muriel', and his current fiancée Marie-Do (Martine Vatel) is unable to intervene or make contact with him from her world of the living.[4] Like Jack and Bernard, Geoff seems to need to dwell outside time (he does not wear a watch for this stated reason), in a darkness populated only by nostalgic images of the past (interestingly, he loses his erection as soon as Kate tells him to open his eyes).[5]

Patricia Polledri argues that envy is most destructive and self-annihilating in people who, for psychical reasons linked to their early experiences of relationality, lack internal images of themselves in relationship with an other. 'Sally was left without a picture, or a symbol of herself, in relation to a life-sustaining object', she notes in an extended discussion (69) of her psychotherapeutic work with one particular patient. Polledri goes on:

> I added that as she had no picture in her mind of herself in an interaction with a maternal figure, she was attached to her experience of being in a black hole, confused and frightened, fearing the hooded messenger of death [...] When I [as her therapist] was not available, all she could discern within herself was the 'lost' part and the feeling was about death and violence [...] At this stage, she went into the bathroom, vomited and retched. She went into the waiting room and remained there, sitting on the floor, with her head in her hands, sobbing, like a frightened child. (74–75)

What I find most useful about Polledri's clinical discussion of post-traumatic envy is the challenge it leaves us with: a challenge to find ways of dynamising and replacing internalised deadness, or 'encapsulated containerlessness', as Polledri puts it, with something alive and real. Such a replacement is not effected merely by swapping one person for another. There is, in any case, no original person to swap, merely a ghastly internalised phantasy of one (or rather the absence of one). Polledri's account of this particularly transformative session with her patient evokes a miraculous finding of words – in the form of an especially vivid interpretation – which seem, no matter how painfully, to disrupt the frozen representations and nonrepresentations of Sally's unmirrored, envious psyche. She literally retches out of self-recognition.

One way we might experience the viscerally unforgettable final scene of *45 Years* – Kate's visible emotional disintegration on the dance floor with Geoff at their forty-fifth wedding anniversary party as they move together to The Platters' 'Smoke Gets in Your Eyes' – is as a cinematic enactment of a mutative psychoanalytic interpretation. The film has been building to this climactic *snap* throughout its deadly mounting of horror, and it is only when the musical break finally comes – after the pictures of the hitherto pictureless marriage the 'fascist' friend Lena so helpfully provides as an anniversary gift; after the desperately awkward words Geoff has just spoken in tribute to his wife; and, significantly, after Kate, like Polledri's patient, has had to flee to the bathroom – that I think we can genuinely feel the frozen, gnawing deadness melting, giving way, like a glacier under the influence of climate change, to a living, flowing pain. Jed Sekoff describes the process beautifully, even though he is writing long before the film was made, because he too is describing the psychical process of disinterring an internal ghost:

> If we keep in mind that it is not death *per se* that we are contending with, but stasis – the freezing of movement across psychical pathways – then we are not left to peddle the necromancer's art [...] The therapeutic task is to raise the possibility of constituting absence, in place of an adherence to deadness. Yet, this absence must constitute an opening out, up, or into a potential presence. In Green's language, the some-thing of absence must take the space of the no-thing that the dead mother 'unpresents'. (122–123)

As Kate shivers, trembles and, spectacularly, 'loses it' on the dancefloor, pulling further and further away from the obliviously performative Geoff, the viewer at last is granted a sense that something is moving. It is not pleasant, and as we watch Rampling's face filling Kate's with a sort of intolerable, physical panic, it seems as if we are witnessing the emotional equivalent of falling backwards off a mountain. But the spell has been broken; the haunting is over. Kate and Geoff may not be granted the sort of disinterred rediscovery of each another that is afforded Ingrid Bergman and George Sanders at the end of that earlier cinematic exploration of English marital deep-freeze, Rossellini's Pompeii-set *Journey to Italy*

(1953); but something no less real and alive has begun to flow.[6] The song changes. 'Smoke' is replaced by The Moody Blues – 'Go Now!' – and the film suddenly ends. Music has featured as one more aspect of Kate and Geoff's life that is nostalgically frozen throughout *45 Years'* retro soundtrack, as we are treated to everything from Dusty Springfield's 'I Only Want to be with You' to Lulu's 'To Sir, With Love' in the background of the film's various scenes. And when, earlier in the film, we hear Kate on the phone to the anniversary DJ, suggesting simply 'The Moody Blues' to him, almost as a hurried afterthought before she hangs up, it strikes the viewer as strange that she does not specify which particular Moodies track she intends him to play. When 'Go Now!' finally comes, it falls like a thunderbolt; another oldie, to be sure, but somehow, uncannily imbued with the divinely new.[7]

Notes

1. The final paragraph from the online review of *Weekend* by blogger Adam (2014) gives some flavour of this: 'Who knows, perhaps after a few years, Glen will return to Russell and they will finally be able to complete each other. We should all be so lucky.'
2. *45 Years* seems also to mirror *The Shining* in its construction around intertitles announcing each successive day of the week as a further stage of spectral breakdown.
3. *45 Years* places so much emphasis on Geoff's slides and their impact on the protagonists' psychical landscape that the sounds of them being changed are grafted onto the opening credits.
4. It is hard not also to think of Resnais's more famous film *Hiroshima mon amour* (1959), when watching *45 Years*, another cinematic narrative about finding that one is the replacement for a traumatically preserved, 'living-dead' German: 'C'était mon premier amour!'
5. Tom Courtenay shot to fame, of course, playing an incorrigible fantasist (*Billy Liar*, Schlesinger 1963), whilst Charlotte Rampling's re-booted career has often seen *her* cast in the role of ghoulish and (literally) masturbatory fantasy-addict (see *Under the Sand* (Ozon 2001); *Swimming Pool* (Ozon 2003); *Heading South* (Cantet 2005)).
6. For a fascinating discussion of this film's aesthetics of the couple in terms of aliveness and deadness, see Mulvey (2006).
7. I am grateful to Naomi Segal for her privately communicated thoughts on the film's God-like deployment of 'Go Now!'

REFERENCES

Adam, 2014, 'In Search of a Gay Film Review – *Weekend* (2011)', *In Search of Adam – How One Gay Man Left His Closet* (https://insearchofadam.wordpress.com/2014/01/19/in-search-of-a-gay-film-review-weekend/, accessed 30 April, 2017)

Cantet, Laurent, dir., 2005, *Heading South*

Fairbairn, W. R. D., 1952, *Psychoanalytic Studies of the Personality* (London: Routledge)

Green, André, 2005, *On Private Madness* (London: Karnac)

Haigh, Andrew, dir., 2009, *Greek Pete*

Haigh, Andrew, dir., 2011, *Weekend*

Haigh, Andrew, dir., 2015, *45 Years*

Kohon, Gregorio, 1999, ed., *The Dead Mother: The Work of André Green* (London: Routledge)

Kubrick, Stanley, dir., 1980, *The Shining*

López-Corvo, Rafael, 1995, *Self-Envy: Therapy and the Inner World* (Northvale: Jason Aronson)

Mulvey, Laura, 2006, *Death 24x a Second* (London: Reaktion)

Ozon, François, dir., 2001, *Under the Sand*

Ozon, François, dir., 2003, *Swimming Pool*

Polledri, Patricia, 2012, *Envy is not Innate* (London: Karnac)

Resnais, Alain, dir., 1959, *Hiroshima mon amour*

Resnais, Alain, dir., 1963, *Muriel ou le temps d'un retour*

Rossellini, Roberto, dir., 1953, *Journey to Italy*

Schlesinger, John, dir., 1963, *Billy Liar*

Sekoff, Jed, 1999, 'The undead: necromancy and the inner world', in Kohon (1999), 109–127

CHAPTER 16

'She was the most beautiful creature I ever saw': visualising replacement in Hitchcock's *Rebecca*

Laura Mulvey

In this chapter, I consider the topic of 'replacement' through Alfred Hitchcock's 1940 film adaptation of Daphne du Maurier's 1938 novel *Rebecca*. Astutely suggested by conference coorganiser Naomi Segal, the film works well as a drama of replacement and its attendant anxieties. How can the rich and aristocratic widower, Maxim de Winter, replace his charismatic, glamorous first wife, Rebecca, with the young and naïve narrator/protagonist of the novel and film? To dramatise the dilemma: the first Mrs de Winter is embodied in the very name of the novel while her successor remains nameless throughout.

But while I was thinking about this chapter, I realised, more acutely than ever before, that there is another aspect to the concept of 'replacement' at stake here. A film adapted from a novel is always itself a replacement and, indeed, often also suffers from attendant anxieties in relation to its original. Although I cannot follow up this point here, I would like to fill in a few background facts to the adaptation of *Rebecca*. From the moment

L. Mulvey (✉)
Birkbeck, University of London, London, UK

© The Author(s) 2018
J. Owen, N. Segal (eds.), *On Replacement*,
https://doi.org/10.1007/978-3-319-76011-7_16

that he read it, Hitchcock saw *Rebecca* as his next project. The novel had been an immediate bestseller, and, although he commissioned a screenplay, Hitchcock was unable to afford the rights. David O. Selznick, the maverick Hollywood mogul, picked *Rebecca* as a suitable, if less grandiose, successor to his production, *Gone with the Wind*. And it was with the rights to the novel secured, and the prospect of working for the first time in Hollywood, that Selznick lured Hitchcock across the Atlantic in 1939. He dismissed Hitchcock's screenplay, most particularly on the grounds that it took liberties with the original, and replaced it with a 'faithful' adaptation. However, as usual, fidelity had to be compromised in order to secure the approval of the censors. It was not possible under the strict censorship rules for the film's protagonist to have committed a murder and 'got away with it' or for its heroine to have colluded with the coverup. The film thus attributes Rebecca's death to an accident, not to her husband, and glosses over the novel's implicit depiction, or even accusation, of class collusion in Maxim's final exoneration.[1]

The film follows the novel closely and both revolve around the heroine's overwhelming sense of her own inadequacy as a replacement for Rebecca in Maxim's estimation and affection. She finds herself in the 'place' of her dead predecessor in the de Winter stately home, Manderley, but is unable to take her place. Although there are rational reasons for this – for instance, her comparative youth, her clumsy naiveté, her middle-class rather than aristocratic origins – the strength of the story lies in its irrationality. Rebecca's ghostly presence haunts Manderley. She persists, as it were, in her own right: she is an emanation of a past not yet laid to rest that also puts up a resistance to the claims of the pretender to her husband, her mansion and their world. But Rebecca is also a figure of her successor's imagination, as an unavoidable presence in the surreal everyday life at Manderley who can be conjured and reconjured by the sinister keeper of Rebecca's flame, the housekeeper, Mrs Danvers. The story's world thus exists on two levels: the surface of everyday life and its nether side, an uncanny verging into an unconscious. The two cannot, of course, be kept separate, and throughout the young protagonist clumsily allows the nether to penetrate the surface world (as I will discuss below). However, the resolution of the story, which will enable the process of replacement to finally take place, can only be achieved by bringing another kind of repression to light: the truth, that is, about Rebecca, her madness and her badness, and the underworld of dissolution and decadence that she had inhabited. In a sense, Rebecca's ghostly presence is also an emanation of her cruelty, of which Mrs Danvers is the willing puppeteer, finding in the pretender's very innocence both a compliant victim and an insult to everything her predecessor had stood for. The resolution depends on an exorcism, an end to Rebecca's hold over her replacement's imagination, and a talking cure, in which Maxim finally acknowledges his wife's right to know about his past and the truth about his relationship with Rebecca. The story's initial situation and its perpetuation into the narrative depend on Maxim's silence, on what cannot be spoken between the husband and his new wife.

The silence at the heart of the *Rebecca* narrative is predicated on inequalities of class and gender. In the opposition between its male and female protagonists one represents sentiment and the low culture of feminine fantasy and the other an upper class, high culture of English aristocracy. While the female protagonist is in a constant state of heightened imagination about all aspects of her husband's past, he is under no obligation to 'fill her in' about anything. At the same time, the silence also belongs to the irrational in the story. The repression of the past only evokes more vividly the woman who cannot be spoken, investing her with a force of the unconscious, the monstrous feminine, with its connotations of rapacious sexuality, from promiscuity to lesbianism. As Rebecca seems to have understood, this femininity is anathema to patriarchal law and order. With her claim to be pregnant by another man, with her intention to impose the child on the de Winter line, the confrontation becomes clear. Rebecca's replacement, of course, belongs to the other extreme of femininity and presents no threat whatsoever to Maxim's world order. From another perspective, Rebecca and her replacement stand together: the story belongs generically to women's fiction and while Rebecca represents its gothic side, her replacement represents the sentimental and the family romance. Aristocracy, in the last resort, is subordinated to female fantasy.

Hitchcock uses the subtlety of cinema, its power of visualisation, to weave the 'Rebecca web' around its heroine. He sets up his scenes very carefully. Over and over again he uses a 'punctuation' device: a line delivered at the end of a scene, as it fades to black. This merging of word and image, a dramatic pronouncement and a specifically cinematic effect, seems to envelop the protagonist, as Rebecca's image is almost literally 'impressed' on her. This device is introduced on the film's first evening in the hotel in Monte Carlo. The narrator is working as the paid companion to a rich, intolerable American woman who corners Maxim into having coffee. Mrs van Hopper's words to her young companion seem to impress her as much as the actual presence of Maxim himself: 'He hasn't got over the death of his wife, you know. They say he simply adored her'. The fade to black seems to conjure up both Rebecca's ghost and the protagonist's fantasy of her. There are other examples. At the end of the protagonist's conversation about Rebecca with Frank Crawley, her husband's agent and best friend (in which they achieve a certain intimacy and rapport) she asks him about Rebecca. He says: 'She was the most beautiful creature I ever saw', followed similarly with a fade to black. And then the same device accompanies Bea's resonant comment on Mrs Danvers: 'Didn't you know? She simply adored Rebecca'. These punctuation points, as I have called them, are mixed with more tableau-like 'end of scene' images: the camera holds for an extended moment on the heroine, alone on the screen, evoking her isolation, discomfort, and humiliation, before the fade to black. Thus the second Mrs de Winter's internalisation of the unbalanced power relationship between herself and Rebecca is woven into the film's aural and visual rhetoric.

These rhetorical points are gradually dramatised through the figure of Mrs Danvers, the central site of the film's emotion or affect. Mrs Danvers, as it were, acts as a materialisation of the replacement fantasy. In the first instance, Mrs Danvers impresses an image onto the film and onto the heroine's imagination, so that the dark silhouette and the forbidding close-ups spread anxiety and, indeed, fear. (Repeated by Maxim: 'You're not afraid of Mrs Danvers are you?' From Bea: 'You mustn't let her know that you're afraid of her'.) Once again, the visual rhetoric draws the spectator into the protagonist's point of view.

Mrs Danvers sets the narrative traps in which the second Mrs de Winter repeatedly enacts her incapacity to replace Rebecca, tipping everyday situations towards melodramatic failure. But at the heart of the relationship between the two is Mrs Danvers' erotic fixation on Rebecca, with an implication of lesbianism that pushed against the limits of Hollywood censorship. Rebecca's apartments have been meticulously preserved after her death. Mrs Danvers draws the second Mrs de Winter into the west wing of the house, luring her into her own fascination with Rebecca while also illustrating the hopelessness of her aspiration to replacement. The scene is staged theatrically: the semi-darkness is filled suddenly with light as Mrs Danvers sweeps open the curtains. Furthermore, the scene unfolds around a key trope of the uncanny: the dead are kept alive in the exact preservation of their living environment. At one and the same time, a denial of death suggests an imminent return to life. The scene revolves around a materialisation of Rebecca: Mrs Danvers and the camera trace her nightly rituals and embody her through the fetishised 'things' that conjure up her powerful, sexualised presence. The intensity and bodily intimacy of the scene, its gothic atmosphere, in fact, its madness, seem to bring the second Mrs de Winter back from the brink of her obsession, giving her a resolve to attempt to escape the traps laid for her and her unconscious by Rebecca.

In three sequences in the film, Rebecca's ghostly hold over the present makes itself especially manifest, successfully intruding between Maxim and his new wife. These take place particularly at times that are set up to be ones of married 'happiness'.

1. The first walk: Maxim showing Manderley, specifically the legendary Happy Valley, to his new wife. The sequence begins in harmony as the two set off with the dog Jasper. At a crossing of paths, Jasper heads off in one direction and, although Maxim forbids her to follow, the second Mrs de Winter follows the dog as he runs towards Rebecca's cottage on the beach. Rebecca's ghostly presence is conjured up through the dog's memory, leading his new mistress into forbidden territory, stirring up the past forcefully into the present. Maxim's explosion of rage brings the moment of potential happiness to an end.

2. The broken cupid. This slip on the part of the second Mrs de Winter is woven carefully across a section of the film. It starts as she sits at Rebecca's writing table, looking at Rebecca's things, all marked with the R monogram. Clearly 'out of place', she looks anxiously through Rebecca's address book, only to knock over a small china figurine of a cupid. Just before, the camera had shifted position, moving to the side and looking up as though to suggest that the address book itself had caused the accident. Panicking and guilty, the 'pretender' shoves the statue's broken bits to the back of the desk drawer.

This attempt at repression returns, once again, to disrupt a scene of happiness. The couple are watching their honeymoon movies, laughing and in harmony, when Maxim is asked to resolve a below-stairs quarrel about the disappearance of the cupid. In Mrs Danvers' presence, the second Mrs de Winter is forced to confess not only to the breakage but also to its cover-up. Her humiliation and Maxim's irritation lead on to her shyly voiced speculation on their marriage; her mention of 'gossip' precipitates another of Maxim's rages. Once again, the unspoken, the presence of Rebecca as an unconscious force, disrupts the scene. Here the film uses the dramatic potential

of the projector in the couple's confrontation: its light is blocked by Maxim's close-up, with only a small, frightened fraction of his wife's face visible in the darkness. As the home movie runs on, the poignancy of the happiness on the screen contrasts with the wreckage left by Rebecca's presence.
3. The costume. On the face of it, Mrs Danvers engineers Rebecca's return through the medium of Lady Caroline de Winter. It is, however, Rebecca's most effective intrusion into the present, that is, into narrative consciousness. For a fancy-dress ball, the second Mrs de Winter joyfully takes up Mrs Danvers' suggestion that she should dress as Maxim's ancestor Lady Caroline. She realises the trap as she appears at the top of the stairs. Bea whispers 'Rebecca!' and Maxim stares in horror; she has clearly succeeded too well, and her gesture shrinks into pathological absurdity. For a moment, no longer the 'replacement' she brings an image of death into life. With the triple figuration of Lady Caroline, Rebecca and her 'replacement', Rebecca literally finds embodiment, if only for a moment, in the body of her replacement.

The film eclipses time after this moment. That night, the past returns but is no longer so ghostly and forceful. During the rescue of a wrecked ship, Rebecca's scuppered boat is found, containing the remains of her body. Rebecca's physical return diminishes her power; the fantasy no longer holds as the ghostly figure turns into the material abjection of the body in decay. At the same time, the narrative shifts into an investigation of the circumstances around, and Maxim's possible involvement in, Rebecca's death. Rebecca emerges into the surface of narrative consciousness and the silence is broken by Maxim's confession. No longer either pretender or replacement, the second Mrs De Winter is reborn as Maxim's 'wife'.

The film and the novel end with Manderley in flames. The film's final shot lingers on a delicately monogrammed garment consumed by flames, implicitly suggesting the end of Rebecca and her myth. But in many ways, this is a victorious moment for her: her replacement will never live in Manderley and Maxim will lose forever the greatest emblem of his status. The book makes Rebecca's victory more brutal: the couple will spend the rest of their lives in a small hotel somewhere in Europe, and the relationship between the second Mrs de Winter and her husband, while deeply affectionate, is seemingly as deeply asexual. And he, Maxim, in his complete dependence on his wife and her subordination to him, uncomfortably conjures up the memory of Mrs van Hopper and with it a sense that the role of wife has been replaced by the role of companion, from which Maxim had originally rescued her in Monte Carlo.

NOTE

1. https://www.telegraph.co.uk/culture/film/starsandstories/6346991/Alfred-Hitchcocks-Rebecca-rowsrivalries-and-a-movie-classic.html

CHAPTER 17

Married to the Eiffel Tower: notes on love, loss and replacement

Agnieszka Piotrowska

Married to the Eiffel Tower (2008) is the piece of work that I am probably best known for as a filmmaker. I do not particularly like this fact, given that I have done much interesting work since, but this still appears to be the case. Maybe it is the reason why I have never written about the film, even though at least some of my academic writings deal with my film work. My monograph *Psychoanalysis and Ethics in Documentary Film* (2014) mentions it in passing, while it has a whole chapter devoted to another film of mine entitled *The Conman with 14 Wives* (2007) – a relatively obscure piece of work.

Psychoanalysis and Ethics is about the relationship between the filmmaker and the subject of her/his films. In it I named the strong attachment that can develop in that relationship, an attachment I have called, following psychoanalytic clinical practice, 'transference'. Transference is a feeling similar to love, which must accompany an analyst/analysand relationship for the work in the clinic to go on at all. The notion of transference, once taken out of the clinical context, is controversial and in my book I discuss it at length, following the work of Freud himself as well as Jacques Lacan and other psychoanalysts and thinkers (Freud 1958 [1915]; Lacan 1998;

A. Piotrowska (✉)
University of Bedfordshire, Luton, UK

© The Author(s) 2018
J. Owen, N. Segal (eds.), *On Replacement*,
https://doi.org/10.1007/978-3-319-76011-7_17

Gueguen 1995). What I did not write about, either then or since, is a negative transference that can also happen occasionally. Is my best-known piece of work an example of such an occurrence?

Since that first monograph I have written extensively about my practice research in Zimbabwe (for example Piotrowska 2014, 2016) and referenced other film work such as *The Best Job in the World* (Piotrowska 2013) using psychoanalysis. However, I still have not mentioned *Married to the Eiffel Tower*. There are many reasons and in this chapter I will reflect on some for the first time. Before I do this, I want to turn to a theoretical article – which I have mentioned elsewhere (Piotrowska 2014), but which needs evoking here. What is relevant in Comolli's essay for my writing is the emphasis on the positive and the creation of something special between the filmmaker and the subject of her film. It confirmed my whole thesis; what it did not do was note that another situation can sometimes occur – as it did in *Married to the Eiffel Tower*.

In 1999, Jean-Louis Comolli published an important article titled 'Documentary Journey to the Land of the Head Shrinkers' in *October* – a journal of art and critical theory. The article was written at a specific moment when the French government was about to introduce tighter controls regarding the use of images by filmmakers and broadcasters, including the right to decide how one's image is used. In essence, Comolli is violently against such a notion, as he feels that it would encroach on the delicate process in which the filmmakers and the filmed are united, as he puts it, in a 'community of desire' (47).

The article was published some twenty years after the heyday of *Cahiers du cinéma*, in which documentary featured only marginally. Despite the historical trend, Comolli insists that documentary projects deserve proper attention – 'The cinema began as documentary and the documentary as cinema […] *Contempt* is a documentary of Brigitte Bardot's body' (36) – and that any film has the key documentary component, which is the relationship between a 'given time (that of recording) and a place (the scene), a body (the actor) and a machine (responsible for recording)' (36). It is the filmed encounter of body and machine, he says, that will be recorded and viewed again by at least one spectator. For Comolli 'this reproducibility of the encounter' (36) is the warrant of its reality. It attests to its existence – it is documentary.

He also makes a potentially important point from a psychoanalytical viewpoint: that this recorded encounter is offered to the viewer as 'the scene in repetition' (37) because the viewer knows that there is a possibility of seeing it again, somehow, somewhere. There is a sense of sharing space and time – the viewer shares it with the creators of the encounters, with the technology and with those who are in it. Comolli is fascinated by technology: 'Life goes on, and the machine remains' (37). In a collection about replacement this is important. Long before I or anybody thought of transference outside a clinic in the documentary encounter, Comolli talks about the relationship between the filmmaker and the subject of the film, and the relationship between the spectator and the documentary text, as a replacement of a kind – of other relationships, present and past – which the documentary experience – both the actual experience of the production process and that evoked in its reproduction and subsequent viewing – makes it more possible to control, to tame. I would argue therefore that it becomes a replacement for an actual lived experience – rather than just a memory of it.

Comolli further argues that in a film the work of the cinematic scene is actually the prefiguration of the moment of absence,

> intensifying through it this moment of presence, so as to intensify, finally, the presence of bodies through the promise of their coming absence. The image of the actor's body, absent but represented, finds a response, and possibly a hidden correspondence, in the real body of the spectator – a presence, certainly, but as if absent from itself in projection toward a screen. (37)

Comolli sees the whole notion of the rights of potential subjects of the films as part of an attempt to commodify everything in a capitalist system. Far from empowering the subject of documentary, he controversially pronounces such a claim 'senseless and dangerous' (44). I am mentioning it here for a reason and will return to it in due course.

Comolli views the key issue as the question of freedom. He emphasises the special nature of the relationship between the filmmaker and her subjects: 'It's fairly clear that the link between documentary filmmakers and those who agree to be in their films is essentially undefined and undefinable. A "two of us" is created, an ensemble that's not stated as such' (45). He then goes on to define this relationship 'as a community of desire; those who are filmed, whether from Africa, Paris, or Quebec, clearly *share* the film with the one who shoots it. *Sharing* means that they're wholly present, without reserve, that they are giving what they have and also what they don't have' (45, my emphasis).

For Comolli the process of filming is a fragile and precious gift for all those involved: the filmmakers end up with a film, but the filmed ones are also privileged because the process of filming 'involves a break, the ordinary becoming extraordinary' (47). He evokes the famous Lacanian phrase 'To give what one has not, that is love' (45), without referencing Lacan.

Comolli stops short of actually spelling this out but he seems to be clear enough: documentary encounter is not just a discourse of desire; it may well be a discourse of love. I cited this extensively in my 2014 monograph supporting my argument about transference love – however, very clearly there are circumstances where the argument does not work.

If my whole notion that transference in documentary is like love confirms Comolli's writings about the importance of shared experience with the people one works with on a documentary, then my experience of *Married to the Eiffel Tower* denies it. The women in the film were heavily traumatised – in one way or another – and my work with them aimed at presenting them well, as human beings who have found another way of being 'normal' – not as a defence. I also wanted to present the film as a political gesture against heteronormative ideas about what relationships ought to be like, and neoliberal values influencing emotions. I respected the women I worked with here and I respected their desire to tell their stories. In the film, one of them says very clearly: 'this is the first time that I am given the voice to talk to the human race – I want to be listened to. I want people to listen to me, to really listen to me and see what I have to say'. And so, I think they did – the film is continuously commented on as one of the most important documentary pieces created in the last twenty years.[1] It has been screened all over the world. Its semi-illegal Vimeo site has had hundreds of thousands of views and it has recently (2016) been rescreened on Netflix. Whatever my intentions might have been, people watch the film because of their curiosity about how these women take care of their sexual and emotional needs. I stand by my film – it is well made. It is satisfying to have created a film that is still relevant and moves so many people.

However, inside the production process, the relationships were not easy – the women we featured really did not like other people and neither I nor my associate producer Vari Innes, who has since gone on to become a reality TV producer-director, were completely exempt from these reservations. Almost all of these women had been traumatised in one way or another by their difficult relationships with those who should have been the guardians of their health and wellbeing – their parents or, more specifically, their fathers. The large objects the women fell in love with replaced the security and safety of those who let them down – in their childhood but also more recently – in their daily encounters with the outside world. The 'replacement' part of it was very clear and very painful – even without any theoretical frameworks, Oedipal traumas or other causal effects. The objects offered a safe haven for the women in the film: they were controlled and controllable, they were fantasies which were nourishing, they offered something the world simply failed to deliver for these individuals. My associate producer and I found ourselves struggling – this was a professional job and we were paid well to make the film on time and on budget for a tough British broadcaster, Channel 5. We were paid to deliver an amusing film and to endure setbacks and difficulties in the course of making it. We struggled but were each other's support and safeguards. We felt sad for the women and questioned why we should be putting them on television. The project certainly replaced something important in their lives: a sense of belonging, a sense of recognition, a sense of being a part of something bigger – like a family, indeed – which fits perfectly into Comolli's schemes, as described above. But the fact of the matter was that to achieve that result we had to put ourselves on the line in many ways – feeling, as we did, that our contributors did not like us at all, that Comolli's 'community of desire' did not quite kick in here, that they wanted to be able to form relationships with other people the way we appeared to be able to do, however difficult our own lives might have been. Simply, we were different from them.

A year before I embarked on my PhD on film and psychoanalysis, I sensed dimly the reasons for our difficulties, without being able to name them: my associate producer Vari and myself were coping but, if truth be told, only just – we had feelings of frustration and anger, we had to field the rage of the contributors, which we were never allowed to disclose or share or do anything about at all. We hired film crews around the world, as the film was technically a mixed-medium project, meaning I shot some of it and used bigger crews to achieve the more glossy beautiful images. These moments with the crews were helpful to us – as we too were beginning to enter the strange world of objectum sexuality and the idea of replacing human relationships by those with objects began to appear fairly attractive to us too. We began discussing the attractiveness of the fences and the bridges – we were laughing at ourselves but both of us had difficult relationships with our fathers too, as it happened – like the women of our film. Ironically, in due course I chose the work of psychoanalyst

Jacques Lacan as my main theoretical paradigm; he identifies the father – and not the mother – as the key holder of a person's identity and sanity.

Vari and I spent a lot of time discussing our own relationships to our fathers. Was the whole process of making the documentary a replacement for a proper therapy or analysis? Perhaps.

And then, in the middle of production, when I was in San Francisco filming the main subject of the documentary, Erica La Tour Eiffel, *aka* Naisho, who declared her strong feelings for the Golden Gate Bridge, my father had a stroke and fell into a coma. I had a text from a close relative in Poland saying 'if I were you, I would get on the plane and come home. Now.' I was furious and it was deeply inconvenient – and I could not believe it as I had spoken to my father only the day before. 'Are you sure?' I said to the relative; 'Are you absolutely sure that he is not just going to wake up tomorrow?' 'He is not waking up. You need to get on the plane and come to Poland, to the hospital. Now', said the relative. I arrived in Poland on a Wednesday morning, my husband and son arrived two days later; my father never woke up, and he died the following Monday.

My father was old. Every father is old but mine was really old – he had had a whole life before he met my mother and had to change everything, for her and me. I should have known he was going to die. But I thought he wouldn't. I felt angry and betrayed, and abandoned.

The funeral took place the following Friday. My father had wanted to lie in state. He was a vain man. 'Make sure I look handsome', he said in his will. 'I can do this', I thought, 'no problem'. On the morning of the funeral I went to the funeral parlour and saw him – in a coffin, wearing an old suit, a white shirt and a navy-blue checked tie. He looked awful – they had lost his dentures in the hospital. His sunken face made him look unlike the father I knew and loved. 'You cannot be serious', I said to the two men who showed his body to me; 'we must fix this – bring some toilet tissue and we will stick it into his mouth to make him look better'. They looked stunned and brought it to me and I tried to open his mouth and could not, and so I cried, and then with rage I started rummaging in my handbag, looking for make-up, foundation and blusher to put on his face, tears streaming down my face. The two attendants stopped me then, looking horrified: 'lady, please leave this now and wait in the car – we will call you when we have prepared him better'. And so they did. At the funeral, on 17 March, there was a military band playing salutes, as he was a war hero. There were unexpected crowds: mourners coming up to me whispering condolences I was unwilling to accept. I thought I should give a speech but felt I might not be able to. As Poland is such a patriarchal society, I would have been excused if I had been unable to perform – women are weak. I was his only child. My two cousins, who were my father's nephews (and like adopted sons), were supposed to speak, but couldn't. They were sobbing uncontrollably instead. 'Oh for goodness sake', I said and gave the speech. I vomited straight afterwards.

On Monday I called my executive producer Justine Kershaw from Blink Films and said I was flying back to resume the production. 'Are you sure about this?' 'I am perfectly sure', I replied confidently. Replacing mourning with a production seemed an excellent plan.

And so Vari and I met in Sweden to work with Frau Berliner Mauer – who talked a lot about her father, the model-maker, who passed on to her his love for objects. I remember standing on the bridge in Sweden, crying, and Vari saying 'you shouldn't be here, you must go back'. But I stayed – the production schedule was tight and we had a broadcast date and perhaps the whole project started replacing the need to mourn the losses that are irreplaceable and the gaps which can never be filled. We just keep going because what else can one do?

We went to Paris and Berlin – and our relationships with the subjects of the film were deteriorating – they were annoyed at my sadness, which perhaps reminded them of their own. Naisho was keen to get intimate with the Eiffel Tower and asked for the crew to form a kind of wall around a particular section of it – a section she sat on and talked about how it felt to feel the coldness of the steel against her body. This scene formed a beautiful sequence and the ending of the film, which is – if I may be so bold – a great ending: moving and life affirming.

Naisho was happy with the film – the 'community of desire' as described by Comolli seemed to have worked after all. And then she changed her mind. 'Remove the ending', she said in an email: 'I don't want my intimacy with Eiffel Tower to be seen in this film'. I felt rising panic – this would have destroyed the whole film – the great finale was what made it. My executive producer said to me: 'We are not removing anything, her permission is clear and in fact it was her idea. Let me deal with this'.

The film went out unchanged. Naisho became vitriolic for a time but then made a whole career of her objectum sexuality, giving speeches at conferences and on talk shows. Amy, who was so vociferous about the voice being given to her, left the objectum sexuality chatrooms as there were some internal difficulties – she loved the film but in the end it could never replace her sense of profound loneliness and of being misunderstood by the world at large.

I collapsed after the film was broadcast on television, to great reviews. I cried for a month – and in a way have not stopped crying since, which of course is not quite true, as life has a way of replacing even the most painful memories with better ones. My father, who was an academic, left some money for me in his will: 'do what you want with it of course, but you do have a good brain and are quite tenacious – for a woman. I always wanted you to do a doctorate – would you consider it?'

NOTE

1. See for example https://filmow.com/listas/indiewire-s-stranger-than-fiction-16-documentaries-that-will-blow-your-mind-153668/.

REFERENCES

Comolli, Jean-Louis, 1999, 'Documentary Journey to the Land of the Head Shrinkers', tr. A. Michelson, *October*, 90, 36–49

Freud, Sigmund, 1958 [1915], 'Observations on Transference-Love (Further Recommendations on the Technique of Psycho-Analysis III)', in *Standard Edition of the Complete Psychological Works of Sigmund Freud*, vol XII, tr. & ed. James Strachey (London: Hogarth Press & the Institute of Psychoanalysis), 157–167

Green, André & Gregorio Kohon, 2005, *Love and its Vicissitudes* (London: Routledge)

Gross, Larry, John Stuart Katz & Jay Ruby, 1988, *Image Ethics: The Moral Subjects in Film, Photographs and Television* (Oxford: Oxford University Press)

Gueguen, Philippe, 1995, 'Transference as Deception', in Richard Feldstein, Bruce Fink & Maire Jaanus, eds., *Reading Seminar XI* (New York: State University of New York Press), 77–91

Lacan, Jacques, 1998 [1981], *Seminar XI. The Four Fundamental Concepts of Psychoanalysis*, ed. Jacques-Alain Miller, tr. Alan Sheridan (London & New York: W. W. Norton)

Lacan, Jacques, 2001 [1960–1961], *Le séminaire VIII: Le Transfert* (Paris: Seuil)

Lévinas, Emmanuel, 1981 [1974], *Otherwise than Being*, tr. Alphonso Lingis (The Hague: Martinus Nijhoff)

Piotrowska, Agnieszka, 2013, 'The Horror of a Doppelgänger in Documentary Film', in *New Review of Film and Television Studies*, 302–313 https://doi.org/10.1080/17400309.2013.807208, last accessed March 2016

Piotrowska, Agnieszka, 2014, *Psychoanalysis and Ethics in Documentary film* (London: Routledge)

Piotrowska, Agnieszka, 2016, *Black and White: cinema, arts and the politics in Zimbabwe* (London: Routledge)

CHAPTER 18

'That's my son': replacement, jealousy and sacrifice in *Un Secret*

Naomi Segal

I first presented the book on which this film is based during a Q&A with its author, psychoanalyst Philippe Grimbert, at Jewish Book Week in London in 2009. Grimbert was born in Paris in 1948. He works in a clinic for psychotic and autistic young people and also has a private practice; in addition, he has published both novels and some quirky books on psychoanalysis. His second fiction, *Un Secret* (2004) received much acclaim and many literary prizes. Claude Miller directed nineteen films between 1969 and the posthumous *Thérèse Desqueyroux* (2012). In the Guardian obituary of 5 April 2012, Ronald Bergan notes: 'the typical Miller film has a central figure under a lot of pressure, either self-imposed or coming from others. His is a cruel universe, created with great sensitivity', and suggests that his choice to direct Grimbert's book may have derived from a similar personal history, both being from assimilated French Jewish families.

The plot of *Un Secret* is not just any personal 'crypt' of holocaust history, however, for it focuses in several ways on the intricacies of domestic

---

NB Quotations with page references are from the translation of the book; others are from the film.

N. Segal (✉)
Birkbeck, University of London, London, UK

© The Author(s) 2018
J. Owen, N. Segal (eds.), *On Replacement*,
https://doi.org/10.1007/978-3-319-76011-7_18

replacement, both familial and erotic. The film opens with two intercut scenes. The first, titled 'the summer of 1955', is set in a sports club where, in warm colours, a gawky child, François (Valentin Vigourt), watches his beautiful mother Tania (Cécile de France) dive faultlessly into the swimming pool. Then we see him in black and white in 1985, as an adult (Mathieu Amalric) treating an autistic boy and hurrying to his parents' home where he has been told his father is missing, upset by the death of the family dog. Back in 1955, the shivering boy persuades his mother to take him home; his father Maxime (Patrick Bruel), pausing briefly from a tennis game, represses a look of disappointment; and as they leave, François glances up to the diving-board where, in lighting that veers between pure black-and-white and cloudy, the figure of another boy waves goodbye.

These criss-crossing images set up the initial doubling of two times (childhood and the present, thirty years apart), two representations (the past in sunlit colour, the present monochrome) and two boys (the feeble one fully visible, the energetic one in shadow). The voice-over opens with its inaugurating paradox: 'I was an only child, but for a long time I had a brother'. These three pairs are all versions of replacement, each with something askew: in the first two we might expect the rainbow reality of the present to blot out the dim past, but the reverse is true; and in the third pair we find the familiar ambivalence of the replacement child, with a powerful hint that this sibling has not been so much made as found.

François believes he has invented the brother for whom he lays an extra place at table, who lends him emotional strength at school but who mocks and fights him in bed at night.[1] He adopts a toy dog found in the attic and observes that it causes his father unexplained grief; he calls it 'Si', short for 'Simon', a name that lends the story enough uncanniness to counteract the gathering theme of imagination.[2] For if François is a small Kafka, intimidated especially by his hunky, over-healthy father, what this fiction tells us is that it is not personal creativity but the vengeance of cultural history that brings us our truth; and – psychoanalytically of course – that the present is a black hole out of which the past has to emerge, as another act of replacement.

The mediator of this truth is a family friend, physiotherapist Louise (Julie Depardieu), and it is she who chooses at last to tell the teenage François (Quentin Dubuis) what no one else will but 'what I had always known'. The superiority of the physically 'perfect' which unites Maxime, Tania and the imaginary brother is, by implication, what makes them less Jewish than François or Louise,[3] like the other figures who arise from the past – Maxime's father, sister Esther and brother-in-law Georges, and a whole other family, the Stirns, whose son Robert (Robert Plagnol) was once Tania's husband while their daughter Hannah (Ludivigne Sagnier) was Maxime's wife and the mother of lost boy Simon.

The story of the family past appears in both the book and the film as a revelation, replacing the boy's false belief in his parents' meeting at the sports club, falling in love, spending the occupation years in the pretty village of Saint-Gaultier, keeping up with politics only through the wireless and, once the war was over, coming back to Paris, collecting the keys from Louise and having him. His birth was a disappointment to his father, represented by the words '4lbs 8oz. Not much', which will soon contrast with the exact opposite measurement at the birth of Simon: '8lbs 4oz. He's a strong 'un'. But something else enters the world with this other child: 'the whole family knew. They had all known Simon, all loved him. They could all remember his energy and confidence. And they had all hidden him from me [...] Simon and Hannah, obliterated twice over: by the hatred of their persecutors and the love of their family' (65).

It is at the wedding of Hannah and Maxime that the latter and Tania first meet. Childlike Hannah delights everyone with her magic tricks, but Tania is already the tall glowing beauty she will remain, and Maxime cannot take his eyes off her. Yet we must not ignore the good intentions of all parties, and desire is shown as something to be resisted. We see Simon grow within the extended family, who vary in their Jewish commitment and confidence in France, as when Maxime tears off the yellow star that Louise has sewn on to Simon's jacket with the retort: 'He's my son, I decide. No disguises'.

At the sports club, Tania gives baby Simon the toy dog, and seven or eight years later, after he wins an athletics contest, she photographs him proudly wearing his medal. Then she dives from the top board and as she does another crossing of gazes takes place:

> Hannah applauds, and then looks to Maxime for agreement. All she sees in his gaze is Tania. She knows her husband well enough to recognise wild desire, a fascination he is not even bothering to hide. He has never looked at her like this. [...] She finds support only in Louise, who has understood and tries to reassure her with a smile. She teeters; in a fog she hears everyone cheering some new feat of Tania's. As her sister-in-law climbs out of the pool, her body streaming and shaking her thick hair, Hannah suddenly realises what a perfect couple these two athletes would make. They are at

home here, the sports club belongs to them, they are radiant. [...] She has never been competitive by nature; immediately she wants to disappear, to remove herself and make way for them. The day becomes gloomy and she spends the rest of the afternoon with Simon, kissing and embracing him, closer than ever to her son.[4]

In saying this, the text's narrator – in purely speculative omniscience – directs readers towards a reading of causes and motives. Motives for what? The ultimate secret, hinted at by the silence the family has steadfastly maintained, is how the mother and son disappeared. As Maxime and Georges succeed in reaching Saint-Gaultier, across the border in unoccupied France, they call for the other four – Hannah, Simon, Esther and Louise – to join them.

A certain balance is maintained: Hannah fears Tania despite herself but hopes that Robert will return and she can be happy again with Maxime. But then two things happen. First, she discovers her parents have been seized in an early-morning round-up. After this, her whole demeanour changes: she is half-distracted and, whether deliberately or not, does not tear up her identity paper saying 'Juive' when the other two women destroy theirs. The second shock is a letter from Maxime casually mentioning that Tania has arrived in Saint-Gaultier. Silent and expressionless, Hannah stares out of the window as Louise and Esther pack and prepare, slaps her son, appears unconnected to anything. She says she and Simon will stay in Paris, but is dissuaded. The whole enigma of the film resides in Hannah's face as she sits impassively on the train. Then we see her take her first (and last) decisive action when a German officer at the border demands their papers: Hannah looks straight at him and hands over her Jewish identity paper; Simon comes running out of the toilet, hesitates whether to join Hannah or the other women, and she says 'That's my son'.

The book offers three explanations: the one the family tell themselves, a sudden moment of 'incredible carelessness' (126); or something much more deliberate: a sense of abandonment, first by her parents, then, impending, by Maxime, Tania, and even Esther, who had invited the latter to Saint-Gaultier. And third: 'Timid, shy Hannah, the perfect mother, had turned into a tragic heroine; the fragile young woman suddenly became Medea, sacrificing her child and her own life on the altar of her wounded heart' (107).

An action that transforms lives may take an instant and we view it in an instant, dwelling on Hannah's face but uncertain whether her fatal choice of ID was planned or impulsive. They are marched away. The rest of the film completes the love story of Maxime and Tania, underlain by guilt and secrecy, and closes on the present day, in which Maxime falls into greater grief at the death of his dog, it seems, than at the loss of his first child; in the 'Epilogue' (filmed in warm colour) dogs appear again when François takes his daughter to a graveyard, on the estate of President Laval's daughter, where animals replace humans as objects of mourning and names like 'Madou' or 'Grigri' give way to a closing recitation of the Jewish dead.

Every time I have shown this film, including at the *Replacement* conference, the subsequent discussion has focused on Hannah's motivation. Few members of my audience have read the book, so it is not there to preempt their judgements. Most agree that Hannah is motivated by sensing she has lost Maxime to Tania but the trigger is the capture of her parents; it is these two combined that make her both 'want to disappear' and cling on to her child. Nagihan Haliloğlu argued that Hannah was making a positive if fatal choice to assert her Jewishness in a way the other characters did not. When the discussion moved to the question of what she was choosing, Naomi Tadmor reminded us that at that time in France – indeed the film shows this – people did not know exactly what capture would mean. What remains is the suddenness of an action whose cause can only be imagined. As André Gide puts it at another autobiographical turning-point, 'the motivation of our acts – I mean, our most significant acts – is unknown to us, not only in our recollection of those moments, but even at the time' (Gide: 279, my translation).

The difference between verbal and visual media shows itself most powerfully in this question. On the DVD, in the film's 'The making of...' Claude Miller comments: 'what's beautiful in making films is that you only film the outside of things, but you try to show what's inside. My ambition is to go inside the intimacy of human beings. I think it's good that people like you and me have lots of secrets'. Indeed, this story presents a spectrum of motivations for secrecy, not all negative – Simon not told about the gathering terror; Maxime and Tania's effort to keep their desire hidden even from themselves; the adolescent François protecting his parents from what he now knows about them. In a variety of ways these ruses turn falsehood into something more subtle.[5] But it also raises questions about the fictionality of things. Grimbert describes how he used the 'few sentences' his relatives and parents eventually told him as 'pillars' of a bridge between which he supplied the 'arches' of made-up details, transforming Hannah's parapraxis into a suicidal wish-fulfilment. He adds: 'I often felt

[...] that the fiction I had invented was in fact real. Like a police inspector, I thought: "I'm sure that's the way it happened, it can't have been otherwise". I was absolutely convinced I had discovered the truth through the fiction. Strangely enough [Curieusement]'. As both psychoanalyst and author, perhaps he is bound to believe this. But what is most curious is that in these comments he does not mention Hannah's choice to take Simon with her – how it happened, or why. Was that a truthful invention too? Why is he so intent (both in the film and in the book) on likening Hannah to Medea?

In most versions of Medea, a wronged wife chooses to displace her impotent anger from the husband she cannot harm to the children she can. In Grimbert's text, a kinder view likens Hannah's choice to an act of embracing rather than harm: Simon is 'all she has left'. But what is at stake in his assertion that fiction is, after all, truer than the scraps of 'specific facts' that his parents gave him? The brother who disappeared by the fault both of cruel history and of all the adults who failed to control their passions, falls back after all into the grip of imagination and of the wish-fulfilment of the replacement child as author.

Notes

1. In the book this ambivalence grows, once he has learned of the existence of his real predecessor, into a mixture of 'a dull anger of which I already felt ashamed' (62), 'the fierce bite of jealousy' (62), compounded more perversely by 'inherited shame' (65) and 'the pleasure I derived from this defeat' (65).
2. In the original text the name is even more direct: 'Sim' (23*ff*).
3. The Louise of Grimbert's book – an invented character – is 'in her sixties' (19), club-footed, pale-skinned, with bags under her eyes and 'a ruined face' (20), and addicted to alcohol and tobacco; in the film only the last trait remains, together with a gentle hint that she may be a lesbian. Her goodness is thus not dependent on a lack of the physical beauty that distinguishes the lovers.
4. Grimbert 2004: 105–106; my translation. 'Radiance/éclat' is the word used of Maxime's first impression of Tania at his wedding, just as 'fog/brouillard' and 'gloomy/assombrit' were used of the shock effect on him.
5. This despite Grimbert's punning assertion in 'The making of...' (just after he has punned 'all humans secrete secrets') that silence can kill: 'ce qui est tu peut tuer'.

References

Bergan, Ronald, 2005, *The Guardian online* (5 April) https://www.theguardian.com/film/2012/apr/05/claude-miller, last accessed 23 Oct 2017

Gide, André, 2001, *Souvenirs et voyages*, eds. Pierre Masson, Daniel Durosay & Martine Sagaert (Paris: Gallimard)

Grimbert, Philippe, 2004, *Un Secret* (Paris: Grasset)

Grimbert, Philippe, 2007, *Secret*, tr. Polly McLean (London: Portobello)

Miller, Claude, dir., 2007, *Un Secret*

PART VI

The Holocaust

CHAPTER 19

Replacement as personal haunting in recent postmemory works

Susanne Baackmann

In this chapter, I focus on how ghosts from the past – in this case dead or lost siblings and lost homes – haunt narrators in several postmemory texts. These texts articulate the effects of parental trauma in the subsequent generation and signal a transgenerational return of traumatic knowledge. My main example is Hans-Ulrich Treichel's *Der Verlorene* (1998) [*Lost*, 1999], a text that features a brother who was first said to be dead but then declared 'lost'. Similarly, a 'host-brother' haunts Art Spiegelman's narrator in *Maus II: A Survivor's Tale: And Here my Troubles Began* (1986). And in a different, yet related way, Angelika Overath's *Nahe Tage: Roman in einer Nacht* [*Near Days: Novel in One Night*] (2005) describes the ghosting of the past by portraying the daughter of a mother traumatised by postwar flight and expulsion as the replacement for a lost home and sense of belonging. I shall argue that this haunting of the present by the past is characteristic of recent postmemory works, which trace experiences of transgenerational trauma across different subject positions. Many critics have noticed 'remarkable similarities […] between the case histories of the children of the oppressed and those of the oppressors' (Santner: 35, also see Hoffman and Epstein).

S. Baackmann (✉)
University of New Mexico, Albuquerque, NM, USA

© The Author(s) 2018
J. Owen, N. Segal (eds.), *On Replacement*,
https://doi.org/10.1007/978-3-319-76011-7_19

The narrators of *Lost* and *Nahe Tage* articulate the paradoxes and impasses experienced by children who are born into the perpetrator legacy. While they are grappling with being an inherently insufficient replacement of a lost brother and a lost home, children of survivor parents, such as Art in *Maus*, face an impossible task: they have to replace dead relatives or children who have perished in the wake of a genocide (see Hoffman and Pellicer-Ortin). Such 'replacement logic' does not differentiate between the children of perpetrators or children of survivors; in other words, psychological symptomology does not know, and thus cannot register, foundational differences of historical cause and effect. This, in turn, raises two questions: do postmemory texts written from the point of view of children born into the perpetrator legacy run the risk of levelling irrefutable differences between perpetrators, victims and bystanders that need to be acknowledged and spelled out in order to forge a path into the future? Or do they, rather, express complex fusions between these different subject positions that articulate the kind of intersections between historical agency and emotional identity that successive generations have to navigate? Do they, in other words, challenge binary and reductive subject positions, along with the conception of the implicated subject, while still acknowledging the particular and irreducible charge assigned to each individual in the historical texture? In what follows, I argue that *Lost* – and in different ways *Maus* and *Nahe Tage* – challenge simplifying and reductive binaries by bringing into play what Michael Rothberg has called the 'implicated subject', a historical subject position that is fundamentally heterogeneous and draws 'attention to how we are *entwined* with and *folded into* ("im-pli-cated in") histories and situations that surpass our agency as individual subjects' (Rothberg, n.p., emphasis in original).

In *Haunting Legacies: Violent Histories and Transgenerational Trauma* (2010), Gabriele Schwab prefaces the chapter on replacement children with a note about her personal life. She writes that late one night she suddenly understood that she 'always felt guilt for owing my life to the death of an infant brother who was killed during the war' (120). When she turned to the body of psychoanalytic literature about replacement children – a phenomenon particularly common after violent histories such as the Holocaust and other genocidal wars – she found that such children share a common problem. 'Children born after such wars may feel more than the burden of having to replace the child or children whom their parents lost during the war: they grow up with a sense that their generation must replace the entire generation that was meant to be exterminated' (120). This burden, while equally pressing, is framed somewhat differently for children of perpetrators, Schwab claims. Children born to perpetrator parents do not feel the pressure to replace an entire generation; nonetheless, they grow up in an atmosphere of silence, denial and splitting off.

How, then, do the works under consideration choreograph the psychological coordinates of replacement children who are born into different historical legacies? While the main focus of this chapter is on Treichel's text, I shall use Spiegelman's and Overath's works as contrasting narratives in order to examine how the complexities of different implications in violent histories can be represented. What allows me to compare these texts is the fact that they are all written from the perspective of children of traumatised parents, who are grappling with their place in a family constellation ruptured by war, displacement and genocide. Describing a family theatre that is composed of silences, denials, rejections and cruelties born of parental trauma, these works confront what Marianne Hirsch has called the 'ghosts of home' (Hirsch 2012: 14). Their narrators seek an understanding of their implication in a wounding and a loss that preceded their birth yet has shaped their life in significant ways. From rather different positions of implication, they are narrating the effects of replacement, a perforation of identity that went before them and marked them deeply, thereby expressing a connection to the past that is 'shaped more and more by affect, need, and desire as time and distance attenuate the links to authenticity and "truth"' (Hirsch: 48). Regardless of their specific focal points, all the texts reveal a '*structure*' of inter- and transgenerational return of traumatic knowledge and embodied experience', performing memory as 'a *consequence* of traumatic recall but [...] at a generational remove' (Hirsch: 6, emphasis in original).[1]

The narrative premise of *Lost* is shaped by a sense of displacement, loss and absence, condensed to the trope of a lost child. Centred on futile but persistent attempts to undo that loss, the parents' revelations about Arnold, the lost brother of the narrator, slide from a dead to an 'un-dead' brother and finally a found one who, sadly, can no longer be acknowledged. Initially, the parents had spun the tale of his death, making the surviving brother believe 'that Arnold had starved to death while they fled the Russians' (6), yet later they revise this story to that of 'loss' during flight and expulsion and Arnold becomes 'the un-dead brother' (17) in the eyes of his confused and irritated sibling. In a moment of panic the mother had handed her baby to a stranger in the trek and later was unable to locate him. The parents remain deeply haunted by 'something dreadful'

(9) at the hands of the Russians (most likely the rape of the mother), but they never explicitly reveal any details to their son. Eventually, they start the process of looking for Arnold, yet without success, since the pseudo-scientific and distorted bureaucratic process – a satire on the perpetuation of postfascist mentalities and procedures – blocks them in their tracks. Ironically, the text ends with the discovery of Arnold but the mother refuses to acknowledge him: he is no longer the baby she lost (135–136). The replacement childhood we witness is focalised through a retrospectively conceived child's perspective (see Baackmann 2017), marked not only by the omnipresent shadow of a lost sibling but also by the legacy of a lost war and a lost home.

The text begins with the description of a photograph of the lost brother in the family album. 'My brother squatted on a white wool blanket and laughed into the camera. That was during the war, my mother said, the last year of the war, at home. At home, that was the East, and my brother had been born in the East' (Treichel: 3, translation amended). This photo is compared to the blurred or incomplete photos of the narrator, a comparison that encapsulates the paradoxical rivalry with a dead sibling. Resentfully, the narrator observes, '[m]y brother Arnold looked not just happy but important even when he was a baby, in most of the photos from my childhood I am either only partly visible or sometimes not really visible at all' (4). Thus, the text opens with a photo of the 'ghost' that haunts the family – that is, it opens with an absence that is articulated as an all-pervasive presence, which is felt as a painful comparison by the replacement child. The brother who squats on a white wool blanket and laughs embodies this family's complicated story of loss and longing. In *Family Frames*, Marianne Hirsch reminds us of Roland Barthes' understanding of presence and absence in photography. The dead brother on the white blanket is what Barthes has called a 'referent'. 'The referent haunts the picture like a ghost: it is a revenant, a return of the lost and dead other' (Hirsch 1997: 5); '[p]hotographs, ghostly revenants, are very particular instruments of remembrance, since they are perched at the edge between memory and postmemory' (22).

Rather than referring to the end of memory, postmemory 'characterizes the experience of those who grow up dominated by narratives that preceded their birth, whose own belated stories are evacuated by the stories of the previous generation shaped by traumatic events that can neither be understood nor recreated' (22). In Treichel's text, the child-narrator is acutely aware that his 'belated story' is erased by the trauma experienced by his parents. When his mother tells him about how Arnold was left behind and that he may have another name now, he defiantly replies that he might have been lucky and 'they named him Arnold again' (10). His mother's reaction of deep sadness leads him to reflect on his relationship to Arnold:

> But I only said it because I was angry at Arnold. Because I was just beginning to understand that Arnold, my un-dead brother, had the leading role in the family and had assigned me a supporting part. I also understood that Arnold was responsible from the very beginning for my growing up in an atmosphere poisoned with guilt and shame. From the day of my birth, guilt and shame had ruled the family, without my knowing why. [...] I absolutely knew that I felt guilty and ashamed, but I could not explain to myself that the innocent child that I was should be shamed by a piece of meat or a potato or should feel guilty. (10–11)

Such defiance is typical of a narrative that represents the poignant psychological and temporal contradictions that replacement children have to grapple with: the replacement child reminds its parents of someone they have lost.

This competition with an absent brother resonates with the opening passage in Art Spiegelman's *Maus II And Here my Troubles Began*, the second instalment of the well-known graphic novel which chronicles the complicated relationship between the narrator and his parents, but also his 'ghost brother' Richieu. Like Arnold in Treichel's text, a photo of Richieu provides the narrative premise for *Maus*. When trying to introduce his family to his wife Françoise, Art finds himself pondering whether he would have got on with his 'ghost-brother'. When the blurred photograph of Richieu that hangs in his parent's bedroom comes up, we hear Art exclaim resentfully, '[t]hey didn't need photos of me in my room. I was *alive*! [...] The photo never threw tantrums or got into any kind of trouble. [...] It was an ideal kid' (15). These words succinctly trace the dilemma of the replacement child who cannot compete with a dead sibling yet also cannot avoid comparison – what Schwab has aptly termed a 'ghostly competition handed down with parental fantasies. This kind of tacit competition with a dead sibling is a classic syndrome of replacement children' (121). As in *Lost*, the long-term effects of growing up with traumatised parents come to the fore in *Maus* as a sibling rivalry featuring a dead and therefore 'ideal' sibling who cancels out the sense of identity and self-worth of the belated replacement child. But in notable contrast to children born into the perpetrator legacy, children of survivor parents also experience an enduring fear of persecution, which indicates the persistent power of the past over the present. Art is rather aware that, '[i]t's *spooky*, having sibling rivalry with a snapshot! I never felt guilty about Richieu. But I did have nightmares about SS men coming into class and dragging all us Jewish kids away' (15–16, emphasis in original).

The nameless narrator of *Lost* also identifies with victims of the Holocaust. When forced to have his photograph taken to be submitted for comparative purposes, his 'father orders [him] to get a short haircut that turned him into a sort of inmate of a camp' (48, see also 50). This evocation of concentration-camp inmates, along with other covert and overt references to National Socialism, demarcates a blurring of lines, a kind of experiential proximity between the children of victims and the children of perpetrators. In fact, Treichel's narrator feels violated by the measuring procedures undertaken to establish a biological link with 'foundling 2307', the boy his parents believed to be their lost son. Here, the text alludes to the kind of agitation expressed by the second generation who saw themselves betrayed by the silence and denial of their perpetrator parents. Yet *Lost* only brushes against this proximity with victims of the Holocaust. Moreover, it does so in a self-reflexive and laconic way that underscores a subtle yet firm line of difference between these two subject positions. While well aware of the ideology that shaped his parents, in contrast to the mortal fear experienced by the child of a Holocaust survivor in *Maus*, this narrator only evokes the legacy of National Socialism indirectly.

Treichel's text gains poignancy as a self-reflexive narrative that chronicles how replacement children born into the perpetrator legacy are charged with articulating irrevocable loss and unacknowledged feelings of parental guilt and shame. These feelings, transferred onto the replacement son, are presented with irony and dry humour that border on satire at times. No matter how much the laconic inflection of the narrative voice tries to temper an underlying sense of shame, the narrator's body exhibits it in the form of psychosomatic symptoms, from severe motion sickness to a painful trigeminal neuralgia. Repeating his parents' deeply ingrained fear of travel, the boy manages to develop 'a special form of travel sickness [...] its chief symptom was the physical inability to tolerate movement' (13). When he hears how much he looks like his lost brother, his intensely physical reaction translates a manner of speaking into a painful physical sensation. Comparing his two sons, the father remarks, Arnold '"looks as if he were carved out of your face"'. An idea which made me so physically queasy that [...] I got some kind of stomach cramp that reached up to my face, shot through my cheeks, and ended behind my forehead' (40). Here, a metaphor, used clumsily by a parent, turns on itself and manifests as a physical symptom in the son, in effect disrupting the already fragile communication between father and son with somatic protestations. Yet these protestations are nonetheless a language. In her analysis of current theories of cultural memory, Anne Fuchs articulates the limits and distortions of narrativity with respect to trauma and memory discourse. She observes that narration alone

> fails to take into account alternative modes of cultural transmission that communicate through the unsaid, the *sous-entendu*, through innuendo, and silence. [...] this latent type of memory work speaks a language of gesturing that defies representation. [...] This other code upsets the rules of discourse by turning the body into a stage for a performance that offers ghosts and phantoms of the past. (236)

Fuchs engages with the theories of alterity of Emmanuel Levinas and Julia Kristeva as contestations of narrative representation or integration and sees them in dialogue with Freud's understanding of the body as an exquisite stage for unresolved tensions. What becomes visible in her exploration of the edges of postmemory is a somatic underbelly: 'a frightful appearance of bodily phantoms [...] both excessive and elusive: excessive because it punctuates the flow of language, and elusive in that it thwarts signification' (241). This somatic underbelly does not know the difference of historical cause and effect and can thus affect the narrators and parents in both *Lost* and *Maus*.

I shall close this cursory analysis with a brief reading of Overath's *Nahe Tage: Roman in einer Nacht*, a text that also charts the effects of replacement; in this case the child is appropriated as the replacement of a lost home (*Heimat*). Johanna, the narrator, reflects on the pathology of her childhood, a childhood marked by relentless maternal domination due to an unresolved trauma experienced by the mother. Faced with the death of her mother, Johanna reluctantly spends one night 'at home', or rather in the last apartment her mother lived in. Being surrounded by the sights and smells of familiar objects from her childhood, she contemplates the insidious nature of home and notes that 'hells must be familiar places' (7), evoking Freud's thoughts on the uncanny.[2] When she inhales the familiar smells emanating from her mother's clothes, she has to vomit, a visceral reaction (which parallels the psychosomatic symptoms of Treichel's narrator) to a lost childhood reconfigured as a substitute for the lost home in the East. Matter-of-factly, she describes the paradox of her childhood, '[t]he child had become her mother's house' (32). But the 'homes' she inhabited were never safe places of comfort and consolation. Once

> [a] bowl had fallen onto the tiled kitchen floor and broken; it had slipped out of the child's hand. [...] After a moment of silence, her mother had wiped her hands on her apron. You will never be able to make up for that, that was from home. [...] Clearly the cozy, ceremoniously scrubbed apartment, was also a minefield, full of secret time bombs from Back-Then and Home. (127)

Like Treichel's and Spiegelman's narrators, this narrator also struggles to gain agency beyond her designated replacement function. If we define terrorism as the suspension of agency, as not knowing what the rules are, when and from where to expect an attack, Johanna is deeply terrorised. She never knows when the past is about to come home to haunt the present, and yet is shamed for it. She understands full well that she never had a home. 'Maybe home is a place where things can break, Johanna thought. Where one can try things out, where not everything counts for eternity because the present does not count and the future only means to save what was lost' (128). Above all, her memory is not trustworthy. In fact, she remembers that she does not remember ever having been a child. 'The thought had crossed her mind that she was not worthy of having a childhood of her own' (39).

Remarkably, and in contrast to both Treichel's and Spiegelman's texts, *Nahe Tage* leaves the oppressive intimacy of the family realm and probes the larger context of global displacement when Johanna meets Svetlana, a Russian-German who had to flee Russia because of political persecution. Svetlana remarks with great equanimity: 'This is a common story, the media are reporting it all the time' (94). The two women bond over similarities in their biographies. 'You also are alien with German passport' (111), Svetlana notes in broken German. At this point, the suffocating coordinates of a replacement childhood, defined by no social connections outside the domestic sphere, open up to the transnational realm. Johanna feels an unexpected, yet warm connection to a stranger who also experienced flight and expulsion, albeit at a different time and under different circumstances, and in this moment is trying out new meanings of home and belonging across differences of place, culture and language.

All three texts chart the psychological, social and transgenerational effects of replacement from different subject positions, and in different ways, yet without levelling historical specificity based on shared traumatic legacies. While evoking parallels between children born to survivors and those born to perpetrators, *Lost* marks historical specificity through narrative strategies of irony and self-reflexivity. *Maus* also relies on self-reflexivity in order to delineate the complication of being born into a survivor legacy, in this case as a strategy that rests on the layering of various speaking positions and images (see Ketchum Glass). *Nahe Tage*, on the other hand, marks fusions between victim and perpetrator legacies by evoking larger global structures of displacement and replacement. In a sense, then, all these works focalise postmemory by resorting to different modes of temporal layering. Treichel's text points backwards to the *past* as a way to diagnose the present, Spiegelman's text portrays the *present* as laced by fears stemming from the past, and Overath's text opens to a *future* sharply informed by the past across differences of cultures and history. While acknowledging the impasses of an inherited parental trauma, all three texts probe subject positions of implication in a legacy of historical violence. The father's bellowing voice that dominates the replacement son in *Lost* evokes the legacy of the fascist past but resists seamless identification with the victim perspective. *Maus* describes the dilemma of the replacement son by performing what Ketchum Glass has aptly termed a 'palimpsestuous' narrative (21), which articulates the implication in the past through different but interdependent voices: the survivor's son, the teller of a survivor's tale, and the anxious self-conscious narrator. *Nahe Tage* addresses the legacy of replacement by opening up to a dialogue of solidarity with a victim of displacement from a different culture and history. This kind of postmemory work is cognisant of specific historical legacies that locate the parents' trauma within the spectrum of the victim-perpetrator imaginary, yet rather than lamenting a childhood subsumed by this, it acknowledges these differences as different ways in which replacement children are always also implicated subjects.

Notes

1. In Baackmann 2016, I explore the complexities of an implicated subject position in my reading of Rachel Seiffert's text 'Lore'. This text is part of Seiffert's story trilogy *The Dark Room* (2001), which was adapted for cinema by Cate Shortland in 2012.
2. All translations from *Nahe Tage* are mine.

References

Baackmann, Susanne, 2016, 'Between Victim and Perpetrator Imaginary: The Implicated Subject in Works by Rachel Seiffert and Cate Shortland', in *Transit* 10. 2, http://transit.berkeley.edu/

Baackmann, Susanne, 2017, 'The Epistemology of Writing Childhood: Hans-Ulrich Treichel's *Der Verlorene*', in *The German Quarterly* 90. 1 (Winter), 71–84

Bude, Heinz, 1992, *Bilanz der Nachfolge: Die Bundesrepublik und der Nationalsozialismus*. (Frankfurt: Suhrkamp)

Epstein, Helen, 1988 [1979], *Children of the Holocaust: Conversations with Sons and Daughters of Survivors* (New York: Penguin)

Fuchs, Anne, 2002, 'Towards an Ethics of Remembering: The Walser-Bubis Debate and the Other of Discourse', in *The German Quarterly* 75. 3 (Summer), 235–246

Hirsch, Marianne, 1997, *Family Frames: Photography, Narrative and Postmemory* (Cambridge, MA and London: Harvard University Press)

Hirsch, Marianne, 2012, *Generations of Postmemory: Writing and Visual Culture After the Holocaust* (New York: Columbia University Press)

Hoffman, Eva, 2004, *After Such Knowledge: Memory, History, and the Legacy of the Holocaust* (New York: Public Affairs)

Ketchum Glass, Susannah, 2007, 'Witnessing the Witness: Narrative Slippage in Art Spiegelman's *Maus*', in *Life Writing* 3:2. 3–24. https://doi.org/10.1080/10408340308518311

Overath, Angelika, 2005, *Nahe Tage. Roman in einer Nacht* (Munich: dtv)

Pellicer-Ortin, Silvia, 2014, 'Separateness and Connectedness: Generational Trauma and the Ethical Impulse in Anne Karpf's *The War After: Living with the Holocaust*', in eds. Susana Onega and Jean-Michel Ganteau, *Contemporary Trauma Narratives: Liminality and the Ethics of Form* (New York and London: Routledge), 193–209

Raczymow, Henri, 1994, 'Memory Shot through with Holes' ['La mémoire trouée], tr. Alan Astro, in *Yale French Studies* 85, 98–105

Rothberg, Michael, 2014, 'Trauma Theory, Implicated Subjects, and the Question of Israel/Palestine', Presidential Forum of *Profession* (May) https://profession.mla.hcommons.org/2014/05/02/trauma-theory-implicated-subjects-and-the-question-of-israelpalestine/, n. p.

Santner, Eric, 1993, *Stranded Objects: Mourning, Memory, and Film in Postwar Germany* (Cornell: Cornell University Press)

Schwab, Gabriele, 2010, *Haunting Legacies: Violent History and Transgenerational Trauma* (New York: Columbia University Press)

Spiegelman, Art, 1986, *Maus II: A Survivor's Tale: And Here my Troubles Began* (New York: Pantheon Books)

Treichel, Hans-Ulrich, 2000a, *Lost* [*Der Verlorene*, 1998], tr. Carol Brown Janeway (New York: Vintage Books)

Treichel, Hans-Ulrich, 2000b, *Der Entwurf des Autors. Frankfurter Poetikvorlesungen* (Frankfurt: Suhrkamp)

CHAPTER 20

Embodying her ghost: self-replacement in Petzold's *Phoenix*

Monika Loewy

A phoenix is a mythological bird that continually dies by fire and is reborn; arising from its ashes, the phoenix endlessly replaces itself. Accordingly, Christian Petzold's 2014 film *Phoenix* is about re-creation, about arising from the ashes of the Second World War. *Phoenix* is loosely based on Hubert Monteilhet's novel *Le Retour des Cendres* [*Return from the ashes*] (1961); taking place in Germany in the mid-1940s, it traces the journey of Nelly (Nina Hoss), an Auschwitz survivor, her attempt to replace her postwar reality with her prewar self, and of the impossibility of doing so. The film opens with a close-up of the face of her friend Lene (Nina Kunzendorf), shadowed in darkness, thus setting the tone for the characters' shadowed understanding of themselves, each other and the aftermath of war. We soon discover that Nelly's face has been severely damaged in the camps and that although she can be, as the surgeon states, 'reconstructed', she can never look the way she desires to look: 'exactly how I used to'. Once the surgery is complete, Nelly seeks out her husband Johnny (Ronald Zehrfeld) to reclaim her former life and identity. However, when she finally finds him he fails to recognise her, though she bears a striking resemblance to his 'former wife' (Nelly prior to the surgery).

M. Loewy (✉)
Goldsmiths, University of London, London, UK

© The Author(s) 2018
J. Owen, N. Segal (eds.), *On Replacement*,
https://doi.org/10.1007/978-3-319-76011-7_20

Driven to obtain her inheritance by proving that she is still alive, Johnny convinces Nelly – whom he believes to be a stranger – to take on his 'former wife's' idealised identity, and begins to mould her towards this ideal. Here, the similarity between *Phoenix* and Hitchcock's *Vertigo* (1958) comes into focus, as an authoritative male forces his illusory ideals upon an, at times, passive female. This patriarchal overtone, moreover, is presumably reflective of Petzold's view of Germany at the time – as an innkeeper in the film ambiguously states, 'you know how men are these days'. However, Nelly takes on a more discernibly active role than *Vertigo's* Madeline (Kim Novak); although Johnny dictates Nelly's identity, she seeks him out because she wants to conform to her former self. Slowly, Nelly realises that this is impossible, a realisation that is triggered by Lene's suicide and the proof that Johnny betrayed her Jewish background and divorced her before the war. Nelly's realisation is solidified when she refuses to burn off her tattooed number and reveals what I shall argue is her 'True Self' in the film's chilling close. Ultimately, then, this chapter traces Nelly's struggle to replace herself with a ghost of her past. To explore this theme, I shall begin with a brief introduction to Petzold's work and move on to illuminate the film's narrative through Freud's notion of the uncanny. This will be followed by a discussion of Winnicott's concept of the 'True and False Self', as it relates to Nelly's self-discovery and independence.

Christian Petzold's films often explore how personal transitions align with political and economic ones, and how individual and national identities intersect. *Phoenix* is emblematic of this, as it centres on a woman who struggles with a split between her prewar and postwar identity, and how this is figured in a fractured country. As Petzold explains in an interview with Adam Nayman for *Cinema Scope*, the film itself also traverses a split as it takes place 'in the cut' between two generations: between those who experienced the war and those who began to recognise that the German state was 'based on fascistic structures' (n.p.). The Berlin portrayed in the film echoes this double: its bareness paradoxically symbolises both destruction and the capacity for construction. In relation to this, I suggest that Nelly's psychological and physical appearances and experiences dramatise the struggle to navigate this divide. She lives between two worlds and two bodies, plagued by the desire to return to an uncannily present past.

Only eight minutes into the film we are reminded of Freud's notion of the uncanny double, as the bandaged protagonist follows a patient, identical in appearance, down a white hallway and towards a room decorated with photographs of her prewar self. And indeed, the film's narrative is driven by doubles: Nelly's current self and the self she pretends to be. This scene establishes the film, as she is drawn towards images of a past that are both painful and comfortingly familiar. In his 1919 essay 'The Uncanny', Freud describes an uncanny feeling as 'that class of the frightening which leads back to what is known of old and long familiar' (220), a feeling reflective of what plagues Nelly throughout the film. Freud also relates the uncanny double to death, which Nicholas Royle states may 'be construed as a foreign body within oneself, even the experience of oneself *as* a foreign body [...], a compulsion to return to an inorganic state, a desire (perhaps unconscious) to die' (2). Thus, I suggest that Nelly exists as a foreign body, one that she continually attempts to erase by transmuting into an apparition of her former self. This foreign body, I suggest, allegorises and is shaped by the traumatic experience of Auschwitz, an experience that, although it has physically happened, can never be comprehended. The trauma has been registered as a bodily blank (represented by a bandaged face) that Nelly is driven to replace with an idealised past. As I shall discuss shortly, this traumatic blank is further reflected in Johnny and in society. As Nayman suggests, Nelly is 'literally trying to climb back into her old life' (n.p.), a life which no longer exists. This ghostly presence relates, moreover, to a particular kind of uncanny double, which is perhaps initially an assurance of immortality, but becomes the 'ghastly harbinger of death' (Freud: 235). As Royle interprets it, 'one may want one's double dead; but the death of the double will always also be the death of oneself' (190). Interestingly, while in several psychoanalytic theories it is often the past self that haunts the present, and which the individual is driven to erase, Nelly is also haunted by her current self. She wants to be replaced by the ghost of her past. To do so, she must vanish; the death of her haunting double *is* the death of herself. However, as we learn throughout the film, she cannot be replaced because the image of herself is, and in a sense always has been, false.

This becomes increasingly apparent when Nelly finds a broken mirror in the rubble and is confronted with a doubled reflection of her altered face. Visibly traumatised, she says to Lene 'I no longer exist' and turns to a photograph, thus indicating that it is her image, rather than herself, that she believes to be real. Lene explains that the photos were needed for her facial '*Rekonstruktion*' (reconstruction) only to correct herself with the 'right word' – '*Wiederherstellen*' (re-creation). A reconstruction might suggest an obliteration of the old, while a recreation shapes it anew, thus allowing both to exist at once. Perhaps Petzold's attention to this word is also related to Lene's desire to move to Palestine to 'found a Jewish state; to take back all they [the Nazis] took away'. Here Lene is referring to the Zionist dream of a Jewish homeland; but some Jews were determined to rebuild their lives in Europe, like Nelly who initially rejects these concepts – of both the Jewish state and her new appearance. In response to her objection, Lene says, 'Nelly you're beautiful'. But for Nelly '[t]hat's not the point'; it is not beauty she desires, but a return to her old self. Throughout the film, Petzold subtly portrays the idea that her re-created face *is* beautiful, precisely because it is uncanny – both foreign and familiar. As Royle writes, the uncanny can 'involve a feeling of something beautiful but at the same time frightening' (2) and, as Petzold tells Nayman in the *Cinema Scope* interview, 'she's pretty because of the experiences that she's had' (n.p.). There is something tragically beautiful to be captured in the wake of war.

This kind of beauty is depicted in Petzold's dark and delicate shots, offering an uncanny experience for the viewer, which is reflected in the scene in which Nelly cloaks her bruised faced with a black veil to wander the seedy, grey streets of Berlin in search of Johnny. Abruptly, the camera cuts to a vibrant red sign reading 'Phoenix', the name of a carnivalesque nightclub where she finds him. Johnny fails to recognise her. This horrifying moment is juxtaposed with an image of Nelly gazing into a mirror at such an angle that her reflection is invisible. It is almost as though Johnny's reaction has concretised Nelly's own absence: his failure to recognise her means she is unable to recognise herself. In 'Mirror Role of Mother and Family in Child Development' (1971), Winnicott quotes a question asked by one of his patients: 'wouldn't it be awful if the child looked into the mirror and saw nothing?' (5). In his essay, Winnicott explains how the mother is a metaphor for a baby's mirror, that if a baby looks at a mother who rarely looks back, it may in turn be traumatised. The child may not psychically see its reflection; though the child exists, it may not feel real. Similarly, when Johnny does not recognise Nelly, she does not feel real. Or as she later explains to Lene, 'when he did not recognise me, I was dead again', a statement I shall return to later.

For Winnicott, this concept of feeling existent or non-existent is related to the 'True' and 'False Self'. More specifically, Winnicott believes that a baby begins life completely dependent on its carer. The baby, in other words, is not a full human being because it cannot differentiate itself from the other, it is not independent, does not understand language, and cannot form cohesive thoughts. Thus, the baby cannot remember or comprehend this stage in life. However, what has happened to the baby has been experienced by and remains part of the growing individual, forming a non-linguistic (bodily) core upon which it develops. Since the baby cannot form conscious thought at the time, this part of the individual cannot be accessed, remembered or understood, and this is reflective of the way in which Nelly has physically experienced a trauma that can never be comprehended. This prelinguistic stage, he writes 'belongs to being alive' (Winnicott 1965b: 192). It is the place where spontaneous gestures are primitively felt. Although it 'forms an intermediate space through which the individual and the world communicate' (Jacobs: 40) it can never be completely expressed through language because the experiences are not linguistically comprehended. It is this core that comprises what Winnicott refers to as the 'True Self'. It is, Adam Phillips writes, 'a feeling of existing and feeling real' (Phillips 2007: 133). However, if a child undergoes a traumatic experience it will form a 'False Self' and this, in turn, will create problems when it comes to finding, expressing and satisfying its needs; it will retain a feeling that it is not entirely real. It will be left with an inaccessible void similar to the uncanny foreign body that, in Freud's thought, haunts the conscious individual. This 'True' and 'False Self', Winnicott believes, exists in varying degrees within every individual and can fluctuate throughout life. In general, as individuals become increasingly independent, they begin to feel more real and the 'True Self' grows robust. I shall now examine the way in which Nelly and Johnny unconsciously foster Nelly's 'False Self' to protect her truer self.

This is caused by Johnny's demand that Nelly conceal her truer self with a false one. After Nelly has agreed to pretend to be his 'former' wife she is hidden in his basement, where he begins to mould her into the former imaginary self she desires to embody. Reflective of the filmmaker himself, Johnny shapes the protagonist: her movements, appearance, and self-narrative. This enactment, Petzold indicates, symbolises Germany's need at the time to repress and deny survivors' painful stories. Petzold explains in an interview with David Jenkins in *Filmmaker Magazine*: 'I wanted a movie about hiding collective trauma' (n.p.). As Johnny begins the transformation, he forcefully grips Nelly's arm, commanding, 'you have to play my wife. I'll instruct you. You'll return as a survivor'. She must play the role of herself (a survivor), albeit dressed in the shadow of Johnny's perception. Her 'False Self', in other words, is to replace her truer, traumatised one. For Winnicott, '[t]he False Self has one positive and very important function: to hide the True Self, which it does by compliance with environmental demands' (Winnicott 1965a: 146–147). Nelly must conform to Johnny's image in order to hide her embodied trauma. When Johnny asks her name, she replies 'Esther', a character who, though absent, looms over the film. Early in the film, Nelly asks Lene about Esther, a person of unknown origin who we later learn died in Auschwitz (she is marked in the photograph as having died). Since the only thing we know about this character is her absence, the viewer is, much like the characters and *Phoenix*'s cinematic aesthetic, left in the dark. However, while an ambiguous lack permeates the film, Esther is a specific lack, one that Nelly supplants. In this way, Esther represents what the viewer cannot know; we cannot, implies Petzold, ever comprehend annihilation, but we can attempt to approach understanding through partially fictional recreations, such as the film itself. By naming her 're-created' self Esther, Nelly, it seems, is attempting to sink back into that photograph; as she, in a sense, replaces Esther, she both deletes and revives the dead.

For now, I shall refer to the postwar protagonist as Esther, and to her prewar self as Nelly. Johnny soon becomes frustrated by Esther's inability to become Nelly, and decides to forgo the plan unless Esther can replicate Nelly's handwriting, which, of course, is identical. Although the writing ensures that Esther will take on the role of Nelly, it also, I suggest, reveals a truer self. As Winnicott states, 'the gesture indicates the existence of a potential True Self' (Winnicott 1965a: 145). There is a possibility, in other words, that her 'True Self' exists and may begin to resurface. At this point in the film it is clear that Johnny is denying something. How can he not suspect that Esther is Nelly? There is no proof of Nelly's death, there is a close resemblance between the two, and Esther duplicates her handwriting. Perhaps Johnny is repressing the recognition that she is a Holocaust survivor, in part because he betrayed her, and in part because the reality is too overwhelming. The overtness of this denial, I argue, emphasises Petzold's message: that Nelly and Johnny, like Germany at the time, are participating in a fetishistic disavowal. Although Johnny may unconsciously know that Esther is Nelly, he believes that she is not, just as, although those in Germany knew of the Holocaust survivors, they denied their existence. They have, it seems, created a fantasy version of Germany – as Johnny has created a fantasy version of Nelly – in response to a traumatic experience. For Freud, the concept of disavowal, though it changed in the course of his writing, can be defined as a common 'mode of defence which consists in the subject's refusing to recognise the reality of a traumatic perception' (Laplanche and Pontalis: 118), and this, I contend, is what Johnny and Nelly partake in here. For Freud, this arises when a (male) child perceives that his mother is 'missing a penis' (the castration complex) and becomes traumatised.[1] At times, this absence is replaced with an object to maintain the delusion that the penis still exists, which Freud calls a fetish. 'Only one current in a person's life', writes Adam Phillips, 'had not recognised the disturbing fact of there being two sexes, while "another current took full account of the fact", the two states of mind "exis[t] side by side"' (105). The fetish, therefore, involves a simultaneous denial and recognition of a traumatic experience. From this perspective, Johnny and Nelly, who have different traumas, have fetishised the prewar Nelly, to both recognise and deny her existence. The 're-created' Nelly acts as a delusion that works to protect them both from (different) overwhelming traumas.

This fantasy is further depicted when Johnny demands that Esther wear one of Nelly's dresses, which he complains is too long. A distorted memory is revealed here, suggesting that he does not, in fact, want Esther to be the prewar Nelly, but an ideal reflection of her, a 'False Self'. For Winnicott, the 'False Self' is 'set up as real and it is this that observers tend to think is the real person' (1965b: 148). However, now her past identity is beginning to unravel, she can no longer hide her truer self: a fragmented victim. This falsified image additionally allegorises Germany's reaction to the Holocaust, as indicated in the scene wherein Johnny dictates to Esther how she will pretend to be Nelly returning from the camp, this time in the red dress. In other words, she will have to relive her experience of having returned to Germany as a survivor, this time disguised as her former, idealised self. However, at this point she begins to recognise that this is disturbingly false. 'I'll be in a red dress and shoes from Paris?' she asks. 'You think anyone leaves the camps like that?' Johnny responds, 'you've seen all the returnees. All the burn wounds and shot-up faces! No one looks at them. Everyone avoids them. But we want them to look at you and say, it's Nelly! Nelly made it! She's back!'. However, Nelly cannot *come* back, first because she always was an illusion, and second because she is one of those 'returnees'. Or, as Petzold tells Nayman, survivors 'want to go back [...] But no, it's impossible to go back, because everything has changed'. The scene continues:

214 MONIKA LOEWY

'I can't come from a camp like that.'
'They want Nelly, not a ragged camp internee. That's what we're working on here.'
'If I'm coming from a camp someone is bound to ask me what I experienced there.'
'What?'
'How it was there and I'll need a story.'
'What kind of story, what?'
'Something or other, like, how we sat on a beam naked and went through the clothing of those who had just arrived. And then this girl, this girl, she looks at me. She looks at me.'
'Where does this story come from?'
'She's got her mother's dress.'
'Where?'
'I read it.'
'Then tell it. If anyone asks. But I assure you, no one will.'

Here it seems obvious that she is relating something that has happened to her, and his reaction suggests that he unconsciously knows this. Reflective of Petzold's view of Germany at the time, Johnny disavows what occurred. Nelly also protectively clings to a delusion, as depicted in a scene wherein she explains to Lene, 'I'd not have survived the camp except for Johnny'. A doubly uncanny trauma comes into focus here: she survives the camps through a necessary ideal; upon her return, this ideal is shattered. She attempts to remove one trauma only to find another, or as Josh Cohen writes, 'in the uncanny, one's veil conceals a veil [...]. My face, as I both know and don't want to know, is a black veil, disguising the uncanny other that "I" is' (75). Nelly attempts to replace her current face with a veil of her former one, only to discover its absence. Or, to return to the statement I quoted earlier, she not only did feel dead, she felt dead *again*. 'And now', she tells Lene, 'he's made me back into Nelly again'.

At this moment, Lene turns on a light to expose Nelly's manicured face and hair, a striking yet subtle image of her false veneer. Nelly then states that she will stay with Johnny because with him 'I'm myself again. When he speaks of her...' 'Of "her!"' Lene interrupts angrily. The pronoun 'her', I argue, foregrounds a double, suggesting that Nelly's split self is approaching consciousness. Though it may seem as though she disowns herself, perhaps this linguistic differentiation also signifies a movement towards self-definition, towards (in Winnicott's terms) independence. For Lene, however, this pronoun confirms Nelly's total submission to Johnny and to the Germans, to those who betrayed her. In response to Lene's judgement, Nelly stubbornly exclaims, 'I know he [Johnny] loves "her". I don't believe he betrayed "her"'. I contend that although this statement is seemingly naïve, while Nelly clings to the hope that he loves her, she also paradoxically reveals what is creeping towards consciousness: that he does not love the person she is now, he loves 'her' – another, non-existent Nelly.

Soon after, a more definitive change occurs, as she discovers that Lene has committed suicide, and has left proof of Johnny's divorce papers, along with a note stating that Lene felt 'more drawn to our dead than to our living'. Nelly in turn begins to realise, it seems, that for her too, the living are dead; the person she wants to be, and those who prop up this identity, are only apparitions. The change is solidified when she responds defensively to Johnny 'accidentally' calling her Nelly (rather than Esther). He then commands that she burn her arm to prove that she had removed her camp number – a final erasure of her identity as a Holocaust victim, the last step to becoming her 'old self again', to replacing herself definitively. This time, she refuses.

Nonetheless, she must reenact her return from the camps, costumed in her red dress. Her expression reveals, however, that now she is removed, the prewar Nelly she has finally become is merely a phantom. In this way, her return is paradoxically her death, and from its ashes she begins to embody a truer self, as a Holocaust victim and survivor. When Nelly 'returns', she is taken to a house, where an audience of old friends coldly observes her. As she timidly takes the stage to sing with Johnny as she used to, she closes her eyes and exposes her camp number, thus shattering her fictional identity, her 'False Self'. To return to Winnicott's statement, in the 'True Self', 'communication is like the music of the spheres, absolutely personal. It belongs to being alive' (Winnicott 1965b: 192). In this way, Nelly is reborn as her truer self, one that cannot return to the past because everything has changed, one that cannot, and should not, be replaced or erased.

Note

1. The castration complex is itself a disavowal, as it is founded upon a false assumption that women are anatomically structured through a lack.

References

Cohen, Josh, 2005, *How to Read Freud* (New York: W. W. Norton)
Freud, Sigmund, 1955 [1919], 'The Uncanny' ['Das Unheimliche'], *The Standard Edition of the Complete Psychological Works of Sigmund Freud*, vol. 17, ed. & tr. James Strachey *et al* (London: Hogarth Press and Institute of Psychoanalysis)
Hitchcock, Alfred, dir., 1958, *Vertigo*
Jacobs, Michael, 1995, *D. W. Winnicott* (London: Sage)
Jenkins, David, 2015, 'Survivor's Song: Christian Petzold on Phoenix', in *Filmmaker* (accessed 11 Feb 2017)
Laplanche, Jean and J.-B. Pontalis, 1996, *The Language of Psychoanalysis* tr. Donald Nicholson-Smith (New York: Karnac)
Monteilhet, Hubert, 1961, *Le Retour des Cendres* (Paris: Éditions de Fallois)
Nayman, Adam, 2014, 'The Face of Another: Christian Petzold's Phoenix', in *Cinema Scope* http://cinema-scope.com/features/face-another-christian-petzolds-phoenix/ (accessed 11 Feb 2017)
Petzold, Christian, dir., 2007, *Phoenix*
Phillips, Adam, 2007, *Winnicott* (London: Penguin)
Phillips, Adam, 2010, *On Balance* (New York: Farrar, Straus and Giroux)
Royle, Nicholas, 2003, *The Uncanny* (New York: Manchester University Press)
Winnicott, D. W., 1965a, 'Ego Distortion in Terms of True and False Self', in *The Maturational Processes and the Facilitating Environment: Studies in the Theory of Emotional Development* (New York: International Universities), 140–152
Winnicott, D. W., 1965b, 'Communicating and Not Communicating Leading to a Study of Certain Opposites', in *The Maturational Processes and the Facilitating Environment: Studies in the Theory of Emotional Development* (New York: International Universities), 179–192
Winnicott, D. W., 1991 [1971], 'Mirror Role of Mother and Family in Child Development', *Playing and Reality* (London: Routledge)

CHAPTER 21

Replacement or ever present: Jerzyk, Irit and Miriam

Anthony Rudolf

A new child cannot replace a child who has died – in this case Jerzyk, my second cousin once removed, whose diary I edited and published in 2016 under the title *Jerzyk*. He killed himself aged eleven and a half. A child is not an object, a child is irreplaceable; the loss of a child irreparable. The very concept of replacement in such a context is distasteful: there was a child; then there was not a child; then there was another child. This child is a new life in his or her own right and represents or rather creates new life for the parents: their own life is renewed. At the same time, the deceased child is ever-present. There is no contradiction. More subtly, contradiction or ambiguity is built into the state of affairs. It is permanent, imprescriptible, to use Jankélévitch's term.

During the lifetime of her parents, Sophie and Izydor Urman, this ever-presence was the lived experience of Jerzyk's sister Irit. Born on 29 October 1945, she was conceived in the town of Drohobycz, where the family had been in hiding, six months after it was liberated by the Red Army. '"We cried with joy that we had an aim in life again"' (Rudolf: 69), wrote her mother. Conceived in love, Irit was wanted. This was almost

---

A. Rudolf (✉)
Writer, London, UK

© The Author(s) 2018
J. Owen, N. Segal (eds.), *On Replacement*,
https://doi.org/10.1007/978-3-319-76011-7_21

two years after Jerzyk had died: 'Only son / Innocent victim of thugs, under the banner of Hitler' (128), reads the epitaph on his tombstone.

It was not easy for Irit to cohabit with the ever-presence of her dead brother, especially during the early years when she lived at home in Tel Aviv. Fearful of losing a second child, her parents were overprotective throughout her childhood and teenage years; they always had to know where she was going and what she was doing. In an email received on 11 November 2016, she writes:

> I didn't feel like a replacement child even though that might have been my parents' original intention. Indeed, my first baby clothes were blue in anticipation of a boy. I may have not felt like a replacement child because I was a girl and I had my own name. My parents were always proud of my scholastic and musical accomplishments and never compared me to anyone else. Of course whenever they reminisced about my brother he was perfect in every way. There is no way you can compete with that so I just accepted it.

Outwardly, Sophie was tougher than Izydor, and she was far more forthcoming than him when I came on the scene in the 1980s. In the same email, Irit recalls her father's eyes welling up with tears whenever Jerzyk's name was mentioned (Figs. 21.1 and 21.2).

The 1988 photograph of the couple reprinted here tells us that even a tragedy on the scale of Jerzyk's death can coexist with the life force as exemplified by Sophie's writings, which are included in *Jerzyk*. It is a hugely powerful photo, post-catastrophe. The sadness in their eyes interrogates us – as do, in a radically opposed way, the innocent prewar photos of Jerzyk, where our hindsight now reads death.

Jerzy Feliks Urman was born on 9 April 1932 in Stanisławów (now Ivano-Frankivsk) in East Galicia, Poland (now western Ukraine). During the German occupation of his homeland, he kept a diary from 10 September to 12 November 1943, the day before he died. The four adults in hiding – his parents, his paternal uncle Emil, and his paternal grandmother Hermina Vogel Urman – survived, and all of them, except Hermina, ended up in Israel.

Jerzyk's diary is written in Polish. It spans only two months because of the boy's tragic death. Although Jerzyk was extraordinarily precocious, clear-sighted and sharp-witted, the diary is not a work of literature. It is, however, a document of considerable interest beyond the heartrending fact of its existence. It is an intelligent child's truthful account of experiences

Fig. 21.1 Sophie and Izydor in the late 1980s, by permission of Anthony Rudolf

and states such as threat and rumour, nervous energy and fear, pain and insight. He kept the diary, he said, because he wanted people afterwards to know what happened. The fragile original is on my desk as I write.

I was the only person in the world close enough to Jerzyk's parents to obtain moral and legal permission to translate and edit his diary. My relationship with his parents, whom I visited several times in Tel Aviv, was complicated – inevitably so. On my first visit, Izydor directed me to the documents in Yad Vashem, where I would study in the library several times over the years, and told me what he could not bear to tell. He supported my project but understandably wanted no further involvement, angrily forbidding his wife from future discussions. I tried my best to persuade him that if I was to do my job properly, eyewitness accounts such as Jerzyk's were crucial to the historiography of the war against the Jews. I needed to know everything that could be known; I also knew it would cast Izydor and Sophie into a pit of sorrow.

Fig. 21.2 Jerzyk aged about eight, with initials on his pullover, by permission of Anthony Rudolf

Nonetheless, Izydor listened to reason and yielded to my entreaties that his son's diary be translated into English and published. (It has yet to appear in Hebrew or the original Polish.) However, we had reached the point when he could not take it any more. He willed the end and not the means. I feared the project might never be completed. Then Sophie phoned me at my hotel: we arranged to meet secretly.

Henceforth, she and I were involved in a conspiracy, albeit a benign one, serving the interests of history and memory. Fortunately, Izydor did not find out. Sophie answered my questions in person, as well as in letters and phone calls after I returned to London. She understood, I know, that as a writer – who had been born in 'the safety' of unoccupied London in September 1942, that is after the Blitz and before the V-1 and V-2 attacks in 1944/1945 – and as a relative of Jerzyk, one who actually looked like Jerzyk when I was young, I was committed to an accurate representation of the truth about his life and death.

I made a later visit in April 1991, shortly before my long-desired pilgrimage to Stanisławów and Drohobycz, including seeing the room where Jerzyk died and the cemetery where he was reburied. The Israel visit was an emotional necessity, but I also wanted to clarify with Sophie some of the remaining obscurities and problems in the diary. Jerzyk himself wanted it to be published, even though, in his words, 'I'm not a professional writer. I'm not even a grown-up' (101).

In an interview following the diary's first appearance, Sophie appears to blame her husband for Jerzyk's death by implying that he alone had allowed the boy to have the cyanide pill; she does not emphasise the extraordinary and desperate circumstances in which solo possession of cyanide by each individual had been agreed with Jerzyk. She shifted her ground because people had criticised her after reading the diary. Izydor always felt guilty about the agreement that the boy would be allowed to keep a portion of cyanide. The truth is that Jerzyk would not have gone into hiding without it.

Survivor guilt is a well-documented phenomenon. The double burden on the parents lay not only in Jerzyk's suicide but also in their survival, a direct result, they believed, of their son's death. It was a survival that enabled the birth of Irit and her future life in Israel and the USA. So, why did the boy have the cyanide on him? Some time between April and August 1942, when the family was living in the Stanisławów ghetto, Jerzyk, then aged ten, had witnessed an atrocity: a child's eye was gouged out with a red-hot wire by an SS man, because the child had been caught smuggling. After witnessing this sadistic action, Jerzyk, already precocious, suddenly grew up. His parents must have realised he understood everything. Although he was well aware of the perilous situation of the Jews, up to that point they would have doubtless tried to protect him from the terrible reality on the streets and in their hearts; he, perhaps, would have derived comfort from the thought that all of them might survive and reach Palestine after the war.

Haunted by the atrocity, he refused to leave the ghetto and go into hiding without the promise of a personal portion of cyanide: he was afraid that if caught he would give away, under torture, information such as the hiding places of friends. 'I will never let them take me alive' (31), he said when the family was discussing the possibility of leaving. As a doctor and gynaecologist, Izydor had easier access than most to the product. And it could be obtained on the black market: its ready availability saved the Germans money on bullets. That the boy, rightly (or if not rightly, understandably), had his own cyanide, and that it had been agreed with him they would all take the cyanide if captured, exemplifies the Nazis' rules of engagement in their cruel and cowardly war against the Jews.

By October 1942, Izydor knew he must not delay his decision to organise a hiding place for his family, if they were to avoid deportation to Bełżec death camp. Jerzyk was collected from Stanisławów and hidden with a Polish family outside the Drohobycz ghetto. In November, Sophie too was brought to Jerzyk's hiding place. That night Jerzyk's Uncle Artur, an engineer who had lived in Drohobycz for some years, brought round a fake identification card for Sophie and a work permit, confirmation that she was employed at his plant. Sophie's appearance was sufficiently 'Aryan' to enable her to pass as a Polish Catholic woman, though of course this remained extremely risky. After a few days, three members of a local militia with a dog searched the house where Sophie and Jerzyk were hiding but somehow failed to trace them. The Gestapo had already arrested the landlady's two grown-up sons. Distraught, the landlady asked Sophie and Jerzyk to leave.

In late December, and on the edge of the town, they obviously could not head for the centre and therefore set off through the snowy fields. After about an hour, Jerzyk was tired and wanted to lie down. Sophie resisted this mortally dangerous idea. Instead, they wandered all night. Next morning, however, with no alternative, they returned to the house. The landlady begged forgiveness. She gave them tea and bread and asked them to pray to St Mary who had saved them.

Shortly afterwards, Jerzyk's father arrived from Stanisławów on a farm truck sent by Uncle Artur. By March 1943, Jerzyk, his parents, his paternal grandmother, and his uncle Emil were in hiding in the apartment of Artur's former housekeeper on 10 Górna Brama Street. Jerzyk's diary and Sophie's memoir recount what happened during the last few months of the boy's life.

The death of the unknown child in the ghetto undoubtedly contributed to his state of mind during the tense and dangerous time in hiding. This does not detract from his heroism. Jerzyk died because he misinterpreted a knock on the door. Thinking all was lost, Jerzyk made the wrong call at a particular moment. According to his parents, he must have assumed it was the Gestapo following a tip-off about the hiding place, and this was the last straw. 'The Kripos [local collaborators, perhaps ethnic Germans] came in'.

> Now we knew our neighbours [whom they had trusted] sent the murderers. They spoke Polish. 'You are Jews'. 'No we're not'. One of them hit me behind the ear with the butt of his pistol. I fell, covered with blood. Jerzyk immediately put the poison in his mouth. 'Daddy, cyan...', and he fell to the floor. They were shocked and left. (32)

Probably blackmailers, the Kripos did not kill or remove or even report the parents. The Kripos saw Jerzyk take the pill and were so shocked that they ran off, saying they would return later. Jerzyk's mother remembers her son saying: 'Mummy, I took the cyanide' (66). There is no contradiction, only heartbreak: maybe he said 'mummy/daddy'. The parents buried their son in the garden shed during the night, digging the grave with hands, forks and spoons. The opportunistic collaborators returned a week later. They allowed the four adults to live, perhaps because they sensed their war was going to be lost and feared retribution. Many people, including Izydor and of course his family, were aware that the tide of the war had turned nine months earlier, at Stalingrad.

Jerzyk had been in hiding for more than a year when he died. Even if one makes allowances for his age and for the terrible stresses and strains involved in being cooped up in one room under those circumstances, even though he judged the situation wrongly, the event under description permits me to suggest that he was in command of his destiny, unlike the tortured child and so many others. It suggests that his suicide – a proactive albeit, in hindsight, mistaken decision – was resistance of the noblest and most tragic kind, just as the keeping of the diary must be accounted a form of non-violent resistance.

Although the family had agreed in principle that they would survive together or die together, when it came to the crunch, in Sophie's words, they 'hadn't the strength to take the poison' (75). Ever since, how could they not believe that they survived because Jerzyk died, even if other factors also played a role? In August 1944, Izydor and Sophie endured the pain of digging up their son and reburying him in the Jewish cemetery in Drohobycz.

When, in 1991, I finally presented Izydor with a copy of the original edition of his son's diary, I could tell he was moved and pleased that it had been published. I do not think Izydor read my book – he was the last person who needed to – and I do not know how he would have reacted to what he could have seen as a betrayal of his wishes on the part of his wife. Or maybe he would have understood. This was a man who had delivered his own son and buried his own son: a rare and tragic symmetry in the life of a father. He and his wife believed their son's death saved their lives. This is a burden. They chose to live, as Deuteronomy 30:19 commands, and the consequence was Irit. Just as Jerzyk's death deserves to be considered an act of resistance to tyranny, the fact that they chose life may be interpreted in the same light.

Czesław Miłosz talks of the pressure of history on experience. In Jerzyk's case the pressure was extreme. Had Jerzyk not killed himself, what would have happened? Perhaps the others would have been murdered in Drohobycz or been deported to Bełżec immediately, or to

Auschwitz, unless they had swallowed the cyanide, as agreed. Or they might all have survived. Perhaps Jerzyk's death did save them, as his parents believed. We should not dwell on this, except to say, given the events described earlier, it is as certain as anything can be that Jerzyk was entitled to have cyanide and his parents were right to allow him to have it. And this on one level is all we need to know about the Nazis.

Sophie too kept a diary, which she began a few weeks after Jerzyk died, and which was discovered by Irit among her papers after her own death. The diary was written over a period of seven months. It is intelligent, observant and outspoken. The most striking impression is of someone determined, after initial and understandable hesitation, to survive, partly in spite of, partly because of, the death of the child. She regularly apostrophises to her son, sometimes calling him 'baby'. She asks herself whether they too should have killed themselves and suggests that his death, his noble sacrifice, saved them. In one entry, the diary page is smudged, we may suppose with her tears. Here is part of the entry for 24 July 1944:

> On the road there were a huge number of front-line troops heading for Sambor. They were very tired, some in nothing but their socks, or even barefoot. Yet they look like an army on the retreat. Apparently they even threw their guns into ditches. And yet I don't believe in that devil's death because there would probably be some signs of mourning on the one hand, and on the other colossal joy, because apparently he [i.e. Hitler] has a lot of opponents in the army. (55)

The circumstances of Jerzyk's tragic death speak for themselves, supported by Sophie's and Izydor's accounts. Intellectual and cultural activities in the Warsaw Ghetto and elsewhere were a form of spiritual resistance, an assertion of humanity against the Nazi definition and treatment of Jews as non-human. Many kept diaries. My introduction to the first edition of the book concluded: 'To stay alive as a moral sentient human being (or choose rational suicide) may in a vortex of evil be the only form of resistance possible. The desperate purity of Jerzyk's act shocks and redeems us even now – on condition we honour him by working to prevent such situations arising again'.

So, after a necessary account of her brother's life, we return to Irit. She is very pleased that my book about her brother exists but, quite naturally, does not dwell on Jerzyk to the extent that I, as the chronicler, am obliged to. It is not for me to probe further into her mind. Jerzyk was ever-present during her childhood and teenage years. This ever-presence does not for one moment mean that she was not loved for herself, but it was surely more difficult and painful than she admits to, perhaps even unbearable at times. Whether her reticence has been out of loyalty to her parents or because it is too distressing to contemplate or because she has moved on, I cannot know. Doubtless, it is a combination of all three. And there is a fourth factor: her parents made the brave decision to face reality, and so did Irit. Izydor and Sophie mourned Jerzyk and celebrated Irit. Mature and clear-headed, they lived in two states at once, as the photograph above reveals. We can say that Jerzyk's death and the way he died – the only child suicide in the records of Yad Vashem – could not fail to involve the hearts and minds of his parents forever and colour their reactions to their daughter. At the same time, they were proud of her achievements: not least her two children, much loved as grandchildren, and her musical gift as teacher and composer. The life of Irit is not a case study in replacement; it is a life lived in plenitude and finitude. Once there was Jerzyk. Then there was no Jerzyk. He will survive us all, remembered in a book, a boy who experienced the worst, and died to tell the tale. The replacement of Jerzyk is not his sister; it is his own words. He has become his words.

Slightly younger than my cousin Irit is my friend Miriam Neiger-Fleischmann, who is from Komarno in Slovakia and now lives in Jerusalem. She is a poet and painter. Maria on her Slovakian birth certificate, Miriam was named after and for her half-sister Marika, the daughter of her father's first marriage. Marika and her mother were murdered in Auschwitz in 1944. Miriam's father survived and remarried another Auschwitz survivor after the war. He lived in Komarno before and after deportation, arriving in Israel with his second wife and the eleven-month-old Miriam in 1949.

In two private emails dated 2 December 2016 and 13 March 2017, Miriam writes that, although a child cannot be replaced as such, the idea of replacement might exist at least in the early years of the new child. This child takes on the 'task' and burden imposed consciously and unconsciously by the mourning parents – Miriam uses Dina Wardi's term – to serve as a 'memorial candle'. The child is required to fill the vacuum left in the parents by the Holocaust, to recreate and continue the family and, by extension, the community. Such children live simultaneously in the past and the present. Miriam took for granted the sadness, which was heavy and stifling and made her choke, like the smoke from her father's cigarettes – a suggestive association, perhaps even a metaphor. Her mother's first child, Miriam not only has her half-sister's name, but as a child she looked like her dead sister, or thought she did. She was encouraged to be a good girl, as good as her father's dead daughter had been. She tells me that when she and her younger sister quarrelled, their mother said: 'in Auschwitz they didn't kill me, but your behaviour will'. It took Miriam years to understand her own feelings of guilt. 'Even now', she writes, 'in certain circumstances I revert to childhood and prefer to take the blame or keep silent, rather than bring back the pain'. She writes in a poem: 'I am compelled / to keep my memory / on full alert'.

Nonetheless, like Irit's parents, Miriam's were over-protective and permanently worried, and this has coloured her feelings about her own children and grandchildren. She writes in the second email:

> In 1994 I revisited my hometown for the first time. My father lived there before and after deportation and until he came to Israel. I met Martha, a non-Jewish woman ten years older than me. She remembered me in my pram, and my father smiling and calling my name. Was it me or my dead sister? I prefer to think it was me. But I didn't forget my 'task' as a 'memorial candle'. In 2014, seventy years after Marika was murdered, I made a memorial exhibition in the local museum, called 'A memento from Marika'. But the bond is not only with Marika, it is with the Jewish community that lived and lives there. I feel obliged to do something to preserve the memory of the past, especially because the young ones are leaving and there is serious doubt as to whether the community has any future at all. I try to collect information and documents about personalities who were part of the community: rabbis, writers, artists and others. My job will not be done until I've explored all these people and the cultural history of my community, and through my research and writings raise a memorial stone forever and ever. This is my 'replacement'.

Miriam has been contacted by two women, unrelated to her and unrelated to each other, whose first and maiden names are the same as hers: 'Miriam Fleischmann'. Their families came to Israel from Hungary, after the war. She asked them about their names. Both, it transpires, were named after their grandmothers. The first grandmother was murdered in the Holocaust, the second died in the Patria disaster.[1] Miriam writes: 'Being a replacement child means to receive messages from women bearing the same first name and family name as your own, and to ask them which murdered relative they are named after'. Miriam's is a more extreme situation than Irit's. Irit did not feel she was a 'memorial candle', and was not consciously encouraged to think she was. But the comparison is instructive.

Note

1. See https://en.wikipedia.org/wiki/Patria_disaster: The Patria, carrying Jewish refugees, was sunk by the Haganah in Haifa harbour in 1940.

References

Jankélévitch, Vladimir, 1971, *L'Imprescriptible* (Paris: Seuil)
Miłosz, Czesław, 1983, *The Witness of Poetry* (Cambridge, Ma.,: Harvard University Press)
Neiger-Fleischmann, Miriam, 2017, *Death of the King and Other Poems*, tr. Anthony Rudolf and the author (Nottingham: Shoestring Press)
Patria disaster: https://en.wikipedia.org/wiki/Patria_disaster (last accessed 15 Sep 2017)
Rudolf, Anthony, 2016, *Jerzyk* (Bristol: Shearsman Books)
Wardi, Dina, 1992, *Memorial Candles: Children of the Holocaust* (London: Routledge)

PART VII

Psychoanalysis

CHAPTER 22

Replacement and reparation in Sarah Polley's *Stories we tell*

Agnieszka Piotrowska

Everybody has a troubled childhood. Psychoanalysis sets up its stall by maintaining that we all carry an originary trauma in us. Colette Soler stresses that Freud highlights the repetitive return of childhood suffering in transference in all clinical encounters (Soler 2015: 12). Transference is both a replication of the early relationship and a replacement of it. Some of us can 'do' something with that suffering through sublimation (which I will come back to in due course) – something artistic or scholarly, that redirects the hurt into a new kind of creation. This in itself, one could argue, is another kind of replacement – replacing love and sexual closeness with writing art or creating theatre or painting; or replacing suffering with writing about suffering. The famous artists' dictum, which was repeated recently by Meryl Streep – 'take your broken heart and make it into art' – has a bittersweet ring to it, of course.[1]

Sarah Polley's documentary *Stories We Tell* (2012) deals with childhood trauma head on. As such it is bold, controversial and inspirational. Its controversy lies in the fact that not all of it is what it seems: parts of it are reconstructed without the viewer being told that this is the case. Some

---

A. Piotrowska (✉)
University of Bedfordshire, Luton, UK

© The Author(s) 2018
J. Owen, N. Segal (eds.), *On Replacement*,
https://doi.org/10.1007/978-3-319-76011-7_22

critics and scholars have been deeply critical of the method.[2] In this chapter, I suggest that the film offers a reparative space for the filmmaker and perhaps, ultimately, for her viewers too, through its use of obsolete technology, or rather, through the filmmaker's choice of using a simulacrum of the technology in question: a pretend super-8 film that never was. In other words, the deception of the viewer enabled by the technology is part of the filmmaker's desire to reclaim the agency that her mother lost.

Stories We Tell considers the notion of lack and loss in a direct and material way: the mother of the filmmaker is dead and the film is a way of dealing with that loss. I suggest that through the 'secret' re-creation of the 'archive' images of her childhood, the filmmaker both takes charge of the past and offers herself and her family the possibility of a different future – a future in which patriarchal might is fractured a little by the filmmaker's repositioning of the power balance. Whilst her mother was either a victim or an ultimately powerless transgressive and promiscuous character, she instead takes charge of the creative process of her film. The process of 'replacing' is therefore a complex one in this film and I shall touch upon some elements of it in this chapter.

The question of the ethics of a documentary text has been debated for decades (see Cooper 2006; Cowie 2011; Lebow 2008; Renov 2004; Rothman 1998, and others). My own contributions to this debate (Piotrowska 2014, 2015) focus on the relationship between the filmmaker and the subject of her/his film and how that 'secret' relationship might influence the way in which the film is perceived by the spectator, without the latter fully realising it. I use psychoanalytic paradigms to frame this process (calling it 'the documentary encounter'). I focus in particular on the parties' unconscious desires, and a deep bond between those who are involved in the documentary encounter, using the clinical mechanism 'transference' which, in essence – as mentioned at the outset of this chapter – can evoke feelings replicating (replacing) those from childhood and be akin to love.

'Transference' – the special bond – is inevitably broken when a filmmaker involves the Third. 'The Third' is a psychoanalytical term used to denote anybody outside a deeply personal bond between the clinician and the analysand. The influence of the Third can feel like a betrayal in a clinical encounter; here, though, the Third is a concrete third party: a broadcaster, a viewing public, or even an editor. Using Lacanian paradigms of the three registers, I have suggested elsewhere (Piotrowska 2014) that one could compare the process of making the work public to the shift from the Imaginary to the Symbolic, which Jacques Lacan calls 'suture' (Lacan 1998: 118), a process that is always a painful movement in a child's development, as much as in culture and society. This shift in a documentary film can amount to an unethical gesture and arouse a sense of betrayal on the part of the participant in the documentary because, in essence, what was given in love is now utilised for a public spectacle. The documentary encounters become even more complex when the filmmaker is a member of the family, as is the case in Polley's *Stories We Tell*.

In recent research on film and the body Davina Quinlivan has introduced the notion of 'reparation' through the film experience. In her *Screen* article of 2014 and her subsequent book, *Filming the Body in Crisis: Trauma, Healing and Hopefulness* (2015) and through her discussion of *Waltz with Bashir* in particular, Quinlivan poses a question about the spectator and her relationship to the film 'as a reparative object and implicated in modes of recuperation in the twenty-first century' (2014: 103). Quinlivan is concerned with the possibilities of 'the film's healing "body"' (2014: 104) for the spectator. To this effect, she discusses the haptic film theories of Vivian Sobchak and Laura U. Marks, before examining the generative potential of Melanie Klein's work on reparation.

In taking up the notion of reparation in film, I will suggest that the reparative work in *Stories We Tell* is done by the filmmaker alone – for herself. For the spectator it offers at best a moment for *reflection* rather than reparation. This hidden and secretive space in which a documentary filmmaker creates her work is still a contested space since it is often too difficult to interrogate. In *Stories We Tell*, some of Polley's tools are on display and therefore more easily analysed.

At the outset the filmmaker shows us the construction of the film, appearing to be making it a kind of performative documentary (see Bruzzi 2000: 155) and evoking the mode of distancing or Brechtian *Verfremdungseffekt*. There is no 'objective' narration in the film and we see the filmmaker and her father settling down to record a commentary for the film. It is here that her father begins to ask Polley whether she could explain why she is filming him in this way and why: 'this is not a usual way', he says, 'is it?'

It is worth recalling that Bertolt Brecht (Weber and Beinen 2010: 32) and the Formalists considered this kind of distancing as empowering for the viewer, since it exposes the process of the making of the work and so enables the viewer to be more than a mere passive spectator. In other words, the viewer sees how a play – or here, a film – is made and therefore becomes a coauthor of its reception (see also for example Den Oever 2010). I also argue elsewhere that not editing yourself (the director) out of a documentary film is, in itself, an ethical gesture, giving the viewer a chance to question the production of knowledge in the text (Piotrowska 2014).

In *Stories We Tell*, the performance by the filmmaker and the performativeness of the piece of work as a whole is a complicated artefact that escapes easy assumptions and categorisations. Indeed, the filmmaker introduces herself and her father at the outset as the key characters of the film, and hence seems to point towards the above-mentioned distancing and performativeness: the father is seen with her in a studio getting ready to record his commentary. He asks her questions about the real motives of her project. By placing her father at the heart of the film as the person who actually writes and records the commentary for the film, Polley is making him a kind of peace offering and an apology for the subsequent dismantling of his world: as the result of the filmmaker's research and the film itself, Polley replaces her own father. Her subsequent efforts to minimise the effects of her work on his world can be seen as small gestures of kindness which can never make up for the spectacular loss he experiences through her film – the loss not only of his belief that he was her biological father, but also arguably the public loss of his dignity as well as the loss of his conviction that his marriage was a happy one and that Polley was a product of a passionate rapprochement between her parents.

In addition, we learn that her biological father, a famous film producer in Canada, also demanded to be allowed to tell the story. Polley refused in a determined way, taking the whole creative power firmly into her hands. We learn this later – though some things are never revealed to the viewer at all – and it renders the initial 'performative' gesture problematic. The gesture of an apparent display of the mechanics of the production of the film thus appears to be unethical, since it is a performance (of being performative). In other words, it is not a Brechtian *Verfremdungseffekt* after all – it is, rather, a staging created by the filmmaker to evoke an emotional replacement for her own sense of loss, but also arguably to provoke a sense of deception and disempowerment in the viewer.

This performance is further mediated and facilitated by the controversial use of the fake archive – the falsity of which is not disclosed until the end, and then only briefly and it is easily missed. When we see the long end-credits of various actors playing the filmmaker's family members, we realise at last that much of the film's supposed and precious home-movies were simply a reconstruction that used actors and cameras. Let us pause here briefly to consider the use of this technology in the film.

In an unpublished lecture on the poetics and politics of obsolescence arising from digital technologies, Thomas Elsaesser draws our attention to the fact that in *Stories We Tell* the obsolete technology, in the guise of the Super-8 camera, has a particular role to play in the rewriting and retelling of Sarah's traumas. It would not have been the same to somehow offer a reenactment of her past without the fake image pretending to be Super-8, matching the original image produced with the now obsolete technology. Elsaesser states:

> I was struck by the way this Super-8 camera, in its precariousness and obsolescence, became a talisman and fetish (in the anthropological sense) charged to document and to uncover what the actual surviving images so carefully hid and concealed, namely the mother's extra-marital affair, of which Sarah turns out to have been the not altogether welcome love-child. It is as if the re-staging and faking is actually Polley's 'working through' and 'acting out' of the trauma of her paternity, for which the Super-8 camera itself as object becomes both the instrument of truth, and the guarantor of authenticity, in the very act of filming the unfilmed, and thus restoring what is missing in Sarah's life narrative. (5)

We – the viewers – are never given enough material to quite understand the complex relationships between the people Sarah introduces as her elder siblings but who, we later discover, are her half-siblings. As we begin to realise that many things are not what they seem, questions are raised in the viewer's mind: did she know some of her brothers and sisters only as occasional strangers? Are they the children her mother left? Are they real people? Or maybe actors? Is there something wrong with the archive? What is this film doing to me? What was the timeline for all this? Why are we not told more? What's going on? Can we trust this filmmaker at all? One could suggest here also that the whole film is, in a way, a reenactment of the confusion and pain the filmmaker herself must have felt as a child – which she is now evacuating into us as we view. It is not an entirely pleasant experience, despite the film's fascinating structure and narrative.

That pain of the lies and early trauma is particularly felt in the interviews in the latter part of the film, when the siblings begin to talk about the violence that had ensued in their families after the mother departed. We realise the reality of the pain the mother too must have felt as the patriarchy stripped her of the right to look after her children (she was deemed an unfit mother because she had left her first husband for another man). How awful all of this must have been (and, indeed, must be) to the rest of the family. But would this pain not be made worse by the filmmaker who makes her family experience their pain as if they were characters on the screen in a public spectacle? Clearly, not all these filmic choices can be considered as friendly or empowering gestures vis-à-vis her family or the viewer.

Through the filmmaking process Polley here appears to be replacing and repairing some things, but she is also *sublimating*, not just her pain but also her *rage* towards the patriarchal world that somehow created those structures in which her mother, her family and she herself have struggled to find their way.

Freud, and Jacques Lacan after him, famously linked sublimation and language – and the process of talking – to libidinal economy. In Seminar XI (1999 [1981]), Lacan presents the idea of sublimation in prosaic terms. Firstly, he reminds us of Freud's position: sublimation is an empowering creative activity that satisfies the libidinal drive. It is a substitute but it gathers the energy of the drive and channels it into something other than sexual activity:

> Freud tells us repeatedly that sublimation is also satisfaction of the drive, whereas it is *zielgehemmt*, inhibited as to its aim – it does not attain it. Sublimation is nonetheless satisfaction of the drive, without repression. In other words – for the moment, I am not fucking, I am talking to you. Well! I can have exactly the same satisfaction as if I were fucking. That's what it means. (Lacan 1998: 165–166)

Simon Critchley suggests another way of thinking about sublimation, drawing upon the figure of Antigone, whom Lacan discusses at length in Seminar VII (1992 [1959–1960]). In some philosophical paradigms it would be easy to call Antigone unethical (many people die as a result of her actions which in the end, one could say, had meaning for her rather than for the world at large). However, she is ethical within the Lacanian paradigm of being faithful to her commitment of 'no matter what'. One could argue that Sarah Polley's film becomes just such a commitment. Critchley (or Lacan?) makes two points: the first is in relation to one's desire and pain, which is given a creative outcome; the second is to do with beauty and sacrifice, which is inherent in the sublimation of desire, at least according to Critchley's reading of Lacan's Seminar VII: 'What is the moral goal of psychoanalysis? "the moral goal of psychoanalysis consists of putting the subject in relation to its unconscious desire". This is why the sublimation is so important, for it is the realisation of such desire' (Critchley 2007: 73).

In Seminar VII, Antigone transforms her trauma through an act that is both beautiful and ethical as she sublimates (indeed replaces) the horror and trauma of death and destruction into the beauty of an act, through a sacrifice. There is no overt sacrifice in Polley's work; and yet something *is* sacrificed, namely the pretended sense of family unity, the fake harmony that nonetheless worked quite well for years, the unknowledge of the truth of her childhood, which did become her driving force, what Lacan would call 'a cause object of desire', her *objet petit a*. But on the other hand, once she arrived at a truth of sorts, the trust in the family was destroyed completely, and in ways that were difficult to articulate. One of her sisters comes up with a startling revelation to the question 'has anything happened since you have learnt that Sarah's father is another man?', which of course happened as a part of the filmmaker's project. She answers: 'No nothing really. Well we all got divorced, yes – we all got divorced'.

In Sarah Polley's story it is also the use of the technology – and here I would argue against Elsaesser – that not so much 'works through' as builds a *replacement* for the void left by the death of the filmmaker's mother and of any fantasy of a happy or at least semi-ordinary family, which was totally destroyed by the filmmaker's effort to get to the truth. The breaking up of the transferential relationships in this film is particularly painful as there are real betrayals we become witnesses to. One cannot deny a certain ruthlessness in the filmmaker's approach. However, in creating her film, Polley is reclaiming the female agency lost by her mother: it is not so much a case of *Nachträglichkeit* as *Vorwärtsträglichkeit* – the move forward to change the future rather than the past.[3]

The filmmaker thus creates a new space, a new body, that connects to Quinlivan's move to link it to the 'reparation', and which advances the notion that a film's body offers or can offer a site for healing ('the healing' is Quinlivan's phrase). Vivian Sobchak writes:

> the 'film's body' is not visible in the film except for its intentional agency and diacritical motion. It is not anthropomorphic, but it is also not reducible to the cinematic apparatus (in the same way that we are not reducible to our material physiognomy); it is discovered and located only reflexively as a

quasi-subjective and embodied 'eye' that has a discrete if ordinarily prepersonal and anonymous existence. (107–108)

Quinlivan reminds us also that Melanie Klein's theory of reparation examines infantile aggression and anxiety in terms of their constituting an ambivalent drive towards the destruction and subsequent restoration of the mother's body. The mother's breast symbolises the most important object the infant encounters: the breast is at once a source of plenitude and frustration, an object of love and hate. One could argue, therefore, that in *Stories We Tell* the filmmaker's decision to create the film, her own 'good object' and a new body, replaces her infantile sense of hopeless impotence, and that her own transference, her love, shifts from her powerful parental figures to her own knowledge and creativity. A passage that is brutal but necessary.

It is important to point out that Polley partly recreates her mother's position between the two men. Polley finds herself torn between the very same men – her fathers – but this time uses her film and its language as a vehicle of not just her defence but, arguably, aggression vis-à-vis the patriarchal might. This time the woman is in charge, this time she is not a pawn moved about between men. In the Oedipal triangle of *Stories We Tell* it is the storytelling, the filmic language chosen, including the deception of the fake archive, which is the tool that enables Polley to build another identity. One could argue therefore that for the filmmaker the work offers a replacement for the loss of her mother and the loss of the mother's power. For the rest of us, once we have worked through our annoyance at being deceived, the film offers a valuable space for contemplative reflection about the nature of truth and lies, and love, betrayal and family.

Notes

1. See https://www.bustle.com/p/the-carrie-fisher-quote-meryl-streep-spoke-at-the-golden-globes-is-the-inspiration-all-creative-people-need-28919 accessed 26 October 2017.
2. See for example http://cinema-scope.com/currency/stories-we-tell-sarah-polley-canada/ or https://beta.theglobeandmail.com/arts/film/film-reviews/stories-we-tell-in-sarah-polleys-doc-self-congratulation-gets-in-the-way/article4604474/?ref=http://www.theglobeandmail.com) accessed 24 October 2017.

3. I have written about Nachträglichkeit in documentary previously (Piotrowska 2015). The term 'Vorwärtsträglichkeit' was used first at a session of the Nordic Summer University in 2016 in a discussion with Rafael Dernbach that followed a presentation of an earlier version of this chapter.

REFERENCES

Bruzzi, Stella, 2000, *New Documentary: A Critical Introduction* (London: Routledge)
Cooper, Sarah, 2006, *Selfless Cinema? Ethics and French Documentary* (Cambridge: Cambridge University Press)
Cowie, Elizabeth, 2011, *Recording Reality, Desiring the Real* (London & Minneapolis: University of Minnesota Press)
Critchley, Simon, 2007, *Infinitely Demanding: Ethics of Commitment, Politics of Resistance*. (London & New York: Verso)
Den Oever, Annie, ed., 2010, *Ostrannenie* (Amsterdam: Amsterdam University Press)
Elsaesser, Thomas, 2014, 'The poetics and politics of obsolescence', keynote lecture at *The Future of Obsolescence*, 9th Orphan Film Symposium, Amsterdam 30 March–2 April 2014
Freud, Sigmund, 1958 [1915], 'Observations on Transference-Love (Further Recommendations on the Technique of Psycho-Analysis III)', in *Standard Edition of the Complete Psychological Works of Sigmund Freud*, vol 12, tr. & ed. by James Strachey *et al.* (London: Hogarth Press & the Institute of Psychoanalysis), 157–167
Lacan, Jacques, 1992 [1959–1960], *Seminar VII. The Ethics of Psychoanalysis 1959–1960*, tr. Dennis Porter (London: Routledge)
Lacan, Jacques, 1998 [1981], *Seminar XI. The Four Fundamental Concepts of Psychoanalysis*, ed. Jacques-Alain Miller, tr. Alan Sheridan (London & New York: W. W. Norton)
Lebow, Alisa, 2008, *First Person Jewish* (London & Minneapolis: University of Minnesota Press)
Marks, Laura U., 2002 [2000], *Touch: Sensuous Theory and Multisensory Media* (Minneapolis, MN: University of Minnesota Press)
Piotrowska, Agnieszka, 2014, *Psychoanalysis and Ethics in Documentary Film* (London and New York: Routledge)
Piotrowska, Agnieszka, 2015, *Embodied Encounters: New Approaches to Psychoanalysis and Cinema* (London and New York: Routledge)
Quinlivan, Davina, 2014, 'Film, healing and the body in crisis: a twenty-first century aesthetics of hope and reparation', in *Screen* 55 (1): 103–117. https://doi.org/10.1093/screen/hjt053. Oxford: Oxford University Press accessed in September 2017

Renov, Michael, 2004, *The Subject of Documentary* (Minneapolis: The University of Minnesota Press)

Rothman, William, 1998, 'The Filmmaker as Hunter' in eds Barry Keith Grant & Jeannette Sloniowski, *Documenting the Documentary: Close Readings of Documentary Film and Video* (Detroit: Wayne State University Press), 23–40

Sobchack, Vivian, 2004, *Carnal Thoughts: Embodiment and Moving Image Culture* (Berkeley: University of California Press)

Soler, Colette, 2015, *Lacanian Affects: The Function of Affect in Lacan's Work*, tr. Bruce Fink (London and New York: Routledge)

Weber, Betty Nance & Hubert Beinen, 2010, *Bertolt Brecht: Political Theory and Literary Practice* (Athens, GA: University of Georgia Press)

CHAPTER 23

Replacement, *objet a* and the dynamic of desire/fantasy in *Rebecca*

Odeya Kohen Raz and Sandra Meiri

In narrative cinema the character, as incorporated by an actor, along with the actor's physical attributes and persona, constitutes a fantasy object, a 'filling' of *objet a* – in the works of Jacques Lacan, any object that sets desire in motion ('the object-cause-of-desire'), which can never be attained. Following Christian Metz (1982), our premise is that the cinematic object in general and the actor in particular are part of a fantasy world whose visual and aural richness are meant to veil its physical absence (the screen's lack), and satisfy the spectator's desire to see, the spectator being aware of cinema's imaginary nature. *Rebecca* (Alfred Hitchcock 1940), *North by Northwest* (Hitchcock 1959), *Psycho* (Hitchcock 1960), *2001: A Space Odyssey* (Stanley Kubrick 1968), *Monsieur Klein* (Joseph Losey 1976) and *Her* (Spike Jonze 2013) are rare films in which the protagonists or other

This chapter is part of a research project in process, supported by the Israel Science Foundation.

O. Kohen Raz (✉)
Sapir Academic College, Ashkelon, Israel

S. Meiri
Open University of Israel, Ra'anana, Israel

characters who are crucial to the unfolding of the narrative are not visually portrayed by actors, thus frustrating the spectator's desire to see. We term them 'bodiless-character films'.

We argue that these films are exceptions that prove the rule, namely the paradoxical nature of narrative film. It is precisely the unattainability of the object on the screen, associated by Metz with the imaginary, that makes it possible for spectators to let the camera inscribe them into a fantasmatic space, compatible with an unconscious inscription in the primal scene fantasy – a 'scene of sexual intercourse between the parents which the child observes, or infers on the basis of certain indications, generating sexual excitation as well as anxiety' (Laplanche and Pontalis: 335). This accounts for the origin of the subject, as well as the child's wish to be included in the desire of those who created it. We conflate this inscription with getting access to the Other's desire (getting access to the Other's desire represents a fantasy of wholeness, believing that the Other is complete), which in life is not only prohibited but also impossible. We further claim that when viewing a film this unconscious transgression is a process which is enabled only within a careful economy of desire/fantasy, as exemplified by *Rebecca*, on which we will focus.

Desire in Lacan characterises all human beings, is unconscious, and is manifested as a longing that can never be satisfied. It emerges in the field of the Other as a relation to a lack that can never be filled, encapsulating both the desire for recognition by another and the desire to be the object-cause of another's desire. The Other is Lacan's term for the Symbolic – the order of language and the law – as well as for another subject in its radical alterity. The mother is the first to occupy the position of the Other (see, for example, Lacan 1992 [1959–1960], especially 57–84; Lacan 2006a [1958]). To the extent that desire originates from another, it is also the Other's desire, which is always enigmatic. Thus the subject's fundamental question in relation to the Other's desire is 'What does the Other want from me?' (Lacan 2006b [1960]: 690). The repressed fantasy of incest with the mother, the fantasy of (re)finding the (already) lost object, not only creates the unconscious, but also establishes a mechanism by which the subject will never cease to seek a defence against the lack in the Other by attempting to provide an answer to the enigma of the Other's desire. This mechanism is fantasy, which belongs to the imaginary order – the order of images, appearances, misrecognition, deception, specularity and imagination. Lacan accepts Freud's formulation of fantasy (see, for example, Freud 1955 [1919]) as a visual configuration that stages desire, emphasising the protective function of conscious fantasies against lack, because of their satisfying nature. Moreover, in the neurotic, 'normal' structure, fantasy 'is the support of desire; it is not the object that is the support of desire' (Lacan 1998 [1964]: 185).

In Metz's description of the ontology of cinema in relation to the appeal of classical narrative film to large audiences three facts are essential: (1) the absence of actors and objects from the spectator's space; (2) the role of seeing in spectatorship in regard to this absence; (3) the ability of cinema to embellish its imaginary objects, the latter playing the role of fantasy objects. While the first characteristic taps into the experience of lack and desire, the other two are attributed to the world of fantasy as daydream – Freud's term for conscious fantasy. For Metz, the cinematic object is doubly imaginary because it is both fictional, as in theatre, and absent from the screen, unlike theatre (see especially 129–137).

Thus, when comparing cinema with Freud's notion of the daydream, Metz emphasises its protective function, contending that classical narrative cinema offers the spectator an experience whereby s/he can pretend for an hour and a half that there is no lack. He further argues that although the spectator is absorbed in the sequences of images projected on the screen, s/he is nevertheless aware of the film being only a daydream. Because of film's imaginary nature, as well as the spectator's awareness, Metz sees no substantial gain in developing the contents and manifestations of the *unconscious* engagement with a film, namely with the dialectic of desire/fantasy. In arguing that the experience of viewing a film is specifically oedipal, simulating the fantasy of the primal scene, he goes only as far as to make a structural comparison between the physical conditions of the primal scene and the viewing of film in a cinema (see especially 63–66). We claim that what enables spectators to be so absorbed in a narrative film is engagement with the protagonist's desire, with the anticipation that it be fulfilled in the end, and an unconscious inscription in the primal-scene fantasy, enabled by the imaginary nature of film, as well as its various techniques.

Through its editing techniques and camera movements, cinema uses its temporal and spatial discrepancy (the impossibility of spectators and actors coinciding in the same scopic space) to inscribe the spectator into the spatial and scopic space of its characters. It creates an imaginary presence through which the character's body and that of the actor coalesce into one. The absent presence of the actors in accordance with the techniques of film allows spectators to be where the characters are, as in the theatre;

but, unlike the theatre, they also get to see what they see from the place in space where they are positioned. In short, what film 'realises' is the spectator's desire not only to see but also to be 'physically' included in a space from which as subject s/he was and still is excluded. The filmic scene renders the past and the location (the then and there) as here and now (the setting of the daydream). As asserted by phenomenological film theories (for example, Sobchack 1994), the camera, which imitates the human eye, is present in the space of the scene, transposing our bodies into it as if we were there, allowing us to see what the characters see but, at the same time, preserving our awareness that we are not really 'there'. The spectator's unconscious inscription into the fantasmatic space/scene, facilitated through its affinity with the primal scene fantasy, and enabled by the camera's multiple positioning, is unique to film. It thus transgresses both the prohibited and the impossible.

This unconscious process constitutes, in our view, the appeal of narrative film, regardless of cultural and social constructions and identities. It first addresses the spectator's lack, as s/he is excluded from the space of the actors portraying desiring subjects, as the child is excluded from the setting of the parents' coitus. Second, by minutely showing the spectator how and what/who the protagonist desires, it positions the spectator in a place that aspires to fill the lack in the Other, regardless of the specific content of the protagonist's desire. To our understanding, narrative cinema thus brings together the Freudian desire to occupy the position of one of the parents in the primal scene (the prohibited) and the Lacanian position of a subjective inscription into the Other's desire (the impossible), with the intention of veiling its lack. The prohibited and the impossible within the structure of the primal scene are transgressed due to the imaginary unity of body-actor, time and space.

This imaginary unity explains why the one thing a plot will almost always refrain from omitting in film is showing its characters embodied by actors. The filling of *objet a* with a fantasy object that is conceived in the conjunction of the character with the actor's attributes – a conception that guides casting decisions – is the linchpin of cinema covering over the lack of the screen (see Meiri and Kohen Raz 2017). The actor's body may function as a fantasy object in relation to the spectator, to other characters in the film's diegesis, or both. By 'emptying' this function, bodiless-character films show us that *objet a* can never be filled and at the same time they reveal narrative cinema's great appeal in that it offers a transgressive experience while remaining within the boundaries of the imaginary.

Broadly, we can divide this group into three categories. First, there are films in which we have a dead character never personified by an actor in flashbacks, for example *Rebecca* and *Psycho*. In *Psycho* the voice of Norman's mother is heard, to indicate her omnipresence. Only at the end of the film do we learn that Norman killed her years earlier, used his taxidermy skills to preserve her body in the cellar, and proceeded to wear her clothes and talk in her voice. These films evince the imaginary nature of the unity of body-actor-character, hence of cinema, precisely by revealing the screen's emptiness. Second, there are films in which a character is invented in the diegesis, while the protagonist, as well as other characters in the film, is unaware of its fictional nature. A salient example is Mr. 'Kaplan' in *North by Northwest*, which puts the emphasis on *objet a* as the cause of desire – an emptiness that sets the plot in motion, namely both the protagonist's and the spectator's desire.[1] A variation of this is *Monsieur Klein*, in which the police seek Robert Klein, a Jew in Paris in 1942; he is never seen in a frontal or close shot. Third, there are films in which we do not see the actor but hear his/her voice, as their character is not a subject. In *2001: A Space Odyssey*, H.A.L. 9000, an intelligent speaking computer (Douglas Rain's voice), is a gaze and a voice. In *Her*, 'Samantha' (Scarlett Johansson's voice) is an operating system designed to meet the protagonist's every need. These films put the emphasis on *objet a* as a partial object (voice and gaze), as representing the split subject, as well as cinema's own split nature (the unity or coherence between sound and image in film is in the imaginary). They evince cinema's challenging engagement with our scopic and invocatory partial drives by insisting on the screen's lack. However, *Her* affirms the relevance of the spectator's engagement with the film's fantasy in its capacity to veil the lack in the Other/the screen's void. This is achieved by engaging the spectator with the protagonist's desire, which in the end is satisfied (a satisfaction that is impossible in life) – but not in the way he has chosen to achieve this goal.

Rebecca, too, makes a clear distinction between the heroine's desire to be loved by her husband (which we engage with and which is sustained throughout, until it is finally fulfilled), and the way she pursues it. The latter is rendered in her attempts to replace Rebecca, believing that this is what her husband wants from her. The heroine's failed attempts to replace Rebecca are conflated with the inevitable failure of attempts to guess what the Other wants. The heroine (Joan Fontaine) is a plain young woman whose name we never learn. She feels inferior to Rebecca, the aristocratic dead wife of her husband Maxim de Winter (Laurence Olivier), when she learns that the latter was very beautiful, greatly admired and extremely successful at her role as mistress of Manderley, Maxim's mansion. In Manderley, Rebecca's monogram ('R' or 'R de W') appears on objects that belonged to her, which the heroine repeatedly encounters. The film thus uses objects that metonymically testify to Rebecca's (omni)presence, which make up for her absence, and at the same time reflexively point to narrative film's need to compensate for the screen's lack. Ultimately, *Rebecca* engages us with the heroine's desire to be loved by her husband, which is satisfied at the end of the film, but undermines both the heroine's and the spectator's inscription in the primal scene, that is, in the Other's desire.

The heroine assumes (as does the spectator when first viewing the film) that Rebecca had been the object of desire for everyone who knew her, men and women alike: Mrs Danvers, the housekeeper (Judith Anderson); Jack Favell (George Sanders), Rebecca's cousin and lover; and, of course, her husband Maxim. The immature and sexually inexperienced heroine relentlessly tries to become the object of Maxim's desiring look, a look she imagines Rebecca effortlessly enjoyed (in repeated viewings we still identify with her desire to be loved by her husband). As long as the heroine's desire to be seen and acknowledged is conflated with actions directed at attempts to replace Rebecca, the film draws her, as well as the spectator, into more and more perilous territory. In the scene in which Mrs Danvers walks the heroine through Rebecca's (and Maxim's) bedroom, displaying Rebecca's objects, treating them with care and sexual admiration, she is in fact forcefully inscribing the heroine into a primal-scene scenario. She 'visualises' Rebecca's sensuality for her; she makes her feel Rebecca's furs, given to her by Maxim; she shows her Rebecca's luxurious underwear, and marvels at the sight of Rebecca's transparent black nightgown, simulating how she used to brush her hair every night, while a large silver-framed photograph of Maxim is 'staring' at them from the top of the dresser. She thus lures her to stand in for Rebecca (*objet a*, associated with the unattainable mother; the heroine is motherless). Danvers' actions are malevolent – her sole purpose is to make the heroine feel inferior to Rebecca, whom she adored – but the heroine's reaction suggests more than that. Overwhelmed by what she imagines to have been the sexual relationship between her husband and his late wife – similar to the child watching her parents' lovemaking – she tries to leave the room, but Danvers stops her. By replacing Rebecca with the heroine in the primal-scene scenario, Danvers clearly articulates the heroine's unconscious desire to take Rebecca's place, as well as its lethal aspect. Her words convey that eternal 'bliss' indeed lies in the fantasy of occupying *objet a*, but that such bliss is in effect lethal for both the subject and the object usurped, and that the desire of the m/Other is itself lethal – its (imagined) overwhelming powers will haunt the subject forever. Modleski writes: 'In *Rebecca* the beautiful, desirable woman is not only never sutured in as object of the look [...], she is actually poised within the diegesis as all-seeing – as for example when Mrs Danvers asks the terrified heroine if she thinks the dead come back to watch the living' (1988: 52). As *objet a* Rebecca can never materialise. She represents the gaze, which never coincides with the eye of the subject that does the looking; it is in the field of the Other, the object that sets desire in motion.

By imagining her husband's desire for the sexually mature, beautiful woman the heroine is in fact attempting to answer the question underlying every fantasy: 'What does the Other want?' And, as in every fantasmatic scenario, the imagined answer is erroneous. She thinks that her husband wants her to be like Rebecca, she wrongly conflates her desire to be seen/recognised by her husband with being in Rebecca's place, a conflation that points to the impossibility of occupying *objet a* as well as guessing what the Other wants. Instead of gaining her husband's adoring look, she is reprehended and ridiculed by him. The harder she tries, the more bitterly she fails. This disdainful chain of events culminates in the traumatising costume ball scene. Not knowing that her costume for the ball is the same one that Rebecca wore the year before (by Mrs Danvers' malicious design), the heroine comes down the stairs, radiant with anticipation, positive that she will finally succeed in gaining her husband's admiration (in repeated viewings the spectator's feelings of anxiety and pity persist). But instead of admiration, Maxim reacts violently, insisting that she be out of sight before the guests arrive to see her. Any fantasy that the heroine might have entertained so far by thinking that her husband wanted her to replace Rebecca is miserably shattered. The trauma resides precisely in missing the impossible and unattainable answer to the question 'What does the Other want?'

This becomes clear near the end of the film, when Maxim tells his young wife about the night Rebecca died. While he describes her actions and reiterates her words in minute detail, the camera simulates these actions. As Modleski notes, a different adaptation of this Daphne du Maurier novel might have resorted to a flashback, 'allaying our anxiety over an empty screen, by filling the "lack"' (53). But instead, Hitchcock lets his camera follow a void. We are thus deprived of the satisfaction of seeing Rebecca embodied by a 'larger than life' star (Joan Crawford might have been a 'good' choice). As we listen to Rebecca's words and intonation enacted by her husband, his off-screen voice portrays a spiteful character (his voice, his body, but saying Rebecca's words and keeping her sarcastic tone) that contradicts the heroine's romantic visual fantasy imagined in relation to Rebecca and her husband up to this point. Maxim hated his wife and believes he accidentally killed her. What we have here is an inscription in the primal scene, with an uncanny twist. By refraining from using a flashback, the scene maintains its temporal and spatial coordinates, which enable the heroine's inclusion in a space that is not hers. A flashback, set in the past, not only would have had an actress embodying Rebecca but also would have made it impossible to physically include the heroine.

The scene starts by showing Maxim speaking, then cuts to the heroine, who is situated at the other end of the room, her eyes turning from Maxim to a divan placed between them, rendering a static shot of the divan from *her* point of view. It thus inscribes her, as well as the audience, into Maxim's and Rebecca's intimacy, namely the primal scene. However, when Maxim, his body off-screen, utters the words 'suddenly she got up, started to walk toward me', the camera tilts up and then pans toward Maxim, simulating Rebecca's movement, thus undermining the illusion previously created by the eyeline-match (although what we see is still the heroine's point of view), as if thrusting us out of this intimacy. We become aware of the camera through its movement, the movement of an absence – the gaze in all its uncanniness. This evinces the presence of the camera in an *elsewhere*, as we do not see the camera – which, like the actor, was present on the set – only its movement. The camera reveals here its ability to inscribe the spectator's body into the primal-scene fantasy by undermining the heroine's inscription in it, created earlier by the editing. We are thus more affected by its very movement, simulating a void, than by the knowledge that this movement is supposed to be rendering the heroine's point of view.

The void that Hitchcock's camera evokes suggests that film, through its material absence, draws our desire and, at the same time, impedes the 'materialisation' of a fantasy meant to fill this void. In other words, the filmic object is by definition *objet a* because of its unattainability. The desire for the lost object, which is absent from the visual field and represented by Rebecca, is achieved via a multitude of objects of fantasy, but the fantasy of actually filling the void via inscription in the primal scene is later dissolved. This is how Hitchcock disables the probability of occupying a perverse position (represented by Mrs Danvers) and, at the same time, engages the spectator with the heroine's desire to be loved by her husband, carefully creating a fantasy world that includes closure and a 'happy ending'. This suggests not only that every subject is prone to *fantasise* a scenario without lack, but also that if narrative cinema wishes to engage spectators with a film, it cannot renounce the creation of a fantasy. Hitchcock, the master-weaver of the dynamic of desire/fantasy, always confronts his spectators with the lack of the screen as well as the experience of lack per se by shattering a fantasy that he is first very careful in creating. Unconsciously, we are 'allowed' inscription in the primal scene by identifying with the desire to fill the lack, only to be jolted out of it. This two-faced strategy is Hitchcock's way of evincing the role of fantasy in narrative cinema – the support of desire.

Note

1. On the objects in Hitchcock's films, see, for example: Žižek; Dolar.

References

Dolar, Mladen, 1992, 'Hitchcock's Objects', in *Everything You Always Wanted to Know about Lacan (But Were Afraid to Ask Hitchcock)*, ed. Slavoj Žižek (New York: Verso), 31–46

Freud, Sigmund, 1955 [1919], '"A Child is Being Beaten": A Contribution to the Study of the Origin of Sexual Perversions', in *The Standard Edition of the Complete Psychological Works of Sigmund Freud*, ed. and tr. James Strachey *et al* (London: Hogarth Press), vol. 6: 175–204

Hitchcock, Alfred, dir., 1940, *Rebecca*

Hitchcock, Alfred, dir., 1959, *North by Northwest*

Hitchcock, Alfred, dir., 1960, *Psycho*

Jonze, Spike, dir., 2013, *Her*

Kubrick, Stanley, dir., 1968, *2001: A Space Odyssey*

Lacan, Jacques, 1992 [1959–1960], *The Ethics of Psychoanalysis, The Seminar of Jacques Lacan*, vol 6, ed. Jacques-Alain Miller, tr. Dennis Porter (New York: Norton)

Lacan, Jacques, 1998 [1964], *The Four Fundamental Concepts of Psychoanalysis, The Seminar of Jacques Lacan*, vol 11, ed. Jacques-Alain Miller, tr. Alan Sheridan (New York: Norton)

Lacan, Jacques, 2006a [1958], 'The Significance of the Phallus', in *Écrits*, tr. Bruce Fink (New York: Norton), 575–584

Lacan, Jacques, 2006b [1960], 'The Subversion of the Subject and the Dialectic of Desire in the Freudian Unconscious', in *Écrits*, tr. Bruce Fink (New York: Norton), 671–702

Laplanche, Jean, and Jean-Bertrand Pontalis, 1988 [1967], *The Language of Psychoanalysis*, tr. Donald Nicholson-Smith (London: Karnac)

Losey, Joseph, dir., 1976, *Monsieur Klein*

Meiri, Sandra, and Odeya Kohen Raz, 2017, 'Mainstream Body-Character-Breach Films and Subjectivization', in *The International Journal of Psychoanalysis* 98, 201–217

Metz, Christian, 1982 [1977], *The Imaginary Signifier: Psychoanalysis and the Cinema*, tr. Celia Britton, Annwyl Williams, Ben Brewster and Alfred Guzzetti (Bloomington and Indianapolis: Indiana University Press)

Modleski, Tania, 1988, 'Woman and the Labyrinth: *Rebecca*', in *The Women Who Knew Too Much: Hitchcock and Feminist Theory* (New York: Routledge), 43–55

Sobchack, Vivian, 1994, 'Phenomenology and the Film Experience', in *Viewing Positions: Ways of Seeing Film*, ed. Linda Williams (New Jersey: Rutgers University Press), 36–58.

Žižek, Slavoj, 1992, 'Alfred Hitchcock, or, the Form and its Historical Mediation', in *Everything You Always Wanted to Know about Lacan (But Were Afraid to Ask Hitchcock)*, ed. Slavoj Žižek (New York: Verso), 1–12

CHAPTER 24

Rooms as replacements for people: the consulting room as a room object

Deborah Wright

When people relate to a room as if it stood for a different room or a person, a room can be thought of as a replacement. I suggest that this happens when meaning is projected from the inside of people's minds out onto the external space of the room. In this chapter, I look at this mechanism of replacement in rooms using historical and clinical evidence, including material from Sigmund Freud prior to his invention of psychoanalysis. I also consider psychoanalytic theory. The psychoanalytic concept of transference is a kind of replacement. I argue that, within a clinical setting, rooms and people get transferred onto the space of the consulting room. This spatial room transference can involve the consulting room representing another room or replacing a person projected onto the insides of the room. This is a three-dimensional process in which images land on the surrounding screen of the walls of the room. I shall demonstrate, by means of a clinical vignette, that this spatial room transference can replace an actual room and actual people from the individual's memories and associations within the consulting room.

D. Wright (✉)
University of Essex, Colchester, UK

© The Author(s) 2018
J. Owen, N. Segal (eds.), *On Replacement*,
https://doi.org/10.1007/978-3-319-76011-7_24

There is evidence for the innate, primitive importance of space usage in modern humans, as well as in Neanderthals. What I am calling 'primitive human space usage' is a form of replacement in which internal meaning is projected externally onto spaces such as burial spaces, cave areas marked out with objects like statuettes and tools, paintings and etchings. This gives the space itself a meaning derived from the replaced object. Rob Dinnis and Chris Stringer give the example of the 'stylized female figures' (136) engraved into cave walls, which may denote areas apportioned as female space, or represent female relations or ancestors.

The recent discovery, by Lee Berger and his team, of bones in the Rising Star Caves in South Africa shows the possible primitive human use of space to create meaning in pre-Neanderthals. Jamie Shreeve writes: 'Until now only homo-sapiens, and possibly some archaic humans such as the Neanderthals, are known to have treated their dead in such a ritualised manner' (Shreeve: 53). The space contained the bones and may have been intended to contain the dead or the spirits of the lost individuals.

A similar use of space was excavated more recently. Judith Flanders writes:

> In the 1960s, builders renovating a house in North London found, bricked up behind a fireplace, a basket holding two shoes, a candlestick and a drinking vessel [...]: votive offerings to the house-gods of the 16th century, resurfacing in the twentieth. Houses, according to myth, folk tale and legend, have souls, and possibly even minds. While we may no longer subscribe to these beliefs on a conscious level, many small rituals based on those beliefs were performed until recently: clocks were stopped and mirrors veiled on the death of a member of the household, while on the day of a funeral window-blinds were habitually drawn, covering the house's 'eyes'. (165)

I suggest that this can be thought of as a way of replacing people in the actual walls of a room. The items, such as shoes, which were bricked into the wall of the room could relate to a lost child or other relative felt to be present in the house. The qualities of the person have been incorporated and kept alive in the skin and being of the room, or house. Mary Douglas writes: 'body symbolism is part of the common stock of symbols, deeply emotive because of the individual's experience' (122). When Flanders refers to the 'mind' or 'eyes' of the house she is surely anthropomorphising the space on account of the people indirectly contained in it.

This affords people an opportunity of exerting control over their space and therefore the meanings within that space. Replacing people within the walls – in a sense rendering them immortal – might be a way of dealing with loss and ensuring the safety and security of the inhabitants of the house. Ernst Kantorowicz writes of the case of monarchs, who have many fantasies projected onto them by members of society relating to their position as protectors of the cohesion of that society. When a king dies, his physical body dies and the projected meanings pass onto a replacement physical body – 'the King is dead, long live the King'. There is then an issue of what to do with the physical body as it contradicts the symbolism of the immortal body. Society has to create 'new fictions' (314) to protect against this potential threat to cohesion. One of these fictions involves covering up the dead body with a monument in the form of an image of the body, often in the walls of a chapel in a cathedral or abbey. Here again the walls are marked out with replacement imagery, to maintain control.

Arguably, projection always implies a spatial dimension (see Klein). However, I also believe that people project parts of the self onto spaces to control the spaces and their experience in them, as Freud suggests in his cultural theories in *Totem and Taboo*: 'It is not to be supposed that men were inspired to create their first system of the universe by pure speculative curiosity. The practical need for controlling the world around them must have played its part' (Freud 1955b [1913]: 78). Projection from the mind into the space of a room of 'parts of the self' – which could include memories and the related feelings/meanings of another room or person – are used to control the space and manage the feelings. This resembles the psychoanalytic concept of transference.

Transference is a kind of replacement. As Freud writes:

> the patient sees in his analyst the return – the reincarnation – of some important figure out of his childhood or past, and consequently transfers onto him feelings and reactions, which undoubtedly applied to this model. It soon becomes evident that this fact of transference is a factor of undreamt-of importance – on the one hand an instrument of irreplaceable value and on the other a source of serious dangers. This transference is *ambivalent:* it comprises positive and affectionate as well as negative and hostile attitudes towards the analyst who, as a rule, is put in the place of one or other of the patient's parents, his father or his mother. (Freud 1940: 52)

I suggest that this model is also transferred onto the consulting room, which is 'put in the place of' a person or another room. This is a spatial room transference: there is a replacement of the person or room with the walls of the room.

Rooms and spaces fascinated Freud. He created a meaning in rooms in which he lived or worked and repeatedly used spatial metaphors in illustrating and explaining theory, often in diagrammatic form.

Figure 24.1 is a sketch by Freud of his room in the Zoologische Station in Trieste, which he included in a letter. In Fig. 24.2, Freud 'described and sketched his new room and his furniture' (Freud, Freud and Grubrich-Simitis: 104), in the General Hospital in Vienna. This was the first room he lived in after leaving his parents' home. He wrote: 'The "animal" part of this cavern which fits me as well as a snail-shell fits the snail, is fairly successful, the "vegetative" part (i.e., the one intended for the ordinary functions of life in opposition to the higher "animal" functions like writing, reading or thinking) rather less so' (Freud, Freud and Grubrich-Simitis: 327).

Freud used the metaphor of a box within the space of a room in a letter of 1881 to his fiancée, Martha Bernays:

> I would so much like to give the picture a place among my household gods that hang above my desk, but while I can display the severe faces of the men I revere, the delicate face of the girl I have to hide and lock away. It lies in your little box and I hardly dare confess how often during the past twenty-four hours I have locked my door and taken it out to refresh my memory. (Freud 1961a [1882]: 8)

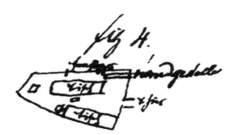

Fig. 24.1 Drawing of Freud's room in the Zoologische Station in Trieste, letter from Sigmund Freud to Eduard Silberstein, 5 April, 1876 (Freud 1990 [1876])

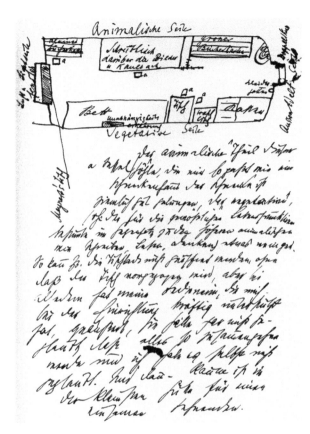

Fig. 24.2 Drawing of Freud's room in the General Hospital in Vienna, in letter to Martha Bernays, October 1883 (Freud, Freud and Grubrich-Simitis 1998)

What is most significant about this early scenario is that it shows Freud projecting meaning onto the room itself and onto the 'box' symbol (object) within the room (see Fig. 24.3). Within this scenario in the letter we can also see a possible transference of the father in the 'household gods' (men) and the box representing the mother and/or Martha (women). The box in the room could be seen as a primitive spatial transference relating to the space of the mother's body. This example shows Freud transferring the

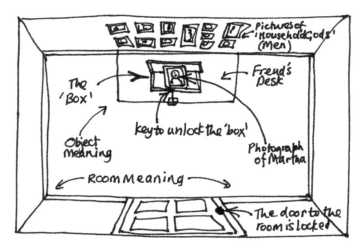

Fig. 24.3 An aerial view of Freud's room (by D. Wright) as described in letter from Sigmund Freud to Martha Bernays, 19 June 1882 (Freud 1961a [1882])

meaning of his mother, fiancée and father onto the space and objects of the room he occupied alone, as a replacement for them. Even before he invented the concept of transference or the consulting room, he transferred the meaning of people onto the space of a room and the objects within it. Freud kept this 'symbol' of his affections safe and concealed within a special box only to be revealed when access to the room was controlled; in the consulting room thoughts and feelings are revealed in safety when the door is shut.

Freud used the 'box' symbol throughout his work. He reports a dream of his mother: 'I saw myself standing in front of a cupboard ['Kasten'] demanding something and screaming [...] Then suddenly my mother, looking beautiful and slim, walked into the room [...] I had missed my mother, and had come to suspect that she was shut up in this wardrobe or cupboard [...] The wardrobe or cupboard was a symbol [...] of [...] mother's inside' (Freud 1960 [1901]: 49–51).

Freud's mother had just given birth to his sister. This dream resonates with his case study of 'Little Hans', in which Hans describes the spatial manifestation of his unprocessed feelings about the birth of his sister. According to Freud, when Hans refers to boxes transported on carts they represent his mother's womb containing the baby sister. 'We can now recognize that all furniture – vans and drays and buses were only stork-box carts, and were only of interest to Hans as being symbolic representations of pregnancy; and that when a heavy or heavily loaded horse fell down he can have seen in it only one thing – a childbirth, a delivery' (Freud 1955a [1909]: 46–74). In the same way, Freud's mother emerges, postnatally 'beautiful and slim', from the cupboard.

A greater insight into Freud's dream about his mother can perhaps be gained from Joseph Berke's observation that Freud experienced his mother as 'emotionally unavailable' and, we might think, possibly physically less available. He writes:

> Amalie became pregnant again with her second son, Julius. This baby also carried the same name as Amalie's brother and beloved companion. Baby Julius died when Sigmund was two years old from an infection and Amalie's brother passed on at around the same time from tuberculosis. Both losses left his mother heartbroken and emotionally unavailable to Sigmund. (xiii)

This may give us an insight into Freud's fascination with rooms. Rooms may represent the mother or a replacement of her care when she is absent emotionally and/or physically.

Another room of significance for Freud was the 'cabinet' he was given when his family moved to a larger flat in 1875, when he was nineteen:

> The 'cabinet', a long and narrow room separated from the rest of the flat, with a window looking onto the street, was allotted to Sigmund; it contained a bed, chairs, shelf, and writing-desk [...] In his teens he would even eat his evening meal there so as to lose no time from his studies. He had an oil lamp to himself, while the other bedrooms had only candles. (Jones: 45–46)

Here Freud was given a special room, unlike his siblings, who had to share rooms, and it also featured special objects. Perhaps the room replaced a special time of just him and mother – it was a room for just him. His drawing and marking out meaning in the space of his room in the General Hospital (see Fig. 24.2), the first room he lived in after leaving home, suggests its significance in replacing the 'cabinet' which substituted for the role of mother. In his foreword to the 1994 edition of Bachelard's *The Poetics of Space*, John Stilgoe writes: 'If the house is the first universe for its young children, the first cosmos, how does its space shape all subsequent knowledge of other space, of any larger cosmos? Is that house "a group of organic habits" or even something deeper, the shelter of the imagination itself?' (Stilgoe 1994: viii).

Donald Winnicott emphasises the idea that in normal development there is a gradual separating as the child matures and becomes independent of the mother. This can only happen if the child feels sufficient 'holding' (Winnicott 2002 [1971]: 111), which is both a psychological and a physical experience. He also writes about the space between the mother and child being an 'intermediate area of *experiencing*, to which inner reality and external life both contribute' (Winnicott 1953: 90). This intermediate area is the space where the capacity to symbolise is learned.

Whilst this may be the case in normal development, when the child has a difficult experience of being with the mother from the beginning, separation becomes problematic. Didier Anzieu writes that the Skin-ego provides 'a containing and unifying wrapping around the Self' (Anzieu 2016 [1995]: 105). When things are more problematic in development, then '[i]t needs strengthening [...] The double wrapping – its own plus that of its mother – is gleaming and ideal; it provides the narcissistic personality with the delusion of being invulnerable and immortal. In the psyche it is represented by the phenomenon of the "double wall"' (135).

I am suggesting that this 'double wrapping', which is a '"double wall"', can be even more cemented and solidified by projecting the mother's part of the double skin onto the actual walls of what Stilgoe describes as the child's formative room. I suggest that later on this can be transferred onto the walls of the consulting room. Bachelard writes:

> If I were asked to name the chief benefit of the house, I should say: the house shelters daydreaming, the house protects the dreamer, the house allows one to dream in peace. [...] Therefore, the places in which we have *experienced daydreaming* reconstitute themselves in a new daydream, and it is because our memories of former dwelling-places are relived as daydreams that these dwelling-places of the past remain in us for all time. (28)

This suggests that the containing mother function is taken up by the walls of rooms.

Freud wrote: 'the dwelling-house was a substitute for the mother's womb, the first lodging, for which in all likelihood man still longs, and in which he was safe and felt at ease' (Freud 1961c [1930]: 91) and 'it seems to me more likely that a room became the symbol of a woman as being the space which encloses human beings' (Freud 1963 [1916]: 156). In the following case study, the consulting room plays the role of a patient's first carer.

Mrs A grew up in a house where domestic violence was constant and when she was three her mother miscarried a baby after being beaten. The only safe place to stay was her grandmother's house. A year and a half before the session from which the following extract is taken, the therapist had building work done to her house, including the consulting room; for a few weeks she had to move to a temporary consulting room, which was in the house of another therapist who lived nearby.

Until then Mrs A's transferential attachment to the consulting room had been positive and unbroken. But now the location was further to walk to and she was not used to the area: the room felt unfamiliar and she felt she was not entitled to be there. She only complained twice about the room being cramped and dark, adding that the couch was very saggy, uncomfortable and unsupportive on the back. She did not want to complain and upset her grandmother – with whom she identified the therapist. The following is an extract from session notes taken eighteen months after the return to the therapist's consulting room.

Mrs A said that she was disappointed: the consulting room used to look so good before the building work. She said: 'A lot of the pictures reminded me of Grandma's; they are all gone'.

She then went on to talk about her anger at the shoddiness of the workmanship: she could not believe that the therapist had paid someone to repaper the walls after the building work and they did such a terrible job. They obviously had grit on their paste brush and it had got all over the paper and it was still there under the paper, making it all lumpy. She said: 'It's really unprofessional and an unnecessary mistake, they could just have been more careful'. Mrs A also reminded the therapist that when she does wallpapering she does a proper job: 'it's not difficult'.

The therapist said that perhaps it was like 'pimples' in their relationship. Mrs A did not respond to this but wondered: 'why haven't the pictures been put back up yet? couldn't you decide where to put them for one and a half years? were you depressed?'

Analysing this case shows that Mrs A associated the safety of her grandmother's house with the consulting room, including the smell of old books (on the shelves), the pictures and the original wallpaper. The curtains, cushions and couch cover reminded her of the bed at her grandmother's house.

Since her grandmother had died (during the course of the therapy) her attachment to the room and her associations had increased, along with her attachment to her therapist. So initially, the therapist replaced the grandmother in the transference, and the consulting room replaced her room at grandmother's house in the spatial room transference.

However, in the course of this session it became apparent that there was another unconscious representation present – that of the mother. Mrs A's attachment to her mother had been unbroken until the latter was hospitalised after her miscarriage. Her attachment to the consulting room was also unbroken until she was forced to leave it (to separate) and go somewhere she did not want to be, and on her return the room felt as if something had been broken.

The walls were left damaged and scarred (like her mother) and the relationship with the mother was like something neglected (by a depressed therapist). She remembered that she had cried at being at her grandmother's when her mother had gone into hospital and how she had been distraught and confused and had not wanted to be there, an association which was the opposite of later safe associations with the grandmother's room. So the temporary consulting room produced the unpleasant, scary feeling of being at her grandmother's when her mother was ill. Then on her return her mother was distant, neglectful and depressed. The room had become 'clinical', the wallpaper had become cream, a lack of care had been taken with the wallpapering and there were no pictures. Mrs A had had no power as a child to make her mother better and now she could not help to make the wallpaper in the consulting room better either. She was experiencing the same feeling of disgust – my mother is still with my father, why is something not being done about this? – manifested in her comments on the shoddy wallpapering. She had no control over the decorator or over what her father did to her mother. She was mourning the 'good' mother and angry that everything had become damaged. The therapist is the mother in the transference who could not prevent the decorator (father) damaging the walls (the mother's body) and Mrs A's relationship with her mother.

This replacement of her mother by the walls of the room was unconscious. The replacement of her grandmother's safe room with the consulting room had been conscious. The change of consulting room presented a rupture in the room replacement mechanism. This rupture brought out the rupture in the relationship with her mother (see Anzieu: 67–69). If the walls of the room were the mother's skin, then it had become damaged.

Primitive spatial room projected meaning can be seen in the caves and the sixteenth-century room. Freud's early letters show a replacement of meaning in the walls of rooms prior to psychoanalysis and the concept of transference. And there is a spatial room transference when other room spaces and people get transferred onto the walls of the consulting room.

References

Anzieu, Didier, 2016 [1995], *The Skin-ego*, tr. Naomi Segal (London: Karnac)

Bachelard, Gaston, 2014 [1958], *The Poetics of Space*, tr. Maria Jolas (New York: Penguin)

Berke, Joseph H., 2015, *The Hidden Freud: His Hassidic Roots* (London: Karnac)

Dinnis, Rob and Chris Stringer, 2015, *Britain – One Million Years of the Human Story* (London: Natural History Museum)

Douglas, Mary, 1999 [1966], *Purity and Danger: An Analysis of the Concepts of Pollution and Taboo* (London: Routledge)

Flanders, Judith, 2014, *The Making of Home* (London: Atlantic Books)

Freud, Ernst, Lucie Freud and Ilse Grubrich-Simitis, 1998 [1978], *Sigmund Freud: his life in pictures and words* (London. W. W. Norton)

Freud, Sigmund, 1940, 'An Outline of Psycho-Analysis', *International Journal of Psycho-analysis*, 21: 27–84

Freud, Sigmund, 1955a [1909], 'Analysis of a Phobia in a Five-Year-Old Boy', tr. & ed. James Strachey *et al*, *The Standard Edition of the Complete Psychological Works of Sigmund Freud*, vol X. [henceforth *SE*] (London: Hogarth Press and the Institute of Psychoanalysis)

Freud, Sigmund, 1955b [1913], *Totem and Taboo*, *SE* vol XIII: vii–162

Freud, Sigmund, 1960 [1901], *The Psychopathology of Everyday Life*, *SE*, vol VI

Freud, Sigmund, 1961a [1882], Letter to Martha Bernays, August 18, 1882, *The Letters of Sigmund Freud 1873–1939*, 25–28, ed. Ernst Freud, tr. Tania and James Stern (London: Hogarth Press)

Freud, Sigmund, 1961b [1923], *The Ego and the Id*, *SE*, vol XIX: 1–66

Freud, Sigmund, 1961c [1930], *Civilisation and its Discontents*, *SE*, vol XXI: 57–146

Freud, Sigmund, 1963 [1916], *Introductory Lectures on Psycho-Analysis*, *SE*, vol XV: 1–240

Freud, Sigmund, 1990 [1876], Letter to Eduard Silberstein April 5, 1876, *The Letters of Sigmund Freud to Eduard Silberstein 1871–1881*, 142–150, ed. Walter Boehlich (Cambridge, MA: Harvard University Press)

Jones, Ernest, 1967 [1953], *The Life and Work of Sigmund Freud* (Harmondsworth: Penguin)

Kantorowicz, Ernst, 1997 [1957], *The King's Two Bodies, A Study in Mediaeval Political Theology* (Princeton NJ: Princeton University Press)

Klein, Melanie, 1946, 'Notes On Some Schizoid Mechanisms', in *International Journal of Psycho-analysis*, 27: 99–110

Shreeve, Jamie, 2015, 'Mystery Man', *National Geographic*, vol. 228, no 4, 30–57

Stilgoe, John R., 2014 [1994], Foreword to Gaston Bachelard, *The Poetics of Space*, tr. Maria Jolas (Boston: Beacon Press)

Winnicott, Donald W., 1953, 'Transitional Objects and Transitional Phenomena – a study of the first Not-Me possession', *International Journal of Psycho-analysis*, 34, 89–97

Winnicott, Donald W., 2002 [1971], *Playing and Reality* (Hove: Routledge)

Index[1]

NUMBERS AND SYMBOLS
45 Years, 2, 9, 23, 161–167

A
Abraham, 28, 127, 132
Abraham Levin, 83–87
Adet, Georges, 27
Adorno, Theodor, 37
Aguerreberry, Rodolfo, 150
A.I. *Artificial Intelligence (A.I)*, 7, 23n3, 67–70
Alfonsín, Raúl, 148
Alfred Allmers, 47–55
Alison, Jane, 7, 57–65, 65n3, 65n7, 65n8
Althusser, Louis, 20
Amalric, Mathieu, 186
Ambrosio, Arturo, 94, 95
Ana [*Un muro de silencio*], 152, 154, 155
Anderson, Judith, 3, 246
Andreas-Salomé, Lou, 20
Antigone, 236, 237
Antoinette Cosway [Bertha Mason Rochester], 113–121
Anzieu, Didier, xvii, 6, 19, 258, 260
Anzieu, Marguerite, 6, 19
Aphrodite, 33, 106, 108
Aristotle, 109
Arnold [*The Lost*], 197–200
Ashenden, Samantha, 8, 125–134
Asibong, Andrew, 9, 161–167
Asta Allmers, 48, 51, 53–55
Auschwitz, 10, 207, 209, 212, 224, 225
Austen, Edward, 125–126

B
Bachelard, Gaston, 257–258
Ball, Eustace Hale, 82, 88n5
Balla, Giacomo, 96
Balzac, Honoré de, 21
Bardot, Brigitte, 178
Barrie, J. M., 6, 10, 19–20, 48, 49, 52, 53
Barrie, Jane Ann, 20

---

[1] Note: Page numbers followed by 'n' refer to notes.

Barthes, Roland, 198
Bedtricks, 7, 25–33
Beethoven, Ludwig van, 6, 20
Bemberg, María Luisa, 148
Benjamin, Walter, 16, 23n1, 154
Bennett, Jill, 147, 149
Bergan, Ronald, 185
Bergman, Ingrid, 165
Berliner Mauer, Frau, 183
Bhatt, Chetan, 137
Bible, xvi, 17, 26, 32, 33, 33n4, 127
Bildungsroman, 114, 121
Birkin, Andrew, 20
Blade Runner, 74
Blood, xvii, 8, 30, 57, 65, 99, 109, 119, 126–132, 133n12, 222
Boccioni, Umberto, 92, 96, 101n3
Booker, M. Keith, 72
Borges, Jorge Luís, 17
Bostrom, Nick, 72
Bourgeoisie, 96, 99, 126, 163
Boxer, Stephen, 71
Bradley, Ruth, 71
Bragaglia, Giulio, 94, 96, 101n3
Braidotti, Rosi, 72
Brecht, Bertolt, 233
Brett, Jeremy, 3
Brontë, Charlotte, 8, 113–121
Brown, James, 7, 35–44, 125, 132n1
Bruel, Patrick, 186
Bruno [*Un muro de silencio*], 148, 152–155
Bruzzone, Gustavo, 150
Burucúa, Constanza, 148, 153
Burucúa, José Emilio, 149–151, 156
Buxton, Richard, 109

C
Callus, Ivan, 72
Cardinal, Marie, 6, 20
Carrà, Carlo, 96

Carroll, Lewis [Charles Lutwidge Dodgson], 17
Cenchreis [Myrrha's mother], 30–32
Chalmers, Damian, 137
Chan, Gemma, 70
'Character and anal erotism,' 33n1
Chateaubriand, François-René de, 6, 20
Chávez, Julio, 152
Chief Sitting Bull, 42–43
Childbirth, 6, 33, 43, 125–133, 257
Childhood, 114, 181, 203, 231–232, 237, 253
Child/ren, xiii, xiv, xv, xvii, 3, 4, 5–6, 7, 9, 10, 15, 18–21, 22–23, 23n5, 25, 36, 39–40, 41, 43, 47–53, 55, 57–66, 67–76, 94, 98, 104–111, 115, 117, 125–133, 140, 142, 143, 145n7, 148, 152–153, 164, 171, 183, 186–190, 195–203, 210–211, 213, 217–226, 233, 235–236, 242, 246, 252, 257, 258, 260
Christianity, 16, 99, 106
Christophine, 116–117
Cinderella, 26, 33n2, 65n5, 88n6
Cinyras [Myrrha's father], 28, 30–33
City, 27, 30, 35, 150, 163
Claudel, Camille, 6
Clifford, James, 121n2
Close, Glenn, 11n1
Cohu, Lucy, 4
Collodi, Carlo, 69
Colman, George, 97
Colonel Chabert, 21–22
Comolli, Jean-Louis, 178–181, 183
Corra, Bruno, 95
Courtenay, Tom, 161, 166n5
Cox, Marian Roalfe, 33n2
Crawford, Joan, 248
Critchley, Simon, 236–237
Cullen, Tom, 162

D

Dalbello, Marija, 8, 79–89
Dalí, Salvador, 6, 18–19
Dance, Charles, 4
Darrieussecq, Marie, 16
Daughters, xvi, 1–2, 3, 7, 19, 20, 21, 22, 25–33, 33n4, 50, 52, 57–65, 71, 83–84, 95, 107, 148, 153, 187, 189, 195, 225, 226
David, Joanna, 3
De France, Cécile, 186
Dearborn, Mary V., 88n6
Demy, Jacques, 7, 25–27, 32
Deneuve, Catherine, 26
Depardieu, Julie, 186
Der Verlorene [*Lost*], 195–203
Derrida, Jacques, 8, 93, 96, 100
Dewey, John, 82, 88n6
Dick, Philip K., 21
Dinnis, Rob, 252
The disappeared, xvii, 9, 139, 147–157, 188, 190
Dolar, Mladen, 249n1
Doniger, Wendy, 31, 33n4
'Donkeyskin' ['Peau d'âne'], 26, 27, 28, 31, 32, 33n2
Doppelgänger, doubles, 8, 9, 16, 20, 29, 59–62, 74, 92, 113, 118, 120, 121, 149, 151–157, 208–210, 215, 258
Douglas, Mary, 25, 33n1, 252
Dubuis, Quentin, 186
Du Maurier, Daphne, 3, 4, 121n3, 169, 247
Durkheim, Émile, 37
Duvall, Shelley, 164

E

Eco, Umberto, 17
Edward Cummins, 57
Edward Rochester, 114, 117–121, 121n4
Electra, 61, 62, 65n7

Ellmann, Richard, 92
Elsaesser, Thomas, 235, 237
Euripides, 8, 61, 104–111, 111n1
Exodus, 17
Eyolf, 47–55

F

Family, xv, xvii, 5, 7, 19–21, 25, 28–29, 32, 33, 36–38, 41, 50–52, 57–65, 67–71, 75, 83–86, 96, 99, 104, 108, 114, 117, 126, 130–131, 139, 142–143, 152–153, 157, 181, 185–190, 197–199, 202, 217–226, 232–238, 257
Family romance, 5, 61, 171
Fatal Attraction, 2, 11n1
Fathers/fatherhood, 5–7, 10, 18, 25–32, 52–54, 57–65, 65n6, 65n8, 70, 86, 98, 104, 105, 109, 115, 120, 126–132, 143, 181–184, 186, 187, 200–201, 203, 218, 222, 223, 226, 233–238, 253, 254, 256, 260
Féret, René, 20
Ferguson, Helen, 84
Finch, Flora, 94
Fineman, Martha, 130
Flanders, Judith, 252
Flaubert, Gustave, 97, 101n6
Flores, Julio, 150
Fondeville, Marina, 148
Foucault, Michel, 126, 128
Fox, Emilia, 3
Fox, Robin, 33n3
Freud, Martha [Bernays], 254–256
Freud, Sigmund, 1, 5–6, 9, 11, 11n2, 11n3, 23n5, 25, 27, 33n1, 61, 73, 151, 177, 201, 208–209, 211–213, 231, 236, 242–244, 243, 251, 253–259, 261
Fuchs, Anne, 201

G

Gatti, Gabriel, 149, 151
Gellner, Ernest, 37, 41
Gemeinschaft and *Gesellschaft*, 38–39
Genealogy, 8, 28, 113–121, 121n2, 121n3
Genesis, 7, 28, 29, 127
Genette, Gérard, 88n3
Geoff [*45 Years*], 161, 163–166, 166n3
Gerty MacDowell, xiv, 8, 91–100
Gide, André, xvii, 22, 23n4, 189
Gilbert, Sandra M., 27, 30, 113, 119
Ginsberg, Alan Robert, 82, 83, 87, 88n7
Girard, René, 23, 23n5
Glasse, G. H., 97
Goodman-Hill, Tim, 70
The God of Small Things, 29
Goudal, Jetta, 87
Graf, Herbert ['Little Hans'], 5, 11n2, 256–257
Graham, Elaine L., 72
Grandfathers, 108, 230
Grandmothers, 150, 218, 222, 226, 259, 260
Gray, Thomas, 100
Green, André, 21, 22, 162, 165
Gretta Conroy, 96
Grimaldi-Pizzorno, Patrizia, 8, 91–100
Grimbert, Philippe, 9, 185–190, 190n3, 190n4, 190n5
The Guardian, 1–2, 185
Gubar, Susan, 27, 113, 119
Guilt, 6, 7, 18, 31, 109, 173, 189, 196, 199–200, 221, 226
Gunn, Olivia Noble, 7, 47–55

H

Hackett, Joan, 3
Hagar, 127, 132
Haliloğlu, Nagihan, 8, 113–121, 189
Hamer, Mary, 8, 103–111
Hamlet, 93, 98–99
The Hand That Rocks the Cradle, 2
Hannah Stirn Grimbert, 187–190
Hanneh Hayyeh, 86
Hanneh Levin, 84–85, 86, 87
Harrison, Kathryn, xvi
Haunting, xiv, 4, 8, 9, 50, 51, 52, 59, 63, 74, 93, 98, 113, 116, 118, 121, 121n3, 148, 149, 163, 170, 195–203, 209, 211, 221
Hayles, Katherine, 73
Heaney, Seamus, 100, 101n7
Hecate, 105–106
Helen Stuart [*Sisters Antipodes*], 57, 58, 62, 65n2
Helios, 108–110
Helland, Frode, 49–52
Herbrechter, Stefan, 72
Hesiod, 104
Hesse, Hermann, 6, 20
Hitchcock, Alfred, 3, 4, 9, 10, 169–175, 208, 241–249, 249n1
Hitler, Adolf, 218, 224
Hoffmann, E. T. A., 73
Holocaust, 10, 150, 185–190, 196, 200, 207–215, 217–226
Homer, 91, 100, 104
Horkheimer, Max, 37
Hoss, Nina, 207
Huggins, David, 3
Hugo, Léopoldine, 22
Hugo, Victor, 22
Human rights, xvii, 9, 72, 137–144, 145n1, 150, 152
Humans, 7, 67, 70–72, 74, 75n1, 75n2
Hungry Hearts, 80, 82, 83–87
Hurt, William, 69, 71
Husbands, 2, 3, 4, 9, 10, 23, 25–32, 47, 58, 105, 127, 128, 131, 161, 162, 170–174, 187, 190, 207, 221, 236, 245–249

I

Ibsen, Henrik, xv, 7, 47–55
Immigration, xiv, 8, 79–88
The Imposter, 21
Incest, xv, xvi, 1, 7, 25–33, 242
Inés, 152, 153
The Infatuations, 21
Innes, Vari, 180–183
Irreplaceability, 1, 39, 40, 163, 217, 253
Ishmael, 127, 132
Israel, xv, xvi, 210, 218, 221, 225, 226

J

Jaime [*Un muro de silencio*], 148–149, 152, 154, 156
James, Geraldine, 163
Jane Cummins [*Sisters Antipodes*], 57–65
Jane Eyre, 3, 8, 113–121
Jason, 8, 104–111
Jealousy, 5–6, 18, 20, 36–37, 58, 62, 109, 185–190, 190n1
Jenkins, David, 211
Jenny Stuart [*Sisters Antipodes*], 57–65
Jentsch, Ernst, 73
Jesus, 17
Jews, Judaism, 17, 87, 185–189, 200, 208, 210, 219–226, 227n1
Johanna [*Near Days*], 201–202
Johansson, Scarlett, 245
John Darling, 49, 52
Johnny [*Phoenix*], 207–215
Johnson, Barbara, 18
Jonze, Spike, 241
Jordanova, Ludmilla, 126
Joyce, James, xiv, 92–100, 100n1, 101n5, 101n6

K

Kafka, Franz, 186
Kantorowicz, Ernst, 253
Kate [*45 Years*], 2, 161–166
Kate Benson [*Un muro de silencio*], 148, 154–155
Katya [*45 Years*], 2, 23, 161–164
Kershaw, Justine, 183
Ketchum Glass, Susannah, 203
Kexel, Guillermo, 150
The Kindness of Strangers, 2
King, John, 156
The Kiss, xvi
Kohen Raz, Odeya, xv, 10, 241–249
Kreider, Tim, 69, 70
Kristeva, Julia, 138, 201
Kubrick, Stanley, 67, 69, 164, 241
Kunzendorf, Nina, 207
Kwiatowski, Nicolás, 149

L

La Tour Eiffel, Erika [Naisho], 182, 183
Laval, Pierre, 189
Law, Jude, 69
Le Colonel Chabert, 21
Lene [*Phoenix*], 207–210, 212–215
Leopold Bloom, 91–100
Les Contemplations, 22
Lesnik-Oberstein, Karín, 48
Lestingi, Tony, 148
Levien, Sonya, 87
Levinas, Emmanuel, 141, 201
Little Eyolf, 47–55
Loewy, Monika, xv, 9–10, 207–215
Longoni, Ana, 150
Losey, Joseph, 241
Loss, 2, 7, 9, 16, 19, 21, 48, 51–53, 62, 65, 68, 71, 73, 96, 110, 120, 138, 139, 143, 144, 183, 189, 197–200, 232, 234, 238, 253, 257

Lot and his daughters, 7, 28–33
Love, 2, 4, 5, 9, 19, 21, 22, 23n3, 26, 27, 29, 31, 36, 41, 51, 52, 55, 59, 60, 61, 62, 68–70, 75, 84, 95–99, 106, 107, 108, 114, 139, 161–166, 177–184, 187, 188, 215, 217, 225, 231–238, 245–249
Luckhurst, Roger, 23n2

M
Madame Butterfly, 11n1
Maggy Cummins [*Sisters Antipodes*], 57–60, 62, 65n5
Maine, Margo, 61, 62
Malte Laurids Brigge, 6
Manent, Pierre, 36
Marías, Javier, 21
Marinetti, Filippo Tommaso, 95, 96
Marks, Laura U., 233
Marriage, 2, 4, 5, 9, 15, 18, 25–28, 30, 40–41, 50, 53, 58, 84, 85, 87, 94, 96, 97, 98, 99, 106, 108, 120, 127–130, 140, 141, 149, 161, 165, 173, 177, 225, 234
Married to the Eiffel Tower, 9, 177–184
Marx, Karl, 39, 42–43
Massey, Anna, 3
Maus II, 9, 195, 199–200, 203
Maxim de Winter, 4, 23, 169–175, 245–248
Maxime Grimbert [*Un Secret*], 186–189, 190n4
McCandless, Julie, 130
McMullen, Ken, 96
Medea, 3, 8, 103–111, 188, 190
Medina, Ofelia, 148
Meiri, Sandra, xvi, 10, 241–249
Méliès, Georges, 101n6
Melissaris, Emmanuel, 137
Menem, Carlos, 148, 153

Metz, Christian, 241–243
Michael Darling, 52
Michael, George, 162
Miller, Claude, 9, 185, 189
Miłosz, Czesław, 223
Mirroring, 7, 21, 31, 57, 58, 59, 63, 64, 83, 119, 130, 153, 165, 166n2, 209–210, 252
The Missing (BBC-TV), 21
Mitchell, Juliet, 5, 59, 61, 64
Modleski, Tania, 247
Möller, Kai, 137
Monteilhet, Hubert, 207
Monti, Félix, 154
The Moody Blues, 166
Moore, Thomas, 97
More, Max, 75n3
Morgan, Hector Davies, 25
Mori, Masahiro, 73
Moss, Carrie-Ann, 71
Mothers, maternity, motherhood, xv, 2, 3, 5, 6, 7, 8, 10, 16–22, 25–33, 47, 50, 52–54, 57, 60, 62, 63, 65n2, 68–71, 83, 86, 103–111, 117, 125–132, 143, 150, 152, 162–165, 182, 186–188, 195, 197–199, 201–202, 210, 213, 217, 222, 232, 235–238, 242, 245, 246, 253, 254, 256–258, 260
Mourning, 6, 9, 18, 48, 50, 51, 54, 55, 62, 71, 73, 98, 100, 110, 156, 161, 182, 183, 189, 224, 225, 260
Mrs Danvers, 3, 4, 170–174, 246–249
'Mrs de Winter', 3–5, 10, 15, 169–175
Mrs Van Hopper, 171, 175
Mulvey, Laura, xvi, 9, 166n6, 169–175
Murúa, Lautaro, 148
Myrrha, 7, 28, 30–33, 33n4
The Myth of the Birth of the Hero, 5

N

Nahe Tage [Near Days], 195, 196, 201–203, 203n2
National Socialism, Nazism, 200, 210, 221, 224
Nayman, Adam, 208–210, 213
Neiger-Fleischmann, Miriam, 10, 217, 225
Nelly [Phoenix], 10, 207–215
New, Chris, 162
Nicholas Stuart, 58
Nicholson, Jack, 164
Nicolson, Vanessa, 1–2
Nin, Anaïs, xvi
Novak, Kim, 208

O

O'Connor, Frances, 68
Oedipus, Oedipus complex, 11n3, 23n3, 23n5, 25, 70, 181, 238, 243
Ogilvy, Margaret [Barrie's mother], 19–20
Olivier, Laurence, 245
Orpheus, 21–22
Osment, Haley Joel, 21, 67
Overath, Angelika, 9, 195, 197, 201, 203
Ovid, 28–33, 65n3
Owen, Jean, xvi, 6–11, 25–33, 57–65

P

Parinaud, André, 19
Parkin, Molly, 20
Parkinson, Katherine, 70
Patricia Stuart [Sisters Antipodes], 57, 58, 60, 64, 65n5
Paul Stuart [Sisters Antipodes], 57, 58, 60, 63, 64, 65n2, 65n5, 65n8
Peau d'Âne, 7, 25, 26, 28, 31, 32, 33n2

Peter Pan, 7, 47, 48, 50, 53
Peter Pan, 20, 47, 48, 49, 50, 52, 53
Petzold, Christian, 9–10, 207–215
Phillips, Adam, 211, 213
Phoenix, 9, 207–215
Pinocchio, xvi, 23n3, 68, 69
Piotrowska, Agnieszka, xvi-xvii, 9, 10, 177–184, 231–239
Pittaros, Peter, 162
Pizzi, Katia, 23n2
Plagnol, Robert, 187
Plath, Sylvia, 61
Plaut, W. Gunther, 17
Polledri, Patricia, 164–165
Polley, Sarah, 231–239
Porot, Maurice, 6, 18, 20, 21
Portela, Graciela, 154
Posthumanism, xvi, 67, 68, 71, 72–75
Psychoanalysis, xv, xvi, xvii, 5, 6, 9, 10, 16, 19, 153, 165, 177, 178, 181, 185, 186, 190, 196, 209, 231, 232, 236–237, 241–249, 251–261

Q

Quinlivan, Davina, 233, 237, 238

R

Rain, Douglas, 245
Rampling, Charlotte, 2, 161, 165, 166n5
Rank, Otto, 5, 26
The Ratmaid, 47, 50–52
Rayor, Diane J., 111n1
Rebecca (Du Maurier), 3–5, 121n3, 169
Rebecca (Hitchcock), 9, 10, 169–174, 241–249
Rebecca de Winter, 3–5, 15, 23, 169–174, 245–248

Redgrave, Vanessa, 148, 155
Redon, Odilon, 101n6
The Replacement (BBC-TV), 2
The Replacement (Redmond), 3
The Replacement (Yovanoff), 3
Replacement child/ren, 6, 15, 18–22, 48, 51, 59, 69, 71, 186, 190, 196–203, 218, 226
Resnais, Alain, 164, 166n4
Revenge, 2, 20, 52, 105, 111, 186
Rhys, Jean, xv, 8, 113–121
Ribeiro de Menezes, Alison, xvii, 9, 147–157
Rigg, Diana, 3
Rilke, Rainer Maria, 6, 20, 22
Rita Allmers [*Eyolf*], 7, 47–55
Rivalry, 2, 5, 6, 7, 20, 23, 57–65, 65n7, 163, 198–200
Robards, Sam, 68
Robertson, Robert, 111n1
Rodríguez, Ximena, 152
Rooms, 10, 31, 47, 51, 60, 65n5, 83, 87, 106, 115–119, 150, 153, 164, 165, 183, 199, 208, 220, 223, 246, 248, 251–261
Rosemary Cummins [*Sisters Antipodes*], 57, 58, 63, 65n5
Rossellini, Roberto, 165–166
Rossini, Manuela, 72
Rothberg, Michael, 196
Roy, Arundhati, 29
Royle, Nicholas, 209–210
Rudolf, Anthony, xvii, 10, 217–226

S
Sabbadini, Andrea, 59
Sacrifice, 9, 36, 98, 144, 185–189, 224, 236, 237
Sagnier, Ludivigne, 187
Salome of the Tenements, 80, 82, 87
Sanders, George, 165, 246

Sarah, 127, 132
Schneider, Rebecca, 151–152
Schwab, Gabriele, 196–197, 199
Sedgwick, Eve Kosofsky, 23n5
Segal, Naomi, xvii, 1–6, 9, 15–23, 23n5, 33n1, 34, 125, 137, 166n7, 169, 185–190
Seiffert, Rachel, xiv, 203n1
Sekoff, Jed, 165
Selznick, David O., 170
The Sense of an Ending, 2
Settimelli, Emilio, 95
Seyrig, Delphine, 27
Shakespeare, William, xiv, xv, 109
Sheldon, Sally, 130
Siblings, 5–6, 7, 10, 15, 18, 20, 21, 57–65, 84, 186, 195, 197–200, 235, 257
Silvia [*Un muro de silencio*], 148–156
Simmel, Georg, 38, 42
Simon Grimbert [*Un Secret*], 186–190
The Sisters Antipodes, 7, 57–65, 65n3
Skapski, Jerzy, 150
Sobchack, Vivian, 72–73, 74, 233, 237, 244
Socrates, 105
Soler, Colette, 231
Sons, 3, 7, 8, 9, 23n3, 25, 28, 30, 33, 47, 48, 50, 53, 58, 68, 69, 70, 71, 74, 86, 105, 108, 110, 129, 182, 183, 185–190, 198, 200–201, 203, 218, 221, 223, 224, 257
Sonya Vrunsky, 87
Spencer, Herbert, 96
Spiegelman, Art, 9, 195, 197, 199–200, 202, 203
Spielberg, Steven, 7, 23n3, 67–70
Springfield, Dusty, 166
Stantic, Lita, 9, 147–157
Stendhal [Henri Beyle], 20
Stephen Dedalus, 95

Stilgoe, John, 257–258
Stirns, Robert, 187
Strachey, James, 11n3
Stringer, Chris, 252
Sublimation, 10, 231, 236–237
Substitution, 1, 7, 10, 15, 16, 17–20, 33n4, 38, 39, 42, 63, 70, 103, 127, 131, 133n4, 147, 202, 236, 257, 258
Surrogacy, 1, 8, 11, 16, 125–132
Suvin, Darko, 72, 73
Sylvie and Bruno Concluded, 17

T

Tadmor, Naomi, 189
Tania Grimbert [*Un Secret*], 186–189, 190n4
Therapy, xiii, xviii, 7, 10, 67, 73, 74, 106, 164, 165, 182, 186, 259, 260
Thiérrée, Jean-Baptiste, 164
Thomas, Jake, 68
Thomson, Stephen, 48
Tocqueville, Alexis de, 7, 35–39, 43
Tommy Cummins [*Sisters Antipodes*], 58
Tönnies, Ferdinand, 38–39
Traffic in Souls, 82
Transference, 8, 10, 15, 16–17, 71, 88, 107, 114, 177–180, 231, 232, 238, 253, 254, 256, 260, 261
Transgeneration, 9, 195, 196–197, 203
Trauma, xvi, 5, 9, 10, 19, 61, 64, 68, 69, 71, 74, 147, 149, 150, 154, 156, 162–164, 166n4, 180, 181, 195–198, 201, 203, 209–214, 231, 233, 235, 237, 247
Treichel, Hans-Ulrich, xiv, 9, 195, 198–200, 202, 203

Trilling, Lionel, 95, 100
Trimble, Lawrence, 94
Trotter, Sarah, xvii, 9, 137–144
True and false selves, 10, 208, 210–213, 215
Tudor, Will, 71
Twinning, 7, 21, 57, 58

U

U*lysses*, xiv, 8, 91–100
Uncanny, 9, 70, 73–75, 95, 115, 121, 149, 151–153, 157, 170, 172, 201, 208–211, 214, 248
Un muro de silencio, 9, 147–157
Un Secret, 9, 185–190
Urman, Irit, 217, 218, 221, 224–226
Urman, Jerzyk, 217–226

V

Van Gogh, Vincent, 6, 20
Vatel, Martine, 164
Vellacott, Philip, 111n1
Vigourt, Valentin, 186
Villages, 3, 39, 83, 84, 86, 187
Villamil, Soledad, 152
Virgil, 22

W

Warner, Marina, 26, 27
Washburn, Bryant, 84
Webber, Andrew J., 151
Weber, Max, 42
Wendy Darling, 20, 49, 52
Wertsch, James, 150
Whitman, Charles S., 88n5
Wide Sargasso Sea, 3, 8, 113–121
Williams, Susan S., 74
Winnicott, Donald W., 9, 107, 208, 210–215, 258

Wives, 2, 4, 5, 8, 9, 10, 11n1, 21–22, 23, 23n4, 25–33, 33n4, 47, 70–71, 83, 84–85, 86, 96, 98, 103, 104–111, 114, 116, 121, 121n3, 164, 165, 169–175, 177, 187, 190, 199, 207–211, 219, 223, 225, 245–248
Wolfe, Cary, 72
Wolin, Sheldon, 38
Wollen, Peter, xvi
Wright, Deborah, xviii, 10, 251–261

Y
Yezierska, Anzia, 8, 79–88, 88n6

Z
Zehrfeld, Ronald, 207
Zelizer, Viviana, 39, 40, 132n2
Zeus, 108, 109
Žižek, Slavoj, 249n1
Zohn, Harry, 16

CPSIA information can be obtained
at www.ICGtesting.com
Printed in the USA
LVHW07*1051100618
580222LV00004B/8/P